A series of student texts in

CONTEMPORARY BIOLOGY

General Editors:
Professor E. J. Barrington, F.R.S.
Professor Arthur J. Willis

CLOUDSLEY-THOMPSON, J. L. Man and the biology of arid zones.
University Park, 1977. 182p ill (A series of student texts in
contemporary biology) bibl index 77-20663. 15.75 ISBN
0-8391-1192-4. C.I.P.
Few writers on this vital topic have had as wide a firsthand knowledge as
Cloudsley-Thompson. He lived, traveled, and studied in an arid area for
years as professor of zoology at the University of Khartoum, and as keeper
of the Sudan Natural History Museum. Discussion of climate, soils,
geology, geography, and man-made deserts is followed by the history of the
expanding Sahara. The physiology of desert fauna and flora is explained,
and their adaptations are examined. The cultures of the human inhabitants
are not neglected but are described with understanding. The book is full of
suggestions for the practical use of our knowledge in using arid lands. All of
this and more is clearly and interestingly written. Photographs, tables, and
many drawings are used to strengthen the appeal of the text. Both index
and bibliography are useful. While the volume could be used as a text, it is
much more and should be of interest to the wide group of readers who are
interested in world affairs. Undergraduate and graduate levels.

Man and the Biology of
Arid Zones

J. L. Cloudsley-Thompson

M.A., Ph.D. (Cantab), D.Sc. (London), F.I. Biol., F.W.A.
Professor of Zoology
Birkbeck College
University of London

formerly

Professor of Zoology
University of Khartoum and Keeper
Sudan Natural History Museum

University Park Press

© J. L. Cloudsley-Thompson, 1977

First published 1977
by Edward Arnold (Publishers) Limited,
25 Hill Street,
London, W1X 8LL

First published in the USA in 1977 by
University Park Press
233 East Redwood Street
Baltimore, Maryland 21202

Library of Congress Cataloging in Publication Data

Cloudsley-Thompson, J. L.
    Man and the biology of arid zones.

    (A Series of student texts in contemporary
biology)
    Bibliography: p.
    Includes index.
    1. Desert ecology. 2. Desert ecology—
Sahara. 3. Man—Influence on nature. 4. Man—
Influence on nature—Sahara. I. Title.
QH541.5.D4C58   1978   574.5'265   77-20663
ISBN 0-8391-1192-4

Printed in Great Britain

Preface

From 1971 to 1973, there was famine in Asia. A pitiless sun baked the parched fields, and prayers for rain apparently went unheeded. When the monsoon finally ended this terrible drought, it came with relentless force. Dried river beds were quickly filled; destructive floods swept across precious paddies and grain fields. The result was an increasingly severe shortage of rice, the staple food of the people.

The year 1973, likewise, witnessed the climax of seven years of drought in the Sahel savanna regions fringing the southern border of the Sahara desert. These also depend on monsoon rains that come when the inter-tropical front moves north during the summer. In consequence, the sheep and cattle of the nomads died in thousands and their owners were faced with starvation.

Periodic disasters of this nature must inevitably follow over-exploitation of the fragile, unstable ecosystem of the semi-arid regions on the desert's fringe. Each of them adds to the relentless advance of desert conditions, which are engendered by human misuse of the environment. Although arid regions are readily degraded into desert, the reclamation of their natural climax vegetation is far less easy to achieve. It is therefore, important that the factors which engender the creation and spread of deserts should be clearly understood.

Whatever its origin, aridity is clearly the primary cause of desert conditions. Low rainfall, although extremely significant, does not, however, invariably produce desert. In the following chapters an attempt is made to assess both the effects of climate and the influence of human activities on the creation of the world's desert regions. In much of the Sahara, for instance, over-grazing by domestic stock and the felling of trees for firewood has probably played a greater part in destroying the vegetation than have any climatic changes since the last pluvial flood.

It is not enough merely to realize the extent to which ignorant exploitation has already squandered the productivity of the land. Not only must the causes of depression and imbalance be removed, but adverse trends will have to be reversed if deserts are to support adequately their increasing human populations. The problem of the world's deserts is not only a scientific one: it is also a problem of sociology and economics. In order that it can be tackled, it should be seen in correct perspective. The aim of the present volume is to assist in this objective. Although special attention is paid to the Sahara, the desert I know best, most of the conclusions have widespread validity.

London, 1976   J. L. C–T.

Table of contents

PREFACE

1 CLIMATE   1
  Desert types   1
  Rainfall   6
  Temperature   7
  Aridity   9
  Wind   10
  Microclimates   11

2 SOILS   13
  Desert soils   13
  Alluvial deposits   13
  Dunes   16
  Semi-desert soils   20

3 DESERTS IN THE PAST   22
  Geomorphology   22
  Palaeoclimates   26

4 MAN-MADE DESERTS OF THE WORLD   29
  The origin of savanna   29
  Shifting cultivation   33
  Forest peoples   38
  Pastoralism   41

5   THE EXPANDING SAHARA—A CASE HISTORY   44
     Climate, past and present   44
     Fossil evidence   47
     Historical evidence   50

6   VEGETATION AND POTENTIAL   55
     Vegetation types   55
     Drought-evading plants   57
     Xerophytic plants   60
     Utilization of desert plants   63
     Food gathering cultures   64
     Exploitation of raw materials   66
     Oasis cultivation   68

7   ANIMAL PROBLEMS OF ARIDITY   70
     Behavioural adaptations: circadian rhythms 71
     Phenology   74
     Similarities between plants and animals   75
     Reduction in transpiration   77
     Respiratory adaptations   79
     Excretory adaptations   83
     Water uptake   85

8   THERMAL PROBLEMS OF ANIMALS   89
     Behavioural thermoregulation   89
     Emergency mechanisms   91
     Hyperthermia   93
     Adaptations for life in sand   94
     Adaptive coloration   97

9   ADAPTATIONS AND EXPLOITATION OF LARGER
     MAMMALS   100
     Camels   100
     Antelopes and asses   104
     Cattle, sheep and goats   106
     Marsupials   107
     Evaporative cooling   107
     Carnivores   109
     Exploitation of desert mammals   110

10   BIOLOGY OF MAN IN THE DESERT   113
     Indigenous animals as human food   113
     Water and electrolytes   115
     Circulatory adjustments   116

Physiological adaptations   117
Acclimatization   119
Pigmentation   119
Technological adaptations   120

11 AGRICULTURAL PESTS   123
Locusts and grasshoppers   123
Termites   129
Other agricultural pests   130
Human influence on the ecology of pests   131
Locust control   132
Prevention of termite damage   134
Alternative methods of pest control   134

12 PATHOGENIC AND VENOMOUS ORGANISMS   136
Plant pathogens   136
Epizootics among mammals   137
Diseases of man   139
Medical problems of development projects   142
Arthropods poisonous to man   143
Venomous reptiles   145
Chemical defence   148

13 THE DESERT COMPLEX AND ITS RATIONAL
    EXPLOITATION   151
Pastoralism   151
Nomadism   153
Preservation of wild life   156
Game ranching   156
Dryland farming   157
Agricultural crops   158
Irrigation   161
Water desalination   163
Hydroponics   164
Dune stabilization   164
Changing the climate   165
Land reclamation   165
Mineral resources   166
Industry and tourism   167
Multiple land use   168

14 EPILOGUE   169
    BIBLIOGRAPHY   172
    INDEX   178

I

Climate

The major deserts of the world result primarily from global, or at least from hemispheric wind patterns, and arise from the whole general circulation.[96] At the same time, while many aspects of meteorology are pertinent to arid regions, few of them are unique to deserts. Arid regions are characterized by low precipitation, which is usually associated with considerable insolation. The greatest deserts (Table 1.1) in which the annual precipitation is less than 25.5 cm (10 in), lie beyond the limits of the swing of the equatorial rainfall belt, at latitudes in which trade winds blow throughout the year. Very few, if any, deserts are completely rainless, however, and low rainfall, although extremely significant, does not, by itself, invariably produce desert conditions.

DESERT TYPES

Arid regions can be divided into five types on a climatic basis.[77, 118] These are as follows: sub-tropical deserts, cool coastal deserts, rain-shadow deserts, interior continental deserts, and polar deserts. In polar regions, water is not available to plants and animals since it is frozen. In the other types of desert, water is deficient throughout most of the year because the amount of evaporation greatly exceeds the annual precipitation. Only these types of desert will be discussed in the present volume.

Sub-tropical deserts are largely the result of semi-permanent belts of high pressure in tropical regions, within which the air has a tendency to descend from high altitudes towards the surface of the land. As it does so, it becomes warmed by compressional heating at a rate of 10K per 1,000 m (K, kelvin ≡ deg C), so that it is hot, dry and completely incapable of producing any precipitation by the time it reaches ground level. Rain, and

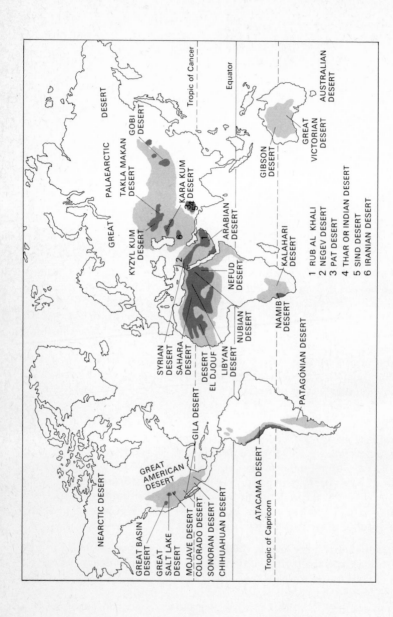

Fig. 1.1 Desert regions of the world.[24]

Table 1.1   The deserts of the world.[24]

	Square kilometres	Square miles
Sahara Desert	9,100,000	3,500,000
Australian Desert	3,400,000	1,300,000
Turkestan Desert	1,900,000	750,000
Arabian Desert	2,600,000	1,000,000
Great American Desert (including the Great Basin, Mojave, Sonoran and Chihuahuan Deserts of south western North America)	1,300,000	500,000
Patagonian Desert (Argentina)	670,000	260,000
Thar Desert (India)	600,000	230,000
Kalahari and Namib Deserts (South West Africa)	570,000	220,000
Takla Makan Desert including the Gobi Desert (from western China to Mongolia)	520,000	200,000
Iranian Desert (Persia)	390,000	150,000
Atacama Desert (Peru and Chile)	360,000	140,000

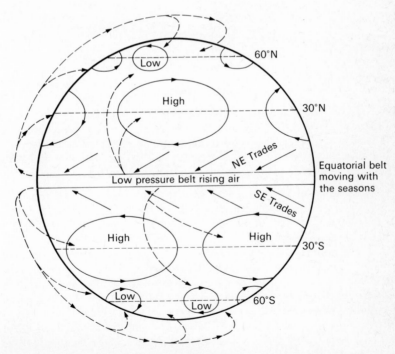

Fig 1.2   Equatorial and tropical wind systems.[29]

thunderstorms of monsoon type, accompany the poleward movements of the inter-tropical fronts in summer.

Cool, coastal deserts, such as the Namib, Atacama, and Baja or Lower Californian, are almost always rainless, yet drenched with chilly moisture. Rainlessness again results from descending air masses, the high humidity and cold from nearby cool ocean currents—in these instances the Benguela, Humboldt and Californian currents respectively.

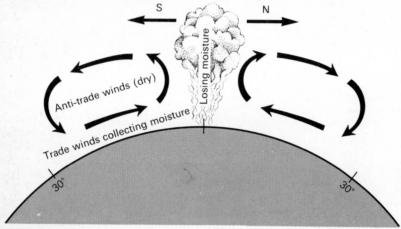

Fig. 1.3 Schematic presentation of the circulatory patterns of the atmosphere between the equator and 30° latitude north and south.[4]

Rain-shadow deserts are situated on the lee sides of mountains which cause the prevailing wind to rise and to drop its moisture on the windward side in the form of orographic precipitation (orographic—related to mountains). Examples are afforded by the Mojave and Great Basin deserts of North America, the deserts of Patagonia and part of the Great Australian desert.

Interior continental deserts are arid through lack of marine influences and other factors related to the massive bulk of the land surrounding them. Much of the Australian desert, of the Great Palaearctic desert and of the North American desert, fall within this category. Nevertheless, it is doubtful whether there is any hot or temperate desert that never encounters precipitation. While driving across the Sahara, in mid-summer 1967, my wife and I experienced a shower in the most arid and desolate stretch, near the frontier between Algeria and Niger. We had driven for over 320 km (200 miles) without seeing a scrap of vegetation—not a blade of grass, not a vestige of *Acacia*—and a similar distance of equal sterility lay ahead. Yet rain drops sprinkled our windscreen, and the fierce heat of the day was momentarily alleviated.

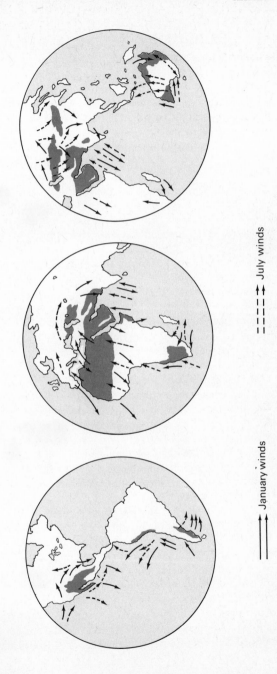

Fig. 1.4 Prevailing winds and the meteorological causes of desert climates.[37]

—— January winds

- - - - July winds

RAINFALL

Desert rainfall is always erratic and, although it sometimes tends to be seasonal, is unevenly distributed in amount and place. For instance, Yuma in Arizona experienced only 25 mm (1 in) of rain in 1899, but more than 280 mm (11 in) fell in 1905. At Tamanrasset, Algeria, 160 mm (6.3 in) fell in one year; in another only 6.4 mm (0.25 in). During the three years following September 1933, only 2 mm, 3 mm and 5 mm, respectively, fell at Helwan in Egypt; but no less than 125 mm (5 in) fell in the year 1945–46. Again, 679 mm (16.7 in) were recorded at Erkowit in the Red Sea Hills in 1951, but only 40 mm (1.5 in) during the following year. The biological significance of average rainfall figures in arid regions is, there-fore, strictly limited. More important is the mean period between storms of sufficient magnitude for some water to remain long enough in some favoured localities for seeds to germinate, grow into mature plants, and re-seed themselves. It is upon such plants that nomadic animals and their owners depend for their food.

Although precipitation does not necessarily occur every year, it is un-wise to be dogmatic about complete drought for any portion of the earth's surface, since rain may fall heavily in one place and not be recorded only a few km away. Thus, the monthly precipitation at Khartoum in July 1946 was 129.5 mm (5.1 in) while Shambat, about 8 km distant, received only 38.7 mm (1.5 in). Rainfall figures for the year in the two localities were 247.7 mm (9.7 in) and 143.1 mm (5.6 in) respectively. The previous year, however, the situation was reversed: Khartoum recorded 90.6 mm (3.6 in) and Shambat 224.8 mm (8.8 in).[41]

On the other hand, the extension of regular air-line services over the Sahara has revealed narrow bands of rainfall extending for hundreds of miles. In 1942, one of these extended from Dakar to southern Morocco. It is to be hoped that photography from satellites may reveal the exact distribution of these zones of precipitation, for this knowledge could be important in human exploitation of arid regions.[120] It also suggests that the climate of the desert may not everywhere be quite so severe as is indicated by meteorological records.

Removal of the vegetation by overgrazing greatly reduces the beneficial effects of rain, because most of the water quickly runs off the surface of the ground. Within a few minutes, dry *wadis* may become roaring torrents, removing any vestiges of top soil and eroding deep gulleys into the ravaged landscape. A *wadi* is a desert watercourse dry except after rain. My wife and I experienced an example of desert rainfall when we were struck by a devastating thunderstorm one evening in northern Tchad. We had only just begun to prepare camp for the night, yet barely had time to secure the primuses, pots and pans from blowing away in the sudden gale before the rain descended. Within minutes the entire landscape, brilliantly illuminated by the continual lightning, was inundated. Looking out from our vehicle, we seemed to be floating in a vast sea, the ripples from the wind giving the appearance of rapid currents. When the rain stopped abruptly at 01.00 hrs we literally had to shout to be heard above the fantastic chorus of croaking toads and stridulating insects. Similar vocalizations follow flash floods in Arizona, New Mexico, Australia and elsewhere. Next morning the water had disappeared and, after 80 km of mud, we reached dry sand.[36]

TEMPERATURE

Like average figures for rainfall, mean temperatures are of little significance in arid regions, where ambient temperatures oscillate greatly between day and night, summer and winter. It is the incidence of high temperatures liable to cause heat damage, and of low temperatures, which limit the growing season, or cause freezing, that affect living organisms. Maximum temperatures are high in arid regions, especially in the

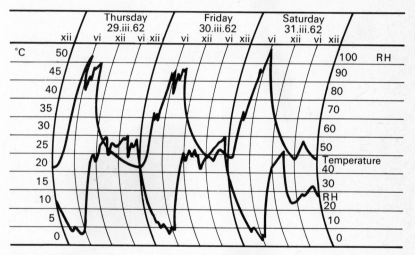

Fig. 1.5 Thermohygrograph recording for three days in March at Khartoum, Sudan.[41]

dry season when there is little cloud or moisture in the atmosphere to absorb the sun's radiation. The mean maximum temperature in summer may reach 43.6°C (110.5°F) in Baghdad, 42.2°C in Bilma and 40.0°C in Phoenix. Maximum shade temperatures, under standard meteorological conditions, of 58°C (136.4°F) have been recorded at El Azizia, Libya, in September, 1922, and at San Luiz Potosi, Mexico in August, 1933; and of 56.5°C (134°F) in Death Valley, California, in July, 1913. Even higher shade temperatures are probably attained in many areas, but recording stations are rather rare in most desert regions. Under such conditions life and work become difficult and one can sympathize with the goats huddled in the scanty shade of the bare rock and sparse vegetation.[37]

Under the influence of intense radiation through a cloudless sky, ground surface temperatures reach extremely high levels during the day, and cool rapidly at night. The world record appears to be 84°C (183°F) registered on the Loango coast near the Equator, but I have equalled this at Wadi Halfa, Sudan. Such temperatures are extremely superficial and do not penetrate for more than a few millimetres into the ground. Nevertheless, they must pose problems of survival to immobile seeds, spores, and the eggs of desert animals. The severity of insolation on desert sand is, of course, greatly enhanced when overgrazing has removed every scrap of vegetation. A cover, even of dry grass, will shade the surface of the soil and ameliorate the intensity of solar radiation.

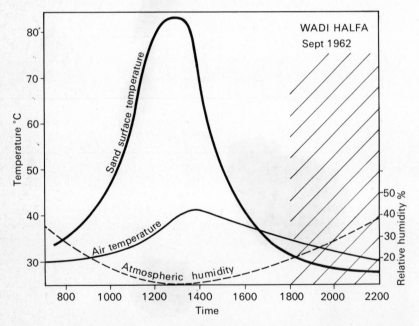

Fig. 1.6 Air and soil surface temperature compared with atmospheric humidity values for a typical September day at Wadi Halfa, Sudan.[41]

The temperatures of hot deserts show greater variation in winter than in summer. They are lower than in the summer during daytime and, at night, they may even drop below freezing point. At Yuma, with a mean of 12°C (54°F) in January, the maxima and minima recorded are 27°C (81°F) and −6°C (22°F). An annual range of shade temperature from −2°C (28°F) to 52.5°C (126.5°F) has been recorded from Wadi Halfa, and a daily range in summer of 29°C (52°F) at In Salah in Algeria. The record fluctuation, however, appears to be from −0.5°C (31 °F) to 37.5°C (99°F) within 24 hours at Bir Mighla, southern Tripolitania, in December.

Similar variations occur in temperate deserts. At Tashkent, where the average January temperature is −1.3°C (29.7°F), the temperature may fall to −30°C (−22°F) during cold periods. In summer, the Turkestan desert has mean temperatures around 30°C (86°F) and absolute maxima very much higher. Such conditions are characteristic of much of the Great Palaearctic desert in Central Asia. The higher plateaux basins and valleys of Arizona, Colorado and New Mexico may sometimes register −17°C (1.4°F). This causes considerable frost damage to the vegetation.[41]

ARIDITY

Not only is lack of moisture in the form of rain the chief factor causing desert conditions, and the absence of clouds responsible for extremes of temperature, but low air humidity in itself has an adverse effect upon plants and animals, because the rate of evaporation is so great at high temperatures. More water is required to saturate a given volume of warm air than to saturate the same amount of cool air. Consequently, at night, when considerable cooling takes place and the relative humidity rises, saturation deficiency may drop to such an extent that the dew-point is reached.

It is often claimed that dew forms a not inconsiderable source of moisture for plants in arid regions where rapid cooling takes place at night, and this seems to be so in some cases. The sand at the bases of the giant candelabras (*Euphorbia abyssinica*), characteristic of the mist oasis of Erkowit in the Red Sea hills, may be quite damp in the early morning. Similarly, the roots of marram grass (*Ammophila arenaria*), which grows in sand dunes around the coastline of Europe, are regularly moistened by dew which runs down the blades of the leaves into the sand and humus at the base of the tuft.

Water can be obtained, even in arid places, by digging holes in the ground and covering them at night with polythene sheets. The moisture that condenses from the air and soil, on the under surfaces of these sheets, drips into containers at the bottom of the holes and is collected in the morning.

Losses of moisture from the ground and from vegetation, often referred to as 'evapotranspiration', are of great significance in semi-arid and arid regions. The transfer of moisture to the atmosphere takes place by turbulent diffusion, and is difficult to estimate because many variable factors are involved. It is influenced considerably by the moisture content and characteristics of the soil. Measurements of evaporation from artificial lakes are subject to several sources of error. Furthermore, a tank cannot act as a natural water surface, as far as evaporation is concerned, nor can it approximate to transpiration from plants. The most promising method for the determination of evaporation consists in accurately measuring the moisture content at two levels and the vertical velocity of the air between them. It is then possible to calculate evaporation directly from these figures.

For purposes of irrigation and agricultural research, it is necessary to know the water balance over large areas. Actual evapotranspiration is difficult to determine, as already mentioned. For this reason, the concept of 'potential evapotranspiration' has been introduced. This is defined as the rate of evaporation from an extended surface of short green crop, actively growing, completely shading the ground, of uniform height, and not short of water. Various methods have been derived for calculating potential evapotranspiration from macrometeorological data.[41]

The analysis of water balance is particularly important in semi-arid areas, because these are situated in a transitional zone between the desert and regions in which there is adequate water for the growth of plants. Information is therefore necessary to determine the needs for irrigation of particular crops. Precipitation and run-off in streams can be measured comparatively easily; soil moisture, fluctuations in ground water, dew conditions, and evaporation are more difficult to assess.

WIND

Hot, strong winds, usually associated with sand storms, are a constant feature of desert climates. They might be quite local, but are frequently associated with large-scale disturbances in the general circulation. They tend to be strongest in spring and early summer, blowing harder during the day than at night. Well-known winds, related to cyclonic disturbances on a large scale, include the *khamsin* of North Africa and the Near East. So-called because it is said to blow for fifty days, the *khamsin* is connected with cyclonic disturbances created in North Africa south of the Atlas mountains and extending eastwards. On one occasion during the war in Libya, in May 1942, the dust was so thick that I could not discern a glimmer from a lighted torch on my tank, at night, from a distance of five paces. In Algeria, this wind is known as the *sirocco* and, in the central Sahara, as the *shahali* or 'wind from the south'. The *harmattan* is a more constant hot wind on the southern fringe of the Sahara, occurring in periods when the north-east trade winds dominate the area. The *simoom* of Iran and Pakistan is a fairly constant, north-westerly summer wind.

The *haboobs* or dust storms of the northern Sudan may also reduce visibility to a few metres, and bring about almost complete darkness in the middle of the day. Equally spectacular and uncomfortable are the *chubaseos* or tropical hurricanes of the North American deserts. Another familiar phenomenon, the whirlwind, 'dust-devil' or *tornillo* results from a sudden, irregular upward rush of heated air on a still day. Such columnar vortices carry sand and other objects from the soil surface to a great height. Throughout the arid regions of the world, the distribution of plants is often determined by the presence or absence of shelter from the wind.[37]

MICROCLIMATES

Although general climatic conditions are important in determining the possibilities for agriculture and pastoralism in arid regions, individual plants and animals usually evade the full rigours of the environment by inhabiting localities with favourable microclimates. Many small desert animals pass the day sheltering down holes in the ground, or in cracks of rocks, where they are insulated from the sun's heat. Violent diurnal and annual temperature fluctuations are characteristic of the upper layers of the soil in deserts. Thus, a diurnal range of 56.5 K, which is nearly the same as the yearly range, has been recorded at a depth of 0.4 cm in Arizona. The effects are not transmitted much below the surface, however, and a relatively moderate and constant temperature is found at 100–200 cm depth, which is well within the range of burrowing animals.[91]

Even mammals that are too large to burrow, and diurnal birds, exploit situations in which climatic extremes are avoided. Large flying species, such as eagles and vultures, soar in the cooler, upper air during the day, while smaller birds such as larks and chats shelter in bushes or in the shade of rocks. Only owls and nightjars are nocturnal. Goats and gazelles, likewise, rest in the shade whenever it is available. Provision of artificial shelter for sheep and cattle is economically important in arid ranches where no natural shade is available, because it results in more rapid growth and increased productivity.

Observations on desert microclimates in the Red Sea hills and coastal plain, for example, show that, given a very small reduction in conditions of extreme heat or dryness, an ecological chain can hang on even such superficially unrewarding matter as dry vegetation. Animal distribution tends to be influenced by extremes rather than by means and, in one series of *jebels* or hills, a surface temperature of 83.5°C (182.5°F) was recorded. The only animal to be seen was a solitary grasshopper but, four hours later, when the temperature had dropped to about 40°C (104°F) some ants ventured out. Low humidities were recorded, even among the roots of grasses, and the primary biological advantage of vegetation apparently lay in the reduction of temperature afforded by its shade.[22]

Dune sands may have a surprisingly high humidity. Even during summer, the air surrounding loose grains at a depth as little as 50 cm in the Sahara has a relative humidity as high as 50 per cent. This moisture can be of vital importance to animals and, when the dunes are stabilized, to plants. It arises from water, derived from rainfall in the Atlas, Hoggar and Tibesti mountains, which underlies much of the desert.[91] Moreover, rain water descends very quickly through wind-blown sand because its permeability is high and it has low anti-wetting properties. Owing to capillarity, a given charge of water applied to the surface of dry sand will only sink to a certain depth, which is about eight times greater than the immediate precipitation. Water that has reached a level of 20–30 cm remains as a moist, unsaturated zone for several years because the temperature is almost constant and there is no ventilation.[6] Exploitation of such microclimates is an essential factor in the survival of many desert plants as well as of animals.

2

Soils

DESERT SOILS

Desert soils are produced almost entirely by mechanical and chemical weathering of rock. Despite uniformly low precipitation and high potential evaporation, they are quite variable in their physical, chemical and biological properties. Fine-textured saline soils of depressions are as typical of arid regions as are upland gravelly surfaces. Chemical weathering is considerable, even in arid climates, because its effect is increased by high temperatures. Although rain storms are rare, they exert a profound effect on bare rock and soil unprotected by vegetation. Furthermore, exposed rock experiences wide and rapid temperature variations. If moisture is present, it is broken up, perhaps by differential expansion and contraction of its mineral constituents, to form screes or *bajadas*, and aprons of rocky waste which, as their tops erode, gradually bury the bases of rocks, cliffs and even hills in the products of their own decay. Finally, rocks are abraded by wind-blown sand and the grinding by torrential desert stream flows.

A striking result of wind action is the shaping of stones so that one or more sides are flattened. Usually three-edged, faceted pebbles, known as *dreikanter*, are produced. These are pitted if the stone is not of uniform hardness.

ALLUVIAL DEPOSITS

The high intensity of precipitation in arid regions, where there is little plant growth to provide protection, leads to high rates of run-off and rapid removal of weathered material. With wind erosion, this tends to prevent the formation *in situ* of soils of much thickness. Conversely, sites of accumu-

Table 2.1 Soils of arid zones.

Extremely arid areas (0–100 mm rain)

Desert Soils Weathered rock, no true 'soil'. Nutrients are present but vegetation is inhibited by drought.

Arid areas (100–250 mm rain)

Soil development limited to short periods annually. Little leaching and very low organic content (c. 1 per cent).

Sierozems The A (surface) horizon is weakly developed, light grey: the B (lower) horizon, if present, is fine textured. Weakly calcareous in surface levels.

Brown soils The A horizon with a distinct crumb structure, grading into a brown B horizon. Calcareous throughout, often overlying a zone of lime accumulation.

Tropical brown soils As above, with even lower organic content in A horizon. Weakly calcareous with accumulations of calcium carbonate or silicate clays in deeper layers.

Semi-arid areas (250–350 mm rain)

Yellow soils A horizon with moderate organic content: B horizon yellowish brown with more clay than C horizon. Usually calcareous.

Chestnut soils As above. A horizon thick (30–50 cm) and granular, its organic content in the form of mull—the humus of well aerated soil. Support low grass steppe or scrub: grade into chernozems or black earths of fertile steppe regions.

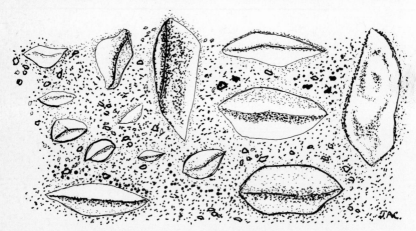

Fig. 2.1 Dreikanter. (Drawing: Anne Cloudsley-Thompson.)

lation tend to have deep deposits. Thus the depressions of rocky desert are frequently filled with deep, coarse sediment. When temporary watercourses (called *wadis* throughout North Africa and the Middle East, *arroyos* in America and *nalas* in Pakistan) terminate in alluvial basins, the sediments they carry become stratified. Gradually they extend until the whole internal drainage basin is filled, forming an immense level plain. Such plains include stony desert with a mosaic surface of gravel, the *reg* of the western Sahara, or of pebbles, the *serir* of Libya and Egypt. In North America, alluvial desert plains are called *playas*, after the Spanish word meaning 'a beach': temporary lakes often form in them after rain. When dry, however, such areas are usually covered with glistening salts whose whiteness reflects the dazzling sunshine. Under humid conditions, soluble salts are leached away forming pedalfers but, where water is scarce, pedocals are formed. In these, calcium and sodium carbonates and sulphates, as well as other salts, remain in the profile.[24]

Saline crusts, covering large areas in enclosed basins, also include the Quattara depression in the Western desert of Egypt, the *chotts* of Algeria and Tunisia, the *sebkhas* of Libya, the salt pans of the Kalahari and many alluvial plains of Central Asia. They can be formed inadvertently through the mis-application of irrigation water (see below). The lakes which develop in the lowest points of *playas* or *sebkhas* are the regions in which the finest sediments are deposited and dissolved salts precipitated. They differ, therefore, from *chotts* and salt pans in which water accumulates and evaporates from artesian sources.[64]

Saline soils offer special problems for subsistence and agriculture. These are not normally possible unless the salt can be washed out by carefully controlled application of irrigation water. Since excessive accumulation of salts is obviously linked with the evaporation of surface water, it can be induced or aggravated by the mismanagement of irrigation water and by unscientific utilization of the land. Moreover, saline ground water may rise to the surface after heavy rain or through excessive irrigation. On the other hand, lowering the level of the saline water-table may leave a high concentration of salt around the roots of fodder plants and cultivated crops.

High salt concentrations may either hinder or assist transport in the desert. The salt flats of Utah in the United States and of Lake Eyre in Australia are associated with attempts on the world land speed record. In contrast, the surfaces of the North African *chotts* are treacherously thin and cover bog in which whole vehicles can easily be swallowed. The salt of the Quattara depression, concealed beneath an apparently firm covering of clay, forms an obstacle to mechanized movement and protected the British southern flank at El Alamein in 1942. Such saline areas could, however, form extremely suitable routes for hovercraft which are easily damaged by rocks and steep *wadi* banks.[120]

Alluvial desert basins, when irrigated, can be very fertile. So may regions of cracking clay or cotton soil, the sites of ancient lakes. Not so the three main types of desert, namely rocky desert (known as *hammada* in the Sahara), stony desert (*reg* or *serir*), and sandy desert (*erg*). *Hammada* is composed of denuded rock plateaux, smoothed and polished by wind abrasion, and flattened by deflation. Libya's great *selima* sand sheet, which stretches for some 7,800 km² (3,000 square miles), consists of a thin layer of sand covering such eroded bedrock. It is not to be expected that much could grow there.

DUNES

Other large desert areas have soils of aeolian origin (aeolian—resulting from wind action). Their dunes may be composed of transported quartz grains, as on the *qoz* soils of the central Sudan, or of carbonate, as in some of the Iranian dunes. In Arizona there are dunes of gypsum; on the plains of Iraq, dunes of finely granulated soil of medium texture; and, in Australia, there are dunes of weathered laterite. Such deposited soils, when composed of wind-blown sand, often take the form of *ergs*—vast, sandy wastes, occupied by great masses of dunes. The Libyan *erg* is as large as France, while each of the two Algerian *ergs* measures at least 150 by 350 km.

Desert dunes may reach a height of 200 m or more in the central Sahara and Rub' al Khali (Empty Quarter) of Arabia. These mountains of sand are known as *draa*, and some of them may have existed for thousands of years. There are two main kinds of sand-dune, *seif* or sword-shaped dunes, and crescent-shaped *barkhan* dunes. *Seif* dunes are caused by strong, uni-directional winds which move both fine and coarse sand, cutting deep troughs parallel with the path of the wind. Transverse dunes result from moderate, one-way winds moving only light sand. Stellar dunes or *rhourds*, with radial buttresses, due to winds that blow from many directions, are found in the great sand seas of the Sahara desert. Dunes of other shapes are sometimes given appropriate names such as parabolic, pyramidal and sigmoidal.[76] In some *ergs*, *rhourds* and *draa* are heaped together with *barkhans* and *seif* dunes between; in others, a more even arrangement is found.

Barkhan dunes occur where sand is relatively scarce and wind direction constant. Their characteristic crescent shape is caused by the fact that sand is blown more rapidly over the advancing horns of the dune than over the central hump. Although relatively rare in the Sahara, they are common in the Arabian and Asian deserts, as well as in North and South America. The gentle, windward slopes (often less than 4°) contrast strongly with the very steep slopes of the leeward sides (about 33°), which correspond roughly to the angle of repose of dry sand. There have been many accidents in the desert when inexperienced drivers have accidentally crossed the ridge of a *barkhan* from the windward to the leeward side.

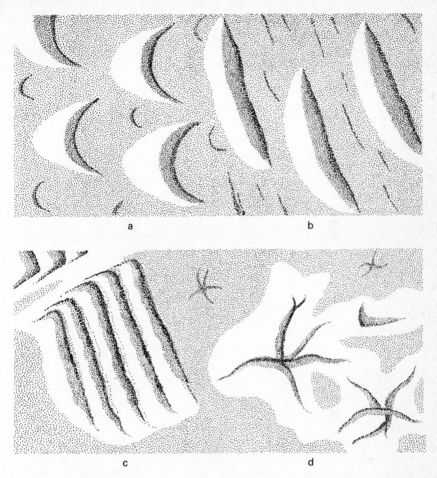

a   b

c   d

Fig. 2.2 Types of desert sand dunes: (a) *Barchan* dunes, (b) Transverse dunes, (c) *Seif* dunes, (d) Stellar dunes.[24, 76]

When *barkhan* and *seif* dunes leave flat areas to join the sand mass of an erg, they lose their distinctive shapes and move slowly in parallel lines known as *anklé* which, from the air, look like a regular pattern of fish scales. When the wind blows, the surface of the sand forms ripples as coarse grains are pushed up windward slopes by the bombardment of smaller, bouncing grains—the smallest sand particles are carried through the air as dust.

Moving dunes impose severe strain on the communications of arid zone countries. Although they can be crossed fairly easily by mechanized vehicles

Fig. 2.3 Wind erosion, central Sahara, Niger.

and prove less wearing than rocky desert on tyres and suspension, they provide an awkward problem for railway engineers. In the first 50 km of the Trans-Caspian railway, between Merv, the Oxus (Amu Darya) and Bokhara, mobile dunes were countered by engineering devices which included soaking the sand with water from the Caspian to give it consistency, covering sections with a layer of clay, and driving wooden stakes into the sand on the windward side of the track so that the dunes could accumulate against them. Other attempts to stabilize the dunes have involved transplantation of tamarisk to the sides of the track from nurseries in the mountains of Iran. Despite these precautions, however, it was still found necessary to maintain labour gangs to keep the lines open. In contrast, construction of the railway across the Grand Erg Oriental, between Biskra and Touggourt, presented no insurmountable obstacles because this huge area of dunes is relatively immobile, and there has been little difficulty in keeping the line open subsequently.[120]

Barkhans rather than *ergs* are the problem of oases, and have caused the collapse of houses, as at Jalo in Libya: it is unknown for *ergs* to bury an oasis. The drifting sand that menaces every desert oasis comes in two forms; slow moving *barkhans* and flying grains carried by strong winds. *Barkhans* tend to travel in clearly defined tracts that are determined by topography, at speeds from about 10 to 20 m per year. When one impinges on a village or cultivated land, the settlement may be overwhelmed unless a belt of tamarisk or other trees is quickly established on the windward side of the dune and as close to it as possible. This prevents fresh sand from reaching it, and also deprives it of its motive force because a new dune arises to windward. This may eventually have to be immobilized in the lee of a second windward belt of trees which, in turn, may require a third.

Flying sand is a more constant nuisance, especially in exposed situations. At In Salah in Algeria the main streets become blocked by drifts of sand several metres deep. Sand also tends to accumulate wherever crops and trees are established so that, as the years pass, all cultivated places rise in level to form low hills which, in turn, cause problems of irrigation. Some protection is obtained by building V-shaped walls in front of important objects such as wells. These walls are given a rough and irregular surface, with large holes left in them, so that the wind is more effectively broken up and the sand deflected to either side. In the endless war against the encroaching sand, which threatens to overwhelm their palm trees, the inhabitants of North African oases contrive complex systems of palm frond hedges. In the Souf, an area 480 km south east from Algiers, the palms are planted deeply in the bottoms of troughs dug into the dunes, so that their roots can reach down to the ground water. In the deeper furrows, the tops of the trees are sunk below the surrounding ground level.[38]

In regions where the rainfall exceeds 150 mm (6 in) per year, sand dunes may be capable of supporting permanent vegetation. Even at the height of the dry season in such areas, the dune sand is moist a short distance below the surface, the rain water that enters the dune being stored from one wet season to the next. Little capillary rise above the water table occurs, and the dry sand on the surface protects the water in the deeper layers from evaporation. If wind removes the surface layers, however, these moist layers become exposed and evaporation is rapid. Such winds also uncover the roots of plants, subjecting them to dehydration and sometimes killing them. Furthermore, the wind-blown sand itself acts as a sand blast and destroys plants above ground. Once vegetation is firmly established, however, the dune surface becomes permanently stabilized; first, because the growing plants provide a natural windbreak which reduces the velocity of the wind near the dune surface and, second, because dead foliage becomes incorporated into the soil and increases its cohesiveness. Thus, the main object of dune stabilization, after the planting of permanent vegetation, is to prevent the movement of sand for a period of 18–24 months, while the plants become established. Conversely, if some of the vegetation stabilizing a dune is removed by overgrazing, the ill effects of this will be sustained and increased by physical causes.

SEMI-DESERT SOILS

The winnowing effect of the wind, sorting out particles of different sizes, transporting and depositing them elsewhere, results in the formation of the various types of desert described above. Sometimes the finest particles of soil are removed so far by wind that they are deposited as loess in the semi-arid steppe lands that border the desert. From the deserts of Asia the wind carries dust to the south and south-east of China; from the Sahara much dust reaches the Atlantic, some is trapped by the Mediterranean and Red Sea, while the remainder is carried to the steppes of Russia and Turkestan. In China alone, there are some 259,300 km² (119,000 square miles) of loess, some of which occurs within humid rather than arid or semi-arid regions.

Although typical yellow loess thus represents an aeolian deposit, its chemical and granulometric composition is by no means uniform. The evolution of loess deposits of central Asia mirrors the development of arid and semi-arid landscapes, under the influence of fluctuating wet and dry climates, in the late Tertiary and Quaternary periods. Consequently, all the morphogenetic processes, including indirect effects of glaciation, will have played a part in its formation. Whatever its ultimate origin, loess has certainly accumulated within historic times; this provides supporting evidence for the human extension of the desert. In northern China, the dead are placed in thick wooden coffins, either resting on the surface of the ground or, sometimes, covered by a low tumulus. The older of these graves now lie beneath deep aeolian deposits of loess.[120]

In semi-arid regions, on the margins of dry desert tracts, where the rainfall varies from 120 to 250 mm (4.7 to 9.8 in) per year, and is of seasonal rather than of sporadic incidence, superficial crusts of lime and gypsum may still occur. But true soils lie beneath. These brown and grey semi-desert soils are known as 'sierozems'. Organic matter is still extremely scarce in them and may comprise less than one per cent of the surface horizon. Nevertheless, sierozems often support low desert-scrub vegetation, including species of *Artemisia*. They, and the climatic regimes in which they appear, are obviously unfit for dry farming except where they are composed of very fine grains on the outer margins of moist flood plains and alluvial fans.

As rainfall increases with increasing length of the rainy season, grassland begins to appear, interspersed at first with low shrubs and bushes. The increased content of humus, which comes from the denser and more luxuriant vegetation, gives rise to darker chestnut-brown soils of the steppe lands. Pedocalic characteristics remain, however, for precipitation is still insufficient to leach calcium carbonate from the soil profile. Chestnut-brown soils are situated in the transition zone where cycles of wet years alternate with years of drought. The former may tempt farmers to extend

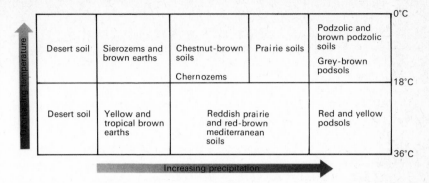

Desert soil	Sierozems and brown earths	Chestnut-brown soils Chernozems	Prairie soils	Podzolic and brown podzolic soils Grey-brown podsols
Desert soil	Yellow and tropical brown earths	Reddish prairie and red-brown mediterranean soils		Red and yellow podsols

Fig. 2.4 Relation between climate and the great soil groups of the world.[4]

the area under cereal cultivation. This invites disastrous crop failures and 'dust bowl' erosion during the period of drought which inevitably follows, sooner or later.

Where annual rainfall exceeds 255 m (10 in), there are found 'chernozems' or black earths, whose humus content may amount to 10 per cent and in which nodules or layers of calcium carbonate occur at or near the base of the 'B' horizon. Chernozems are often developed from loess deposits, and are found in the great cereal growing areas of North America, the Ukraine and of Argentina. Where the rainfall is sufficient to leach away the concretions of calcium carbonate, so that their pedocalic soils become pedalfers, so-called 'prairie soils' like those of the corn belt of North America, are created. These, however, are the products of humid rather than of dry climate, and therefore lie beyond the scope of this book.

Distribution of the various soil types mentioned above is not merely latitudinal. A transect up the slope of a desert massif, rising above its surrounding plains, would grade from desert soils, through sierozems, brown semi-desert and chestnut-brown soils, to chernozems, prairie soils and finally, at high altitude, to leached podsols.[39]

3

Deserts in the Past

Landscapes everywhere are continually changing. The processes of weathering, erosion and deposition are constantly operating on basic geological structures, destroying old landforms and creating new ones. These physiographic processes, induced by arid climates, give the deserts their geomorphic unity, for they do not correspond with any special geological features.

GEOMORPHOLOGY

Some deserts rest upon vast sheets of bedrock that are divided into blocks separated by faults or sharp flexures. Large areas of south-western U.S.A., including the arid regions, for example, exhibit block tectonics. As a result of differential movements between various blocks, there is a basin and range topography with abrupt escarpments between uplands and lowlands. Similar structural landforms are found in some parts of the Gobi desert, the Little Kharas mountains of South-West Africa, and elsewhere.

In contrast, the Sahara is a typical continental platform, a region in which much of the underlying skeleton consists of ancient crystalline and igneous rocks that were subsequently folded and eroded to form a rigid rock shield. (The remainder consists of strongly contorted Pre-Cambrian basement complex, either exposed or covered with sedimentary rocks of Palaeozoic, Mesozoic or Tertiary origin.) Subsequent uprising produced the Hoggar and Tibesti mountains, long before the oldest existing sedimentary rocks were laid down.

Although the Gobi has high mountains, as already mentioned, it also

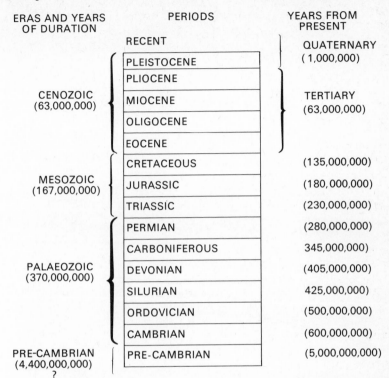

ERAS AND YEARS OF DURATION	PERIODS	YEARS FROM PRESENT
	RECENT	QUATERNARY
	PLEISTOCENE	(1,000,000)
CENOZOIC (63,000,000)	PLIOCENE	
	MIOCENE	TERTIARY (63,000,000)
	OLIGOCENE	
	EOCENE	
MESOZOIC (167,000,000)	CRETACEOUS	(135,000,000)
	JURASSIC	(180,000,000)
	TRIASSIC	(230,000,000)
PALAEOZOIC (370,000,000)	PERMIAN	(280,000,000)
	CARBONIFEROUS	345,000,000)
	DEVONIAN	(405,000,000)
	SILURIAN	425,000,000)
	ORDOVICIAN	(500,000,000)
	CAMBRIAN	(600,000,000)
PRE-CAMBRIAN (4,400,000,000) ?	PRE-CAMBRIAN	(5,000,000,000)

Fig. 3.1 Geological chronology.

possesses platform characteristics, for there are large areas of undeformed Mesozoic sediments in the Gobi basin. Arabia is similar to the Sahara with ranges of rugged mountains on exposed Pre-Cambrian crystalline basement while the Australian shield likewise consists of Pre-Cambrian basement complex bordered by younger rocks. The Thar desert of northwestern India consists largely of a sand plain overlying a peneplain eroded across the basement of the Deccan shield, interrupted only by occasional low outcrops and ridges.

Most of the Sahara was covered by a vast sea throughout much of the Carboniferous period. At this time the sandstone of Adrar and Tassili was deposited. It was followed by a long continental era during the Mesozoic, when the land supported huge marshes, lakes and tropical forests whose fossil remains are associated with those of dinosaurs and other extinct creatures. Sea again covered large areas of the Sahara during the Cretaceous, but there was no continuous flooding this time although the sandstone and limestone of the *hammadas* of Tindouf, Dra and Guir date from then.

24

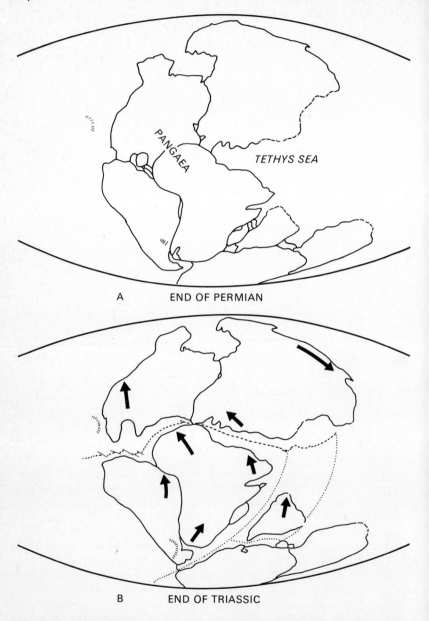

Fig. 3.2 Continental movements during the Mesozoic. It is assumed here that there was a single super-continent (Pangaea) in the Permian (A). The southern and northern continents (Gondwana and Laurasia), separated by the Tethys Sea, appeared at the Triassic (B), by which time South America, Africa and India had broken free from Antartica. By the end of the Cretaceous (C), South America and

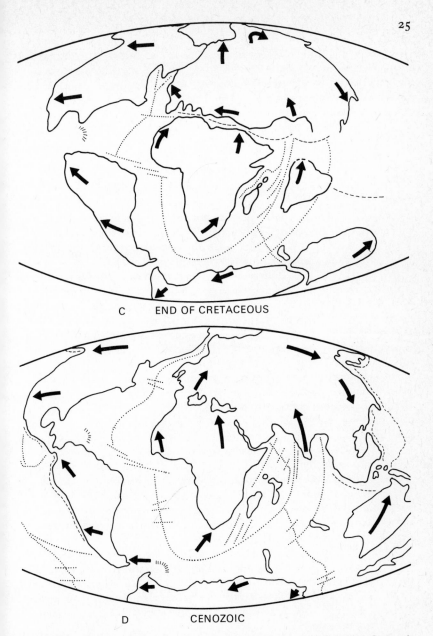

C   END OF CRETACEOUS

D   CENOZOIC

Africa had drifted well apart and India was approaching Asia. The Cenozoic
distribution of the continents is shown in (D). Rifts and ocean ridges, from which
sea-floor spreading is occurring, are shown by dotted lines: arrows indicate
directions of continuing movement patterns[39] (after R. S. Dietz and J. C. Holden).

At the present time, active volcanoes are rare in arid regions, but extinct volcanoes are important in several desert landscapes. There are volcanic mountains and lava flows of Recent age in the Hoggar, Aïr and Tibesti massifs of the Sahara and old ones in Anatolia, Transjordan, Aden and the American deserts. In the neighbourhood of Death Valley, for instance, there are numerous small lava flows and cinder cones.

PALAEOCLIMATES

Desert conditions have occurred more than once during the succession of geological ages, and have played an important role in evolution. The late Silurian and early Devonian periods, for instance, were characterized by increasing climatic aridity. This may have been an impelling factor in the evolution of air-breathing vertebrates, through drying up of the streams, lakes and swamps which harboured their gilled ancestors.

World climates have undergone several periods of great change during the last 1,000 million years for which good stratigraphical evidence is available. Ice ages have alternated with periods when tropical climates extended as far as 50°–60° north and south of the equator, and even the polar regions were quite warm. In these changing conditions, regions that are desert today have sometimes been well watered while, at other times, lands now humid have been dry and barren.

An outstanding example of an ancient desert which can be identified from dune forms preserved in the stratigraphic record is provided by the Botucatú sandstone of South America. This is a fine-grained rock, predominantly quartzite, of which the larger grains are well rounded. They exhibit minute pitting and a veneer of red ferric oxide, sedimentological features typical of aeolian deposits.

Botucatú is but one of several deserts that probably existed in Permo-Triassic times, although it is the only example in which dune forms are both preserved and exposed as sandstone. In some localities, the dunes have been protected by lava flows and are sometimes conveniently exposed in railway cuttings. Today, the Paraná basin, in which this sandstone lies, experiences an annual rainfall of 100–200 cm (40–80 in).

Sands of aeolian origin, containing wind-faceted pebbles or *dreikanter* (p. 13) are fairly frequent in British Permo-Triassic deposits. They are particularly common in the Lower Permian sand sea, where many dune structures are known. Dune-bedded sands are also abundant in western U.S.A., ranging in age from the Upper Carboniferous (Pennsylvanian) to the Upper Jurassic.[18]

No account of arid regions in the world today can omit reference to the relatively recent climatic changes of the Quaternary period. Since the Pliocene epoch there have been several ice ages and interglacial periods, whose effects on living organisms, soils and geomorphology are still with us. Indeed, earlier events of the Tertiary may also be of direct significance since fossil soils of that period are still preserved in the present land surface, especially in arid regions. Moreover, many major geological and geomorphological features of current importance were initiated at that time.

Pluvial periods, during which the rainfall increased in duration and intensity for sufficiently long to be of geological significance, have occurred at intervals throughout the Quaternary era. They affected not only the great desert areas and their margins, but also wide expanses of semi-arid grasslands, from the equator to mid-latitudes.

About five million years ago in Africa, shifting desert sands stretched from the Congo River to the Cape. On later occasions, the present Kalahari desert has almost disappeared. There have been times when regions of Africa supported great lakes where, today, even drinking water is unavailable. The Olduvai Gorge of Tanzania, in which have been found the earliest artefacts and cultural traces of man, is one such site.

The most recent series of pluvial periods began with the onset of the Pleistocene epoch, perhaps one million years ago, when climates changed markedly throughout most of the world. Higher latitudes were subjected to a rhythm of glacial and interglacial periods while, nearer the equator, an even more complex succession of pluvials and interpluvials followed one another. During episodes of glaciation there was a tendency for the rainfall to increase in the interior continental deserts of high latitudes. At such times, the sea-level was lowered by 100 m or more, because so much water was incorporated in the polar ice-caps.

Much of this water was later released during the warmer interglacials, and the sea-level rose. Such fluctuations of sea-level should, therefore, provide good stratigraphic markers of the various glacial and pluvial periods; but they do not necessarily bear any relationship to the fluctuations of interior lakes. There is, moreover, no justification for assuming that pluvials in the tropics and sub-tropics can be correlated directly with glacial periods in temperate regions of the world. Ill-advised attempts to do so have resulted in error and confusion. There have been moist, cool intervals in low latitude dry areas, as well as dry, cool intervals, moist, warm intervals, and dry, warm intervals. In addition, there have been times when there was an ice-mass in the South Atlantic only, and others when there were two polar ice caps. An effect of the northern cap has been to cause the north-east trade winds to blow further south. It has also deflected the temperate climate depression tracks southward, engendering increased rainfall on the northern edge of the Sahara.[39]

During the last interglacial in the Sahara, the climate probably changed from warm and comparatively dry to warm and comparatively moist;

while the last glacial period began cool and comparatively moist, afterwards changing to cold and dry.

It is believed that the maximum of the last Pleistocene pluvial phase dates back to more than 50,000 years B.P. (before the present) and that all pluvial characteristics had ended well before the close of the Pleistocene, some 10,000 years ago. The closed Alexandersfontein depression, near Kimberley, now only an evaporation pan, harboured a lake 19 m in depth and with a surface area of 44 km², a little before 16,000 B.P. Assuming a temperature depression of 6 K, calculations show that rainfall was about double that of today.

From a study of the *qoz* dune systems of Kordofan in central Sudan, it has been deduced that these have been influenced by four different climatic periods. The first occurred during the Middle and Late Pleistocene (*c.* 25,000 B.P.) and was very arid. Wind and rainfall belts were then some 450 km south of their present positions. The second phase (*c.* 11,000 B.P.) was comparatively wet and there was a climatic shift to approximately 250 km north of the present situation. During the third phase (*c.* 10,000–7,000 B.P.) dry conditions were again experienced: wind and rainfall belts were 200 km south of their present location. Finally, there was a second humid period (7,000–5,000 B.P.) when the belts occupied a position 100 km north of their present positions. By this time, the climate of the world's arid zones had approached a mean not unlike that of the present. Although the climate may have continued to fluctuate slightly in Recent times, there have been no very marked changes since man's influence on the terrestrial environment first reached significant proportions.[121]

It must always be remembered that the climate in desert and semi-arid regions tends to be very variable, with erratic rainfall. Unusually long, dry periods may therefore result in the destruction of relict elements of the flora and fauna that have survived since the last pluvial period. Once this has occurred, there is very little chance of the desert being subsequently recolonized from less arid areas. Thus, random climatic variations may have been responsible for progressive elimination of many glacial relics of the desert flora and fauna, so that a steady deterioration has taken place quite naturally. This has been greatly accelerated, however, through bad agricultural practices, the reckless destruction of trees, and overgrazing by domestic animals, especially goats.

In the following chapters, I shall outline the extent to which human activities have been responsible for creating new deserts, and extending existing ones throughout the world.

4

Man-made Deserts of the World

THE ORIGIN OF SAVANNA

A traveller, moving northwards from the African rain-forest, will cross several broad zones of savanna vegetation before he reaches the Sahara desert.[29, 74] Three main types of savanna are generally recognized, but their boundaries are by no means clear. Tropical forest grades into wooded 'Guinea savanna' where the rainfall exceeds 100 cm (40 in) in a year, although the dry season is severe. Characteristic trees are species of *Isoberlinia*, such as *I. doka*, which, unlike the components of rain-forest, tolerate the fires to which they are subjected annually during the course of the dry season. North of the Guinea savanna belt lies a zone of vegetation known as 'Sudan savanna' where the annual rainfall is in the region of 50–100 cm (20–40 in) and the dry season lasts from October to April. Typical trees include *Acacia seyal*, the dôm palm (*Hyphaene thebaica*) and the massive baobab or tebaldi (*Adansonia digitata*), the trunks of which are hollowed out by the people of Darfur to store water during the dry season.

The southern border of the Saharan desert steppe is known as 'Sahel savanna'. This enjoys a rainfall of only 25–50 cm (10–20 in) concentrated in four to five months of the year. The vegetation here is mostly of thorn-land type, consisting of grasses and trees usually less than 10 m high. *Acacia mellifera* is characteristic of clay soil, *A. senegal* of sand. Other species include *A. raddiana*, *Commiphora africana*, *Leptadenia pyrotechnica*, *Salvadora persica* and species of *Grewea*. Grasses are sparse and seldom exceed one metre in height, so that fires tend not to be so fierce and extensive as in the Sudan savanna belt.[92]

Large areas of primary rain-forest are still to be found in the Congo basin and parts of the Cameroons, with smaller patches in Eastern Africa;

Fig. 4.1   Miombo savanna Zambia.

Fig. 4.2 Sudan savanna, with baboons. Dinder.

Fig. 4.3 Sahel savanna, Sudan.

Fig. 4.4 Goats browsing in a *wadi* bed.

Fig. 4.5 Chihuahan desert, New Mexico, an area that supported tall grass and grazing cattle at the beginning of this century.

but extensive regions have been cleared in recent years throughout West Africa. Nigeria has clearly suffered more in respect of forest clearance than Ghana or Côte d'Ivoire, for example, because very little mature secondary forest remains there either. This is probably correlated with the greater density of population in Nigeria. Buttressed forest trees extend through the Guinea savanna of Côte d'Ivoire into the Sudan and Sahel savannas of Haute Volta and Mali, and it seems probable that most of the African savanna exists in its present form as a result of human activity.[36] Guinea savanna, like 'Miombo savanna', its counterpart south of the Equator, was probably originally thick woodland or forest, although its floral composition must have differed from that of tropical evergreen rain-forest, because it would have experienced less precipitation and a longer dry season. Sudan and Sahel savanna have, doubtless, also been profoundly affected by man.[90]

SHIFTING CULTIVATION

Although the range of variation in savanna vegetation is considerable, there is characteristically always sufficient light passing through the canopy of the trees for a layer of grass to develop underneath. This grass may be very tall or relatively short, but its presence clearly distinguishes wooded

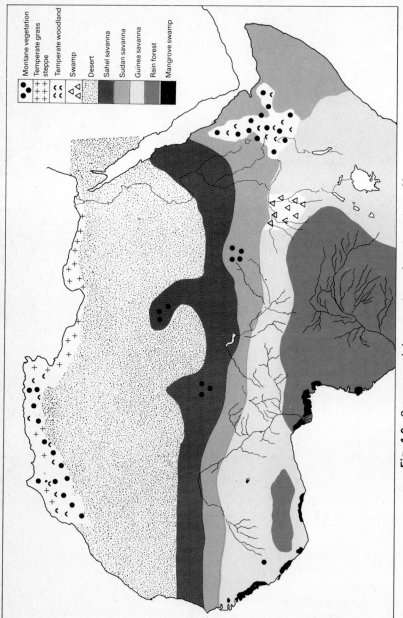

Fig. 4.6 Savanna and desert regions of northern Africa.[36]

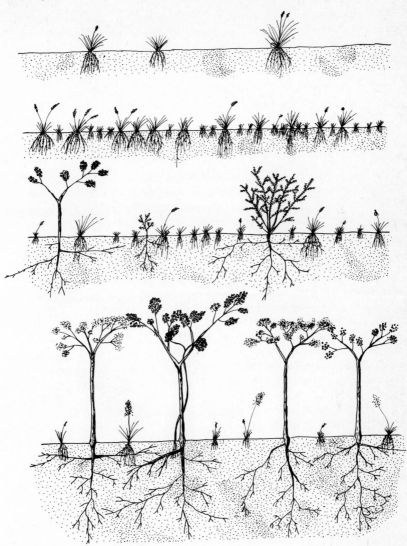

Fig. 4.7 Schematic profiles of desert, grassland, Sahel and Sudan savanna. (Not to the same scale.)

savanna from true forest, where grass is practically absent apart from a few specialized, broad-leaved species. Savanna usually begins where the rainfall is about 115 cm (45 in) per year, but there are areas of savanna in which rainfall exceeds 150 cm (60 in).[57] Even in these, however, precipitation is markedly seasonal so that grass fires can occur at regular intervals. For, it seems, much of the savanna is maintained by regular burning. If protected from annual fires, it soon becomes closed woodland.[90]

The destruction of the African forest and the resulting savanna doubtless began when man first acquired the use of fire. This was probably well over 50,000 years ago; for already, between 50,000 and 60,000 B.P., hearths were being used systematically by Acheulian peoples at lake-side sites by the Kolambo Falls, near the south-east corner of Lake Tanganyika.[122] Fire is an essential tool in the shifting cultivation by which so much of the forest has been destroyed.

Although fires must occur naturally from time to time, deliberate firing by man has a far greater effect upon the vegetation. This is because a man-made fire covers the same ground more frequently and, moreover, is not associated with thunderstorms, the rain from which may quench the fires that lightning has started.[89]

Fire does not usually spread continuously over whole tracts of vegetation. Normally, small patches are burned and, later, neighbouring patches, so that a mosaic pattern is produced. Some areas may even be burned twice annually, while others escape from one year to the next. Fire favours perennial grasses with underground stems, which regenerate rapidly and produce new green shoots. These may even be stimulated by the burning. In contrast, trees are always more or less damaged by fire. Their trunks become twisted and gnarled, and many of the species that survive best have stems covered with thick, protective bark. Others regenerate from suckers produced by their roots. Intermediate types of vegetation tend to be eliminated by constant burning so that stark contrasts are created between wooded grasslands which feed roaring bush fires, and the evergreen forest too humid to support a blaze unless it has first been felled and dried.[36, 89]

Since the savanna belts of Africa have developed contemporaneously with the evolution of man there is, perhaps, little point in trying to reconstruct their possible floristic and faunal composition, had man not appeared to make them what they now are. It is enough to realize that mankind has had a very pronounced effect on the savanna regions of Africa and that probably only remnants of the rain-forest represent an ecosystem as yet untouched by human influence.

Most of the inhabitants of tropical forest today live as farmers. Although they take advantage of any available game or fish (duikers (*Cephalophus* spp.), cane rats (*Thryonomys swinderianus*), and so on, provide 20 per cent of the mean annual consumption of animal protein in rural areas of Nigeria), most of their food comes from cultivation of crops grown in temporary forest clearings. Trees are felled and burned, and crops planted. After a year or two, however, the fertility of the soil decreases, the clearing is abandoned and a new one created. Consequently, shifting cultivation results in the destruction of huge areas of forest. When it is remembered that over 200,000,000 people in Africa, Asia, Central and South America obtain their livelihood in this way, the rapid depletion of the forest is not difficult to understand.

The largest trees are often spared, but the smaller trunks and branches are piled together, and burned as soon as they are dry. When necessary, partly burned wood is gathered up for a second time and burned again. Even so, the ground becomes littered with charred and partially destroyed logs and branches, while dead and blackened stumps cut off a couple of metres above ground level, remain scattered throughout the clearings. Seeds are planted irregularly, with the aid of a hoe or digging stick, but no attempt is made to plough the land.

Although shifting cultivation results in the loss of much of the mineral nutrient in the soil, the land gradually recovers, and new trees create secondary forest which is often quite unlike the original primary rain-forest. These trees are much shorter than the giants they replaced, and are all of relatively fast-growing species. It would probably take centuries for climax primary forest to re-establish itself. With rapidly increasing human populations, and the constant need for more farmland, however, the young forests are seldom left undisturbed for more than 15–20 years, by which time the soil will have recovered sufficiently to support a second food crop. But this process cannot continue indefinitely, and eventually the forest deteriorates into wooded savanna, which is maintained by regular burning of the grass. This has occurred extensively in eastern Africa in particular.[110]

The park-like savanna ecosystem of tropical Africa is not a climax, but is maintained largely by the delicately balanced interaction of climate, soils, vegetation, animals and fire. The association between plant and animal life is extremely complex, and alteration of any of the components of the dynamic equilibrium usually affects the whole ecosystem—that is, the ecological system formed by the interaction of all the animals and plants with their environment. Although frequent fires occur, they are not always necessary for the maintenance of savanna.

In East Africa, however, savanna has long been maintained by regular burning of the grass. Without this, the conditions which used to support such magnificent herds of wild beasts and, in parts, still do so, would never have been created. Protection from fire encourages the growth of trees and causes a retreat of the grass. Consequently, the environment becomes less favourable to the big ruminants and their carnivorous followers, and the fauna changes. The original agriculturalists, who destroyed the forests, were replaced by pastoral people. For centuries, these have regularly burned the grass to provide grazing for their cattle. In so doing, they have created the large herds of game animals which are so characteristic of the savanna. A similar process has been responsible for the conditions under which vast herds of bison arose in much of North America.

Wholesale felling of forests creates extreme changes that destroy the entire forest ecosystem. Much of the fauna and the smaller forest plants that depend on the trees for shade, rapidly disappear. A deep humus layer is seldom to be found in tropical forest. When exposed to the elements, the topsoil is soon eroded: this, in turn, reduces the capacity of the ground to retain water. The flooding along many great rivers, from the Yangtze-Kiang in China to the rivers of California, has been greatly aggravated by heavy logging in their watersheds.

The small quantity of humus in tropical forest soils is occasioned by a combination of moisture and high temperatures that accelerate the activities of bacteria, fungi, termites and other soil organisms which engender its breakdown. Savanna and grassland soils tend to dry out more and, therefore, retain more humus. They are also not affected by burning to the same extent as are forest soils, and consequently are more stable. The vegetation, however, is greatly influenced by burning, as is shown by the prevalence of 'pyrophytic' or fire-resisting trees and shrubs. Of course, burning must have occurred naturally in pre-human times, but not to the same extent: as we have already noted, fires started by lightning may be quenched by rain (see p. 36).

FOREST PEOPLES

Men have not always destroyed the land in which they live. For centuries, tropical forests were the home of primitive peoples, who had no knowledge of agriculture, and used only stone and wooden tools, so that their influence on the environment was insignificant. Few human races today, except African Pygmies and the Punans of Borneo, continue to exist in such a state of equilibrium with their surroundings. The Punans have no permanent dwellings, but construct flimsy shelters from branches and palm leaves. These are inhabited only for a few weeks before their owners move on to new locations. In addition to hunting for wild pigs, monkeys and other game, the Punans extract wild sago from the stems of a palm that grows in swampy regions of the forest. This forms their staple diet. Pygmies, likewise, live mainly by hunting with bows and poisoned arrows, as do some of the more primitive South American Indians.

Few forest tribes today exist in this way, entirely on what they can hunt and gather in the wild. Most forest-dwelling people live in more or less permanent settlements and cultivate food crops in the clearings. They are very assiduous in removing trees, which is not really surprising, because the forest is not an easy place for men to inhabit. Not only is felling and burning necessary to let light into the gloomy depths of the forest and to provide fertile ashes for cultivation to take place, but the forest itself can be a danger. It provides cover behind which predators lurk and enemies can approach unobserved. Even today, many people find that dense forest induces a feeling of claustrophobia: they experience quite a sense of relief on leaving it for more open country.

There are now few terrestrial environments that have not been grossly affected by human activities. Exceptions are the remaining areas of rain-forest in Africa, South America and South-East Asia, the taiga or coni-ferous forest of sub-arctic Eurasia and America, the tundra, and the snow-lands. This does not mean that all the savanna of the world has been produced from forest, or that desert is entirely man-made. Indeed, the Sahara has been constantly expanding and contracting throughout the Pleistocene era, purely as a result of climatic changes, but, as explained in the previous chapter, it has been greatly enlarged under man's influence, especially during the last century.

During the history of mankind, the human stock has passed through four great ecological epochs. The first, and longest, ended when our an-cestors first left the African rain-forest. The second witnessed the progres-sive development of a terrestrial, hunting way of life. As a result of this, the third epoch was one of enormous ecological expansion, and a wide variety of habitats was successfully colonized. The last epoch, in which we are still living, has been one in which man has deliberately controlled and modified his environment.

Early man (*Homo erectus*) in Africa, like the Australopithecines before him, lived an active life as hunter and collector in a hot climate. Fire was probably used for the first time by Pekin man (*H. erectus pekinensis*) who inhabited caves at Choukoutien about 400,000 years B.P., at the time of the second glaciation (Mindel II) in Europe. As already mentioned, fire was not used in Africa until 60,000 B.P. or even later, by *H. sapiens*. Since mesolithic cultures persisted throughout Africa south of the Sahara until a mere 7,000 or 8,000 years ago, it would seem that most of the changes induced by shifting cultivation that we have been discussing, must date from that short time ago.[122]

The introduction of farming everywhere has been a slow process. Cereal cultivation is believed to have been first adopted in Africa, probably early in the seventh millennium B.P., when much of the Sahara was well-watered and covered with bushes, and could be exploited by incoming horti-culturalists. This was during the Makalian wet phase (Table 4.1), and the first cultivators may have arisen from Mesolithic groups who moved north-wards from the densely wooded savanna of west and central Africa. A later, post-Makalian dry phase forced cereal cultivation to spread further south and, after 5,000 B.P., it was progressively taken up by sub-Saharan popula-

Table 4.1 Chronology of Late Pleistocene and Holocene climates in Europe, East Africa, Sudan and the Sahara. Dates in years before the present.

Europe	East Africa[42]	Sudan[65]	Sahara[8]
Sub-Atlantic	Nakuran	Present day climate −1800	Hot
−2700	−2800	Perhaps slightly wetter −3500	−2500
Sub-boreal	Drier	Final abandonment of sites in northern desert −4000	Warmer
−5000	−4500	Cattle-owning people in northern desert −550	−4800
Atlantic	Makalian	Rainfall at Khartoum c. 500 mm	Probably gradually becoming warmer
−7800	−7500	−7000	
Boreal −8700	Makalian I?	Rainfall at Khartoum c. 700 mm	
Pre-boreal	−10,000	−10,000 ? Sand invasions	
10,600	Drier −12,000	of Kordofan −12,000	Temperate −12,000
Late Glacial	Gamblian 3 −14,500	Formation of Gezira plain	
	Drier	Rainfall in the Gezira	Cold
−17,000		c. 70 mm	
Würm Main Phase			

tions. Great discoveries are often made, and re-made, several times independently. Because there was little open savanna, Neolithic food-gatherers in the forest may well have developed shifting cultivation, in different places at different times, without the benefit of ideas first acquired in the Near East. The advances of civilization have not invariably followed along a single path. Ideas and discoveries have tended to crop up independently, like isolated crystals forming in a super-saturated solution of salts. They have not always developed at one centre of nucleation.

During the early stages of agriculture, cultivation was merely an adjunct to hunting, fishing and food gathering. Later developments were based partly on a knowledge of sorghum, probably acquired from Ethiopia, and partly on the local development of yams, oil palms, pumpkins, bananas and pulses. At first, men lived beside lakes and rivers and on the fringes of the forest but, after 3,000 B.P. Neolithic food-producing communities were established at the forest margins and in the savanna. These possessed various tools, such as the adze, axe and hoe, so that, from this time, shifting agriculture must have developed widely. Sorghum provided a basis for the successful spread of cultivation from the zone between western Ethiopia and Nigeria into eastern central and southern Africa.

PASTORALISM

In areas where the soil became so impoverished that agriculture was no longer profitable, cultivation was replaced by pastoralism, which dates from no earlier than 3,000 B.P. The keeping of cattle diffused into East Africa from its main origin in southern Arabia, via Nubia and the Horn of Africa. Not a single fossil of any animal that could be regarded as ancestral to the domestic ox has been found in African deposits older than about 3,000 years.

Introduction of cattle into the tsetse-free pastures created by cultivators has occurred on at least three occasions. The first to be introduced were humpless longhorns such as the Ankole cattle of Uganda which have acquired resistance to trypanosomiasis through their long association with the disease. The second type to be introduced was a humpless shorthorn strain which has also adjusted to tsetse. More recently, waves of Zebu and cross breeds (Sanga etc.) have been introduced wherever there was enough fly-free pasture to permit nomadism, and these have acquired little resistance to trypanosomiasis (see p. 138). There is no doubt that the presence of tsetse flies and trypanosomes has protected much of tropical Africa from the tramping and overgrazing that result in soil erosion and the production of desert conditions.[54]

It has sometimes been argued that the recent expansion of the Sahara may have been caused by a change in meteorological conditions. Rainfall in the Mediterranean and Middle East, in the Sahel zone and in north-west India have been related since the beginning of the century to changes in the general circulation of the atmosphere. Because of the low mean annual rainfall (80–250 mm) and the strong north-south gradient of precipitation in the Sahel savanna, a shift of the climatic zones of only 1° of latitude in 100 years would mean a decrease in rainfall of some 40–50 per cent.[123] In the more humid zones further south, where the mean annual rainfall is up to 3,000 mm, a similar shift of the isohyets corresponds to a decrease in annual precipitation of only 10 per cent. I would not deny that changes of this nature may have taken place, but I do not believe that they can be responsible for the enormous expansion of the Sahara that has occurred in recent times and especially during the last hundred years, and which is discussed in the following chapter.[33, 36] At the same time, removal of the vegetation by overgrazing increases the albedo (reflectivity) of the land surface, and this may inhibit rainfall. Furthermore, fine atmospheric dust can cause an inversion of temperature so that the air is hotter at higher levels over the Sahelian zone, than nearer the surface of the ground. This prevents the formations of rain-bearing cumulus cloud. Perhaps 160 million tons of soil (more than the total silt carried by the Nile) are lost annually from the Sahara and Sahel savanna.

Some idea of the extent to which man has contributed to the creation of desert conditions throughout the world is indicated by the fact that, in 1882, land classified either as desert or wasteland amounted to 9.4 per cent of the total terrestrial environment. In 1952, it had risen to 23.3 per cent. During the same period, land carrying inaccessible forest decreased from 43.9 per cent to 21.1 per cent.[52] Although such figures are of limited value because definitions are not provided, they do give some idea of the magnitude of the problem.

Alexander and his army, during their advance into India, marched through areas of virgin forest where now only desert is to be found. Like the Sahara, the great Thar desert of western India is the result of man's influence. Some 2,000 years B.P., what is now the centre of this desert was a jungle. Not long ago, in Zambia, I met an Indian botanist who told me that he had been born in a village surrounded by forest. He recently returned to his parents' home and found, to his horror, that it is now situated in the desert. The spread of this desert, formed primarily by felling the trees, tramping, and overgrazing, has accelerated in recent years. For nearly a century, it has been increasing at a rate of about 8 km per decade around its entire perimeter. It now occupies about 155,000 km² (60,000 sq. miles).

The use of artesian wells and intensive farming of date palms in parts of North Africa have had a dramatic effect on the water balance (p. 161). Since 1881, the number of palms in the border region of the Tunisian Sahara has increased by more than 50 per cent, reducing the level of subterranean water at a rate of 5 cm per annum. (A well at Azaouad in Mali is over 100 m deep—it has been deepened progressively over the centuries as the water table has fallen.) Even now, however, it may not be too late to take steps to rectify the situation, at least partially. At one farm site north of Nefta, an area of 50 hectares has been protected by barbed wire for the past 60 years. Here, the original vegetation has been restored, with an average soil coverage of more than 80 per cent, a figure which contrasts dramatically with 5 per cent coverage by the degraded vegetation on the other side of the fence.[38]

In Somalia and the Horn of Africa, the creation of desert has proceeded at an alarming rate. As already mentioned, pleasant, park-like country, inhabited by herds of game, has been reduced within living memory to a grim wasteland, without cover and eroded to a serious extent. Only a few dead stumps now show where *Juniperus procera* thrived; lions were common there, and the plains were full of hartebeest, oryx and gazelle. The semi-arid Karoo is likewise estimated to have increased by nearly 50 per cent in recent years; and similar change has taken place in other parts of the world. Much of the Chihuahuan desert around Las Cruces in New Mexico was covered with lush grass at the beginning of the century. Too many cattle were grazed there, however; too many people became rich too quickly. So now the land is desert, and its productivity destroyed. The original vegetation has been replaced by the expansion of Mexican floral species, as has also occurred in the Sonoran desert of Arizona. The Colorado Plateau is likewise by all definitions a major desert area. Various historical records, however, indicate that grazing by domestic cattle since 1870 has been a major factor in shaping the vegetation and edaphic conditions. The floristic poverty of the area could be explained on the basis of the inability of Mexican species to survive severely cold winters.

Even the vast Amazon rain-forest is being ravaged. Trees are felled and the soil dug and cultivated. After a few years of continual rain and the exhaustion of the ground, the coffee plantations are moved to an area where the soil is fresher and more fertile. In South America, the relationship between man and the earth has never been marked by that reciprocity of attention which has been the basis of prosperity in much of the Old World. Yet, even so, the heathland of Britain was formerly forest. The trees were felled to provide pasture for sheep and, after the fertility of the land had been destroyed, bracken, heath and heather took over.

In comparison with the long-established and expanding deserts of Asia and Africa, the dust-bowls of North America are less significant. When the natural grassland vegetation was ploughed up, however, and imported cereals harvested in its stead, the land lost its fertility. The top soil, without cohesion, blew away in dust storms and the land became desert although by no means climatically arid. Consequently more soil was probably lost to the world through erosion between 1914 and 1934 than in the whole of previous human history.[25] The awesome Sistan desert of Iran and Afghanistan was fertile agricultural land as recently as the fifteenth century, when ancient fields supported the large estates of the Islamic period and gave the region the name 'granary of the East'. A good river system existed throughout the arid zone of India during Vedic times, and the Thar desert is estimated as being only 5,000–10,000 years old.

Enough has been said to illustrate the part played by man during the last few centuries in the expansion of existing deserts throughout the world and in the creation of new ones. One has only to travel with an observant eye, to realize how little of the world remains in its pristine state. In later chapters we shall see how plants and animals are able to survive in desert conditions, and consider how they may be exploited for the benefit of mankind.

5

The Expanding Sahara—A Case History

There is plentiful evidence for the existence in North Africa of dry conditions during Cretaceous and Tertiary times, as well as more recently. The presence of an arid zone in northern Africa is therefore almost certainly the direct result of fundamental features of atmospheric circulation. Nevertheless, it is generally agreed that the Sahara was not desert at least during portions of the Pleistocene and post-Pleistocene times, and that the recent extinction of much of the flora and fauna can be ascribed to phases of severe climatic deterioration. The evidence for a change in the climate of the region is undeniable, for the desert is dotted with upper Palaeolithic to Neolithic rock engravings, as well as the fossil remains of elephant, rhinoceros, hippopotamus, giraffe, and even of domestic animals, whose present range lies well outside the areas of the petroglyphs.[43]

CLIMATE, PAST AND PRESENT

The climate of the Sahara today is controlled by a subtropical anticyclone, the explanation of which is not known. This occurs both at ground level and aloft, and the subsidence of dry air (p. 4) caused by it is responsible for the extreme aridity of this part of the world. During interglacial periods, the inter-tropical convergence front, at which the tropical air-masses of the two hemispheres meet, would have moved further north in summer than it does today. Depending upon the depth of its penetration, considerable precipitation could have reached areas which, at present, are arid or semi-arid.

Under present-day conditions, which are comparable with the latter half of an interglacial phase, the meteorological equator is situated 5–7°

north of the geographical equator. This asymmetry is apparently caused by the influence of the Antarctic ice-cap. During interglacial maxima, therefore, the equatorial convergence would have had an even more northerly position than at present, and, during hypothermal periods, a more southerly one. This would have enhanced the precipitation that occurred during pluvial periods, and would have brought summer rains to the highlands of Adrar, Aïr, Tibesti, Ennedi and, perhaps, even to Hoggar.[124]

The general pattern of the distribution of rainfall throughout Africa probably remained largely unchanged throughout the Pleistocene period, although it was to some degree affected by pluvial and inter-pluvial phases during which the climate was successively wetter and then drier than it is today. Even minor changes, however, could have had important local effects. An increase of 25.5 cm (10 in) in the rainfall, providing that it is suitably distributed, can change desert into scrub; although a similar increase in the equatorial rain-forest zone makes little difference, if any, to the vegetation.

The rainfall in tropical Africa may have fluctuated between 40 per cent more than the present at the heights of the pluvials and 40 per cent less at the minima of the dry phases. These estimates do not provide evidence of temperature change, but it has been strongly suggested that air temperatures may have fluctuated between as much as 5 to 6°C from the present.

Raised terraces in various parts of Africa have been attributed to lakes and rivers enlarged by pluvial conditions of varying degrees of intensity. These wet periods could, to some extent, have been caused by decreased evaporation when temperatures were lower, but the differences in size between past and present lakes are so enormous that changes in temperature alone are unlikely to account for them and there must have been considerable variation in the amount of rainfall.[42]

Variations in the high water level of the Nile have left traces which reflect a succession of palaeoclimatic events that occurred in the higher basins of the river.[11] Peaks of high water probably corresponded with the colder phases of the upper Pleistocene and Holocene, depletions with warmer inter-stadials. An alternative view has also been proposed, that pluvial periods would have coincided with the disappearance of the ice-caps. In this case, the last general wet maximum would have occurred around 6,000 years ago. It has indeed been established from geological data that the climate on the southern edge of the Sahara was more humid at that time, but this does not seem to have been demonstrated satisfactorily elsewhere. In the present state of knowledge it would be premature to try to correlate climatic fluctuations in different areas of the Sahara. The northern fringes of the desert are more likely to have been affected by changes in the location of depressions coming in from the Atlantic, while the southern edges were influenced by the tropical monsoon system.[88]

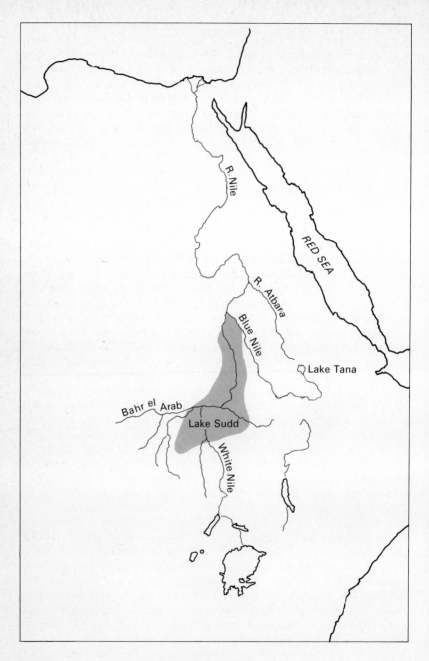

Fig. 5.1 The Nile valley in Pleistocene times.[11]

Pollen analyses show that, during the first pluvial of the Upper Pleistocene, the central Sahara was covered by mediterranean vegetation with
forests of pine, cedar and oak trees on the mountains. A cold and dry
climate, with considerable variations in temperature, accompanied the
last glaciation of the northern hemisphere. At this time the Sahara was
covered by a steppe in which Chenopodiaceae and Gramineae comprised
the dominant vegetation. Afterwards, the climate gradually ameliorated
with a consistent rise in temperature so that, during the Late Glacial in
Europe (Table 4.1, p. 40), there was an invasion of mediterranean macchia in the lower regions and of forests of *Pinus, Tilia, Alnus, Acer, Quercus*
and *Cedrus* in the mountains.[8] In Libya, too, cold or wet conditions continued from about 35,000 to 11,500 years ago, at which time a warmer and
drier climate began and has possibly continued up to the present. Although
animals were probably never able to migrate freely across the whole of the
Sahara in Pleistocene times, periods of higher rainfall would have opened
up a number of possible routes across the desert.

At the end of the Pleistocene, the Sahara south of the tropic of Cancer
was full of lakes and active rivers, from Mauretania in the west to the plains
south of Khartoum. Several of the deposits left by these bodies of water
have been dated, and most of them are between 5,000 and 8,000 years old.
Although the lakes near Khartoum had apparently dried up 7,000 years
ago, most of the others lasted until 3,000 B.P.[11]

As the climate became still warmer and drier the forest trees mentioned
above were replaced by more xerophyllous species of *Cupressus, Juniperus*
and *Olea*. About 4,800 years ago, desiccation increased to such an extent
that the mediterranean flora could survive only on the higher mountains;
while the Sahelian flora, of which *Acacia* is a prominent genus, invaded
the lower regions as far north as the Atlas Mountains. In historical times
real desert conditions set in and the central Sahara became inhospitable to
plants and animals.[33]

FOSSIL EVIDENCE

The climate of Africa bordering the Mediterranean remained cold until
about 10,000 years ago and, from about 5,000 to 2,000 B.P., the humidity
in the north-west of the Sahara increased considerably. It was possibly
at this time that Palaearctic land Mollusca, as shown by the distributions
of their shells, penetrated as far as a line running from about Port Etienne
on the Atlantic coast, south of the Hoggar Mountains, north to the Gulf
of Sirte and then south again to Kharga. The date of Mega-Chad has not
yet been established, but hippopotamus and other swamp animals were
living at Taoudeni, 650 km (400 miles) north of Timbuktu, only 7,000
years ago. Elephant and hippopotamus were also present as far north as

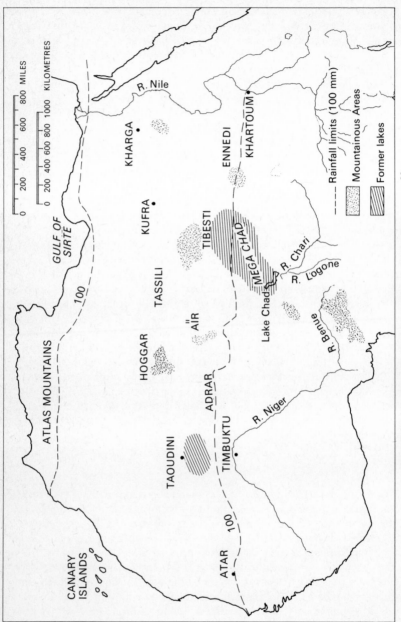

Fig. 5.2 The Sahara, to show some Pleistocene features.[89]

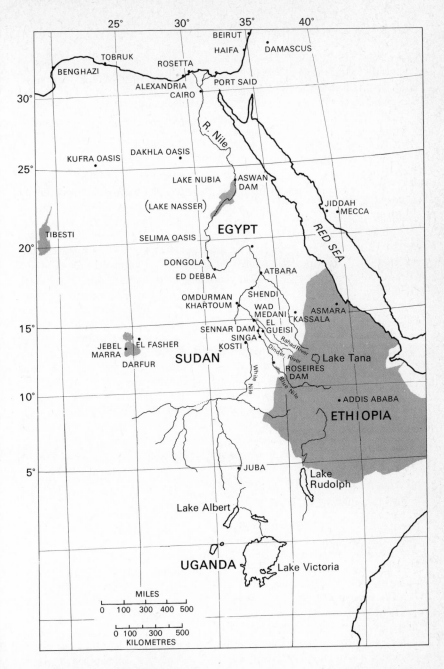

Fig. 5.3 The Nile valley today.

Ounianga near Tibesti. This fossil evidence and that from pollen analysis combine to show that, around 7,000 B.P., reliable rainfall extended some 480 km (300 miles) further north than it does today.[88]

Changes of climate and vegetation in the Sudan are well documented. The presence of land snails (*Limicolaria flammata* and *Zootectus insularis*) in Mesolithic deposits suggests that conditions at Khartoum were similar to those found today in areas where the annual rainfall exceeds 500 mm (20 in). The fauna also included a water mongoose (*Antilax paludinosus*), an extinct reed rat (*Thryonomys arkelli*), a spiny field rat (*Arvicanthis* sp., essentially an inhabitant of bushy or grass country with a plentiful supply of water), the Nile lechwe (*Onotragus megaceros*, a swamp-loving species), buffalo, elephant and hippopotamus.[3] A somewhat different fauna was found at Shaheinab, 50 km north of Omdurman in Neolithic times, about 5,500 years B.P. Desiccation had begun to set in, for the swamp-dwelling animals had disappeared, while the presence of hares, gerbils, ground squirrels, gazelles, oryx and giraffe also suggest somewhat drier conditions than obtained in early Khartoum. In addition, domestic sheep and goats were present in small numbers. Nevertheless, cattle still grazed away from the Nile valley in Lower Nubia. The level of the river at Semna was 7.9 m (26 ft) above that of modern times. The significance of this has been disputed. It may indicate greater precipitation throughout the course of the river. Alternatively, a dam may have been built across the Nile at Semna about 3,800 years ago, thus creating an artificially high water level.

This fossil evidence, supported by Egyptian Dynastic records, suggests that, from 7,000 B.P. until about 3,500 years ago, the climate of the northern Sudan and southern Egypt became steadily drier. Until 3,500 B.P., when modern conditions set in, pastoral tribes inhabited regions, both east and west of the Nile, that are now desert; but the Egyptians were not able to settle away from the river.[65]

HISTORICAL EVIDENCE

From 6,000 B.P. sheep were depicted in rock paintings of upland areas of the central Sahara, and cattle were painted in caves almost everywhere. Well known examples occur in Tassili. In the subsequent 2,000 years, overgrazing destroyed most of the grass cover and wild game became more plentiful. Cattle disappear from Saharan rock paintings of 3,000 B.P. when horses were introduced. It seems probable, therefore, that there have been three main periods of human life in the Sahara before the present. Rock pictures of 7,000 B.P. illustrate wild game being hunted. Between 6,000 and 4,000 B.P. the hunters were replaced by people with large herds of cattle who painted in a superb naturalistic style. In about 3,000 B.P. the Sahara was opened by trade and military expeditions and horses were introduced. Finally these were replaced by camels around 2,600 B.P. and modern conditions supervened.

Until very recently, the fauna in the central part of the Nile valley was comparatively rich. Elephants and lions were frequently represented in the Meroitic art of Nubia and were almost certainly captured and tamed locally. The latter were probably kept in temples as living representatives of the god Apedemek, and elephants were used for war as well as for ceremonial purposes. They were trained at Musawwarat es-Sofra, a day's

Fig. 5.4   Rock paintings from Tassili. *Left*, 7,000 B.P.—game. *Centre*, 5,000 B.C. —cattle. *Right*, 2,000 B.P.—camel. (Drawing, Anne Cloudsley-Thompson.)

camel journey from the Nile, south east of Meroë, less than 2,000 years ago. In those days, elephants also lived among the forests on the foothills of the Atlas Mountains, although the climate of the Sahara was probably not different from that of today.[107]

An ivory tablet engraved with a drawing of a rhinoceros and representations of elephants and giraffes have been found at Kerma in Dongola district where an Egyptian trading post was established about 3,900 years ago. Diodorus (1st century B.C.) described a tribe of elephant-eaters living in regions covered with thickets of trees growing close together, probably on the upper reaches of the Atbara river, and Strabo (c. 63 B.C.–A.D. 23) mentioned a hunting ground for elephants at Ptolemais, near the modern Aqiq. About A.D. 60 the emperor Nero sent an expedition, commanded by two centurions, to discover the source of the Nile. According to Pliny, they found the tracks of elephants and rhinos around Merowe. During the 12th century A.D., the Arab traveller Idrisi found elephants and giraffes near Dongola.[65]

Two thousand years ago, elephants lived among the forests on the foothills of the Atlas Mountains, and Hanno saw them on the Atlantic shores of

Fig. 5.5   Meroitic artefacts[107] (drawing, Anne Cloudsley-Thompson).

Morocco about 500 B.C. Lions, too, were widely distributed: they were common in Algeria, for example, until the time of the French occupation of that country. Cheetahs were plentiful also, and at one time were caught and trained for coursing game.

Most of the Saharan game has been eliminated by indiscriminate hunting during the last century. Antelope, mouflon and ostriches have been exterminated over large areas and even gazelles are becoming scarce. However, it is difficult to imagine such animals surviving today in the barren desert that was able to support them until very recently.

In the journal of his journey up the Nile during the years 1821 and 1822, Linant de Bellefonds commented on the woodedness of the countryside of the northern Sudan and mentioned that he heard a lion roaring at Ed Debba near old Dongola. Away from the river today, that region of the Sahara is almost complete desert, with practically no vegetation. In 1835, lions were plentiful around Shendi, 190 km north of Khartoum, and game was abundant at Kassala as late at 1883. Many other examples could be cited to show how much the flora and fauna of the Sahara have been impoverished in recent times.[26]

The inhabitants of Leptis Magna in Tripolitania were able to draw on the produce of hundreds of thousands of olive trees, and the areas planted probably increased during the Roman period. The beds of the *wadis* were terraced, catchment walls along their sides prevented rain water from washing away the soil, and enough moisture was retained to make possible the cultivation of cereals, dates and even of vines. The Roman amphitheatre at El Djem, the third largest in the world and capable of seating 60,000 people, contrasts with the present small Arab village and suggests how much standards of agriculture have been depressed in recent years, although climatic conditions have probably not changed greatly in North Africa. The land was not fertilized, however, in ancient times. It is said that the sewers of Rome, in the course of centuries, engulfed the prosperity of the Roman peasants and devoured the wealth of Sicily, Sardinia and the fertile lands of North Africa as well. Even today, the chief drawback to development in much of North Africa is not climate so much as the monoculture of wheat, and other bad agricultural practices which, combined with overgrazing, result in destruction of the natural vegetation.

Turkhana tradition has it that the area around Lake Rudolph, now semi-desert, was once lush and fertile. Within living memory, much of Somalia that is now overgrazed and eroded to a serious extent, was forested, with permanent springs and a rich fauna of elephant, lion and other game. Not only do effective summer rains move further northwards in West Africa than in the east, but overgrazing is less acute in the west than it is in the proximity of the Nile. The extension of the desert into tropical Africa is primarily due to the deliberate action of man, in many instances within living memory. Desert encroaches over steppe, steppe over savanna, and savanna over forest. Thus the increase of the Sahara in recent years is part of the man-made, large scale, shift of the vegetation belts.[67]

As in the Sahara, so the present-day vegetation of Somalia shows a variety of effects produced by the heavy hand of man and his stock. The chief way in which overgrazing operates is by the actual eating of the plants to such an extent that they either disappear or die. Young seedlings are also eaten and the species are therefore unable to replace themselves. During the dry season, when the low plants offer poor grazing, it is common for Somali graziers to lop off large branches from *Acacia* trees so that goats and sheep may feed on their leaves and fruit. Grazing herds also cause erosion by loosening the soil so that it is blown away by wind. Their tracks act as avenues along which water erosion begins, and many plants are killed when their roots are exposed.[63]

Such effects are more conspicious in some desert regions than in others, and may be disguised by topography and edaphic factors. For instance, many species of plants require only two thirds as much rainfall on sandy soils as they do when growing on clay. The effects of overgrazing are therefore likely to be greater where clay predominates. Perennial grasses are the first element of the vegetation to suffer under heavy grazing. Their replacement by annual species is associated with a general reduction in the amount of plant cover. Bare ground generally absorbs less rain-water than it would in the presence of vegetation. Thus the amount of water entering the soil and becoming available for plants is reduced. Run-off is increased when the soil is compacted, and shallow rooted plants, such as *Acacia bussei*, die. Soil erosion then becomes steadily more serious.

Man cannot escape responsibility for having created a large part of the Sahara. In regions where the needs of the vegetation are delicately balanced by precarious rainfall, overgrazing and the utilization of firewood can have a disastrous and irreversible effect.[57] Destruction of the *Acacia* desert scrub around Khartoum and Omdurman has taken place to such an extent that charcoal now has to be brought from as far afield as Kosti Wad Medani and El Gueisi.[32] It has been estimated that in the Sahel zone alone, nearly three tonnes of wood are consumed annually by each family— a total of some 50,000,000 tonnes a year.

Even more important in creating erosion and desert conditions are overgrazing and compacting of the soil by domestic animals, especially goats which will even climb trees in order to reach their leaves. Tramping produced desert-like conditions in the northern Ugandan province of Karamoja, where there is an annual rainfall of about 635 mm (25 in). The vegetation recovered, however, when tsetse fly invaded the land, the stock was removed, and the people moved away.

The detrimental influence of man and grazing animals on the natural vegetation has been demonstrated experimentally on a number of occasions, and it has been emphasized that the conservation of soil and plant cover is imperative in arid regions where the unstable balance of nature can easily be tipped towards destruction by a slight disturbance of the ecosystem. The effects of overgrazing are manifold. Construction of additional wells and water-holes may enable grazing to be spread over a wider area, thus reducing the pressure around the original watering points. Unfortunately, such amelioration is usually short-lived, since the additional water made available merely enables the numbers of animals to increase still more, while the level of ground-water almost inevitably drops.[117] There is no possibility that the number of domestic animals in the Sahara will be voluntarily reduced in the foreseeable future, for these represent the sustenance of the nomads and an insurance for the poor farmer against the years of drought when his crops fail. He does not realize that these animals are actually endangering his very existence.

6

Vegetation and Potential

The natural vegetation of arid regions is of vital importance because desert conditions swiftly follow if it is destroyed. For this reason, policies of mechanized agriculture and dry farming on the fringes of continental deserts should be pursued only with the greatest caution, if at all. Vegetation protects the surface of the ground from raindrop erosion: it binds soils and sediments together, preventing their movement down the slopes, and it shades the surface of the land from excessive insolation. At the same time, there is no other element of the landscape which can, so easily, be changed by man and domesticated animals. Vegetation, far more than fauna, is soon modified by short-term and long-term climatic changes, and there is probably no other single factor of the environment which can cause such rapid changes in the appearance and potential of the landscape. Because of the interdependence of these components, however, a slight change in one of them induces a chain reaction which eventually leads to a reorganization of the ecosystem, producing temporary stability until a new series of changes is initiated. It is, therefore, important for ecologists, economists, agriculturists and planners to understand as much as possible about the flora and fauna of arid regions.[84]

VEGETATION TYPES

The vegetation of desert areas may be divided into three general categories:

(a) *Vegetation dependent upon local precipitation only*

Under extreme conditions this may be lacking but, in many cases, the recently discovered phenomenon of subterranean dew may furnish sufficient moisture to support a sparse cover of vegetation, especially on sand, since this has a high capacity for heat, and in areas with great diurnal fluctuations of temperature.

(b) *Vegetation dependent upon the accumulation of local rain in drainage courses and depressions.*

Such vegetation, growing under favourable topographic conditions, need not be as xerophytic in character as must the vegetation of the first category. French workers refer to this as 'mode contracté' when compared with more scattered vegetation, which they term 'mode diffus'. An extreme example occurs in the central Sahara, where the vegetation is contained exclusively in *wadis*. Likewise, a compact rock surface offers little possibility for plant growth, except in pockets of sand which may provide favourable conditions locally.[87]

Fig. 6.1   Desert vegetation on the edge of a *wadi,* Southern Algeria.

Physiography is an important factor controlling local water resources. The lowest portions of desert areas receive water and soil from more extensive drainage and, in consequence, the moisture available for plant growth is considerably in excess of the actual rainfall. Such areas are therefore especially favourable for dry farming and in many arid regions are thus exploited. Slopes and elevated regions retain the least amount of water, so that local differences, although small, may favour one place at the expense of another. Under minimum precipitation only the lower areas may support any vegetation while, with more rainfall, they show qualitative and quantitative differences when compared to higher ground. The distinctions are especially noticeable in the *wadis* of the Sahara and other very dry deserts.

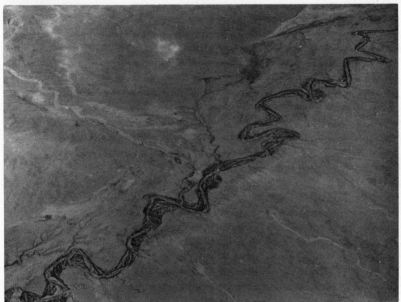

Fig. 6.2 Riparian vegetation beside the Rio Grande.

(c) *Vegetation dependent upon moisture from sources beyond the desert, such as rivers or lakes fed partly from precipitation elsewhere.*

To this category belongs the vegetation of oases (p. 68) and of regions irrigated artificially by man (Chapter 13).

DROUGHT-EVADING PLANTS

Desert plants are able to survive in their harsh environment by virtue of complicated combinations of physiology and anatomy. Many of them, including annual grasses and some small dicotyledons, evade more extreme conditions by completing their life-cycles during the short rainy season, and passing the remainder of the year as fruit or seeds lying dormant in the soil. Such drought-evading plants are not true xerophytes. They are really mesophytic because their activity takes place only when moisture is available. They are sometimes termed 'ephemerals' on account of the brevity of their life-cycles. For example, in the semi-desert northeast of Khartoum, species of *Tribulus* have been found bearing flowers and

Fig. 6.3 Sonoran desert, Arizona, showing luxurious vegetation.

fruits only 25 days after a heavy shower. Plants of *Eragrostis pilosa* and *Mollugo cerviana* grow from seeds to flowers within 30 days. The gama grass (*Bouteloua aristidoides*) germinates from seeds within four weeks in California, while *Boerhaavia repens* of the southern fringe of the Sahara has been observed to germinate, flower and sow its seeds in the space of eight days when moisture is available. A brief life-cycle, however, is related not only to the restricted duration of the season when conditions are suitable for growth, but also to the short period during which insects are available for pollination. Clearly, it is one of the primary requisites for which plant breeders must strive when producing new varieties of arable crops for use in semi-arid regions.

Many species of drought-evading plant produce seeds equipped with dispersal units which aid their distribution. In this way, the offspring have an increased chance of reaching a site that is suitable for germination. The stems and leaves of others are closely curled towards one another when dry, but open apart when moistened. By this means, seeds are scattered only during the moist season. This tends to prevent long distance dispersal of seeds from their parent plant which presumably is already growing in a favourable locality.

Dispersal of some annual grasses involves a large number of seeds becoming entwined to form a dense, rounded ball which is blown over the

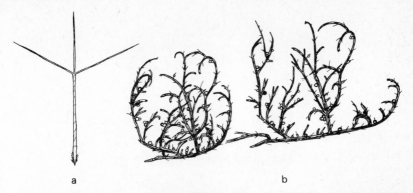

a   b

Fig. 6.4 Dispersal mechanisms in desert plants: (a) Seed of grass, *Aristida* sp. (2 cm); (b) 'Rose of Jericho', *Anastatica* sp., dry (8 cm) and wet (10 cm).

desert surface by the wind. As the sharp points come in contact with the soil, individual units become anchored and detached, until the ball finally disintegrates. Changes in the humidity of the air subsequently cause each seed to twist like a drill, forcing it even deeper into the soil where it remains until the rain falls. Individual seeds may also become attached to the hairs of animals—the legs of goats are sometimes completely covered with them—and are thereby dispersed. Many other plants of desert regions have well-developed barbs and bristles to aid their dispersal by animals. An example is afforded by the spikelets of bur grasses. The fruits of some desert plants are blown about for a considerable distance until they become trapped in a rock or hollow where eventually they disintegrate or become buried in wind-blown sand. When the rain falls and collects in the hollows, the seeds germinate in favourable surroundings.[41]

It is believed that seeds and fragments of wind-blown vegetation form the basis of the food webs in desert regions where no plants grow. Seeds are collected and stored by harvester ants, while accumulations of dried vegetable matter support bristle-tails and the larvae of desert beetles, themselves eaten by scorpions and other predators.[16]

Many desert and savanna trees shed their leaves at the onset of the dry season. Oddly enough, some species of *Acacia* usually retain their leaves, and one actually produces leaves at the beginning of the dry season! Presumably it grows where subterranean water is available and benefits from producing its foliage at a time when there are not so many insects around to feed on it. Some desert plants are always leafless, and others possess only very small leaves: in such cases, the stems are green and used for photosynthesis.

The leaves of desert grasses are often folded or rolled into tubes. Stomata are concentrated on the upper surface, and the lower is thickened

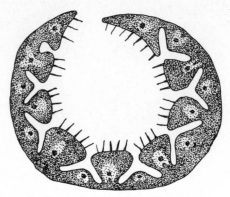

Fig. 6.5   Rolled xerophytic grassleaf in section.[24]

so that water loss is greatly reduced when the edges of the leaves curl up and touch each other. In addition to exhibiting a very small leaf surface and a low rate of evaporation, plants such as the succulent cacti and Euphorbiaceae must depend for their extreme drought resistance upon well-developed water-storing tissues and low surface-to-volume ratio, for they are always thick and fleshy. It is said that even a small cactus would transpire 300 times faster if it were cut up into thin leaves. The fluted stem of *Carnegiea gigantea* expands and contracts like an accordion as moist and dry season alternate.

In periods of extreme drought, some plants are able to survive on moisture from the air. At night, when the temperature drops, dew may condense on their leaves and stems, and then run down into the soil around the roots. *Welwitschia mirabilis* of the Namib desert has two curling leaves, split longitudinally into strips, on which dew condenses, providing water for the shallow roots. By absorbing some moisture from the night air, even when the dew point is not reached, dry vegetation can make water available for snails, insects and other small animals of the desert.

The coastal deserts of Chile, Peru and South-West Africa are caused by cold oceanic currents bringing cool winds that carry fog and mist but not rain. Anyone lost in one of these deserts could find his direction, even when the sun or stars were obscured, by the fact that lichen grows on the seaward side of the rocks. Various animals of these deserts, such as beetles, scorpions, lizards and rodents, are dependent directly or indirectly on fog for water, and on wind-blown plant detritus as a source of food.[37]

XEROPHYTIC PLANTS

Alternative forms of adjustment to life in arid regions are concerned with tolerance and resistance. Either one of these qualities, if not the evasion

Fig. 6.6 *Welwitschia mirabilis*. (Drawing: Anne Cloudsley-Thompson.)

Fig. 6.7 Crushing sunflowers to extricate the seeds, central Turkey.

of drought, is necessary to all desert vegetation and must, therefore, be found in any perennial crop plants exploited by man for dry farming in arid regions. True xerophytes must be adapted to live in conditions of heat, drought and low humidity for long periods of time, and to survive in pedocalic soils rich in calcium but containing little moisture. It may be possible, however, to overcome the growth-inhibiting effect of salinity by growing agricultural crops in atmospheres with high relative humidity when less water is required by the leaves. Where vegetation is sparse, plants become discrete individuals and do not benefit from protection by their neighbours: the opportunity to modify the local environment thus decreases as the degree of aridity increases.

Xerophytic plants experience not only high air and soil temperatures during the day but also low nocturnal and cold-season minima, according to latitude and altitude. The texture of the soil in which they grow is, moreover, frequently open, and its organic content extremely low. To some extent, such problems are countered by the development of extensive rooting systems that serve to increase the uptake of water. In succulents, such roots spread laterally but are seldom more than 3 or 4 cm below the surface of the soil. Thus they exploit to the maximum every shower of rain even if the water does not penetrate far into the ground.

In contrast, many non-succulent desert plants have extraordinarily deep roots. The American mesquite (*Prosopis velutina*) has been found with roots to a depth of over 15 m, and *Acacia* spp. in Africa are equally well endowed: their long tap-roots reach a water table many metres below the surface, while a superficial rooting system exploits the moisture from showers and thunderstorms. These observations suggest that optimum spacing may be important when trees and other plants are established, either for agricultural purposes, or for the stabilization of dunes and desert reclamation. In order to provide mutual protection, they should be planted as close to one another as is possible without crowding their superficial rooting systems.[67]

Xerophytes are drought-resisting plants. They do not benefit from dry conditions, except in that competition from mesophytes is reduced, and they will grow more quickly if well watered, as all cactus growers know. A few are able to survive dehydration of their tissues for long periods without suffering much injury. They are resistant to wilting, and a few species may lose up to 25 per cent of their water content before beginning to do so. In contrast, mesophytes usually begin to wilt after as little as 1 or 2 per cent of their water has been lost. Leaves of the creosote bush retain the powers of growth even after the buds have dried out and become brown.

While the function of transpiration is to limit heat stress, the attainment of this object conflicts with the need for water conservation. In desert regions, where water shortage is acute, the balance between these incom-

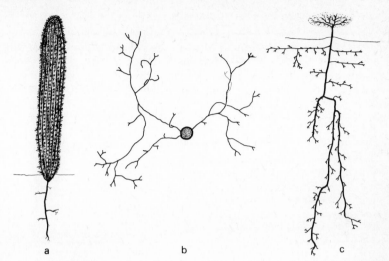

Fig. 6.8 Rooting system of a cactus (a) view from side; (b) from above, and of an acacia; (c) from side. (Not to scale.)

patible requirements swings in favour of water conservation. When wilting does occur, however, heat stress is lessened by the fact that the leaves no longer remain at right angles to the sun's rays, but fold downward, thereby exposing a reduced area to solar radiation.

UTILIZATION OF DESERT PLANTS

In addition to exhibiting a much reduced leaf surface and cuticular transpiration, succulent desert plants, such as Cactaceae and many Euphorbiaceae, depend upon well developed water storing tissues and low surface to volume ratios. These can be utilized by man as a source of moisture, as are gourds and *tsama* melons (p. 65). In Texas, the thorns of yucca (*Yucca* spp.) and of prickly pear (*Opuntia inermis*) have been burned off with petrol torches, in times of drought, to provide food and water for famished cattle. The mouth of the camel is so tough and leathery that no such treatment is required to make prickly pear acceptable to him. Spineless cacti (*O. ficus-indica*) are an important food of livestock in North Africa, and sheep can be fed on them exclusively for up to 12 weeks or more without suffering ill effects.

Although prickly pear thrives in Eritrea and on the Mediterranean coast, where it provides excellent fodder for camels and goats, it is not found extensively along the southern fringe of the Sahara. This may be because climatic conditions there are too extreme, but the possibility of its intro-

Table 6.1   Plants used by desert inhabitants.

Fruits   *Opuntia* and *Agave* spp in America. The succulent euphorbias of Africa contain toxic alkaloids: the berries of many species are eaten, however.

Starch-filled storage organs   Edible roots, rhizomes, tubers, bulbs etc. found in many desert plants. Tender 'hearts' of *Agave*, *Yucca*, etc., roasted as a staple food by many American Indian tribes.

Seeds and nuts   The legume pods, etc., are eaten; the seeds are gathered and used fresh, dried or ground.

Greens and herbs   The young leaves and shoots of many plants are used as salads or condiments.

Drugs and medicines   These include narcotic drugs, stimulants, etc.

Fibres   Desert plants supply fibres with a wide variety of uses. *Yucca* and *Agave* are the principal genera involved.

Miscellaneous   Desert plants supply building materials, weapons, tools, ornaments, dyes, gums, fuel, soap, perfumes, etc.

---

duction into new areas certainly merits investigation. If it were to become established, not only would it provide food for domestic animals, but it might also help to check excessive run off from rainstorms. Although it can become a pest by competing with more beneficial plants, it would hardly do so in the region under discussion.[32]

Whatever their mode of adaptation, desert plants have in common one major problem with which they have to contend. This is the animals which graze on them and the people who burn them for fuel or clear them for cultivation. In response to attacks of this nature, many desert shrubs have evolved painfully sharp and prickly barbs and spikes, as we have seen. These include the stipulate thorns of African species of *Acacia* and *Euphorbia*. In the Australian deserts, where there is more vegetation as alternative food and, consequently, less grazing pressure, the *Acacia* spp. mostly bear phyllodes. Many desert plants, such as *Euphorbia* spp. and Asclepiadaceae also contain poisonous or irritant latex. Others secrete, in the bark or leaves, resins or tannins which can be utilized by man (p. 67). Terpenoids produced by *Commiphora myrrhae*, for example, are responsible for its smell in incense (p. 75) when burned, while the pods of *Cassia senna* are the source of a strong purgative.[24]

FOOD GATHERING CULTURES

Although some desert plants produce edible grains and fruits, few provide an important source of food for indigenous people, unless these are nomadic hunters and food gatherers, like the Bushmen of the Kalahari and Namib, and the Bindibu of central Australia. Such peoples have not advanced materially beyond the Stone Age. They plant no food, have no permanent abode, and keep no domesticated animals except dogs.

Bushmen economize in water, which they store in gourds and empty ostrich eggs, and by avoiding activity while the sun is high. In very hot weather they urinate into pits dug in the ground and lie in these throughout the day, keeping as cool as possible. They wear little clothing, but their pigmented skin shields them from ultra-violet light. At night, they rest in temporary shelters or *skerms* of skins lying across the branches of a thorn tree. The anatomical peculiarity of steatopygia enables them, in time of plenty, to store fat in their protuberant buttocks which shrink during periods of drought. Bushmen are excellent hunters and can hit a moving antelope with a poisoned arrow from a distance of 150 m. The women and children dig the earth with grubbing sticks for their staple diet of edible bulbs, roots and *tsama* melons which are prized as a source of moisture. Although extremely shy, the Bushmen are intelligent, cheerful and good-natured. They have a well-developed sense of art and beauty, as shown by their wonderful rock and cave paintings.[76]

Fig. 6.9 Bushman rock paintings. (Drawing, Anne Cloudsley-Thompson.)

Like Bushmen, the Bindibu are incomparably skilled at tracking game: they are also very courteous and intelligent although their existence is primitive in the extreme. A flimsy windbreak made of sticks or clumps of *Spinifex* grass provides their only shelter: fires and the bodies of their dogs are their source of warmth at night. The womenfolk may trudge long distances daily in search of food and firewood. Since Australia has no counterpart of the water-storing *tsama* melon, the aborigine must camp near water-holes and follow the course of the rare desert rains. He is thus more restricted even than the Bushman. Primitive hunting and food-gathering such as this are believed not to have had much impact on the desert ecosystem.

Other desert people are nomads who depend for food upon their flocks and herds and thus only indirectly upon the vegetation. In the western Gran Chaco, however, with its very long dry seasons, some tubers, such as those of a coriaceous shrub (*Facaratia hassleriana*) are consumed, but mainly for their water content. Except for the vegetation in *wadis* and drain-age basins, extreme deserts have little wood for burning or for any other purposes. Thus, the primitive shelter of desert dwellers is usually of skin or cloth, and dried manure is used as a source of fuel.

In North America, food-gathering cultures in the arid regions were represented in the past by the scattered Shoshonean tribes of the Great Basin. These people lived in family units and, only occasionally, bonded together to hunt rabbits or pronghorn antelope. Normally, each family collected seeds and roots, or hunted rodents separately.

EXPLOITATION OF RAW MATERIALS

In addition to its importance as cover, and as feed for domestic animals, desert vegetation includes some food and beverage plants, substitutes for soap, medicinal plants and sources of oils, waxes and fibres. In the arid parts of Argentina, for example, the pods of several species of *Prosopis* are important as concentrated forage and sometimes as food, especially since these trees fruit most abundantly in dry years. Elsewhere, the pods of *Acacia*, *Zizyphus*, *Geoffroea* spp., and other desert trees are utilized for forage.

In general, the harvest of wild desert plants is centred on arid areas that have low carrying capacity for grazing, and insufficient rainfall for dry farming. *Agave lechuguilla* is the source of a hard fibre known as 'ixtle'. It is harvested in northern Mexico and western Texas, where it grows abundantly in areas with an annual rainfall averaging 150–200 mm (5–8 in). Gum tragacanth is obtained from *Astragalus gossypenus* in Iran, guayuli rubber from *Parthenium argentatum* in Mexico, and candelilla wax from *Euphorbia antisyphilitica* in Mexico and western Texas. This formerly ranked second only to the carnauba palm as a source of hard wax for floor polishes and the manufacture of gramophone records. The demand today is, however, supplied by synthetic materials. The demand for *Ephedra gerardiana*, of which about 1,000 tons were at one time collected annually in Pakistan, has likewise decreased enormously since ephedrine has been synthesized and other synthetic vasoconstrictors have appeared to alleviate the lot of asthma sufferers. The drug ma-huang is, however, said still to be harvested from *E. sinica* in China.

The creosote bush (*Larrea divaricata*) contains nordihydroguaiaretic acid, a powerful antioxidant for fats and oils, but the market for this has now been usurped by cheaper synthetic chemicals. Egyptian henbane (*Hyocyamus muticus*) was at one time gathered in such quantities for medicinal purposes that the plant was almost exterminated but, again, the market has been taken over by synthetic substitutes. These examples show that the outlook is poor for harvesting natural supplies and using arid lands that have little other possible economic potential. Certain xerophytic plants can, however, be used to extend cultivation into semi-arid and arid regions, in which ordinary cultivated crops fail because of drought and grazing gives a low return. These include *Agave sisalona* and *A. fourcroydes* which produce the fibres sisal and henequen, in arid parts of Israel, Tanzania, Kenya, Mozambique, Cuba, Haiti, Brazil, and Indonesia. These are the largest and most advanced desert plant industries in existence. Allied plants of various genera produce smaller amounts of hard fibres locally.

In Mexico the alcoholic drink tequila is distilled from *A. tequilana*, and mezcal from *A. atrovirens*. In each case the central portions are heated in ovens to convert glucoxides into sugars. The juices are then extracted, fermented and distilled. Peasant people in Mexico, North Africa, Eritrea and elsewhere depend on the tunas or fruit of prickly pear and other species of *Opuntia* for much of their carbohydrates and vitamins, and commercial plantations of *Opuntia* spp. have been established in many parts of the world. Gum arabic, the second most important export of the Sudan, is produced from trees of *Acacia senegal*. This grows in areas with rainfall between 300–375 mm (12–15 in). The bark wattle of *A. decurrens*, which grows in Australia, South and East Africa in semi-arid places having a rainfall of 400–500 mm (16–20 in), is an important source of tanning agents; but this crop is threatened by the growing use of synthetic substitutes and of artificial leathers.

In general, the outlook for cultivated arid zone plants is considerably better than for wild species. Nevertheless, economic production of sisal, henequen, wattle and gum arabic is still greatly dependent upon cheap labour. With an increasing world demand for raw materials, however, these products could, perhaps, maintain their value despite competition from synthetic materials.

For many reasons, deep-rooted perennial shrubs appear to have a better potential than grasses for increasing the agricultural productivity of arid regions in which perennial grasses have not been successful. Because drought-adapted shrubs have massive root systems, they can exploit the moisture from a greater volume of soil than grasses can. Moreover, many of them have quite high protein contents and provide excellent food for livestock.[49]

OASIS CULTIVATION

Most of the agricultural produce of arid regions comes from oases. The word 'oasis' is derived from the Coptic *oueh* (to dwell) and *saa* (to drink). In the arid regions of the world, oases are the only sites of permanent human habitation. Nearly all the larger oases of the old world have long been transformed by man, who has destroyed the characteristic local fauna and flora, planted date palms and vegetables, and introduced weeds and insect pests. The oases of Africa and Asia have been so changed in this way that it is extremely difficult to establish what they were like before the advent of man. The original flora probably consisted mainly of tamarisk (*Tamarix aphylla* and *T. gallica*), oleander (*Nerium oleander*) and other shrubs, but these have long been replaced by date palms (*Phoenix dactylifera*), fruit trees and vegetables.

Many oases obtain their water from springs. In North Africa, these frequently mark the natural outflow of artesian supplies. Other oases draw their waters from rivers that enter the desert from nearby mountains where there is heavy rainfall or snow. Oases of this kind are found on the fringe of the Kara Kum desert, at Sinkiang and along the foothills of the Andes. Ribbonlike oases are found along the banks of rivers such as the Nile, Indus, Tigris, Euphrates, Colorado, Rio Grande, and those that flow through the Peruvian desert to the Pacific Ocean. Altitudinal oases, like the Hoggar and Tibesti mountains of the central Sahara, Jebel Marra in Darfur and Windhoek in South West Africa, depend upon local rainfall caused by their elevation. Inaccessibility to man and domestic animals sometimes results in the survival of rare plants in altitudinal oases, such as oleander, olives and *Cupressus dupreziana*, which are found in a few localities of the Hoggar mountains.

The date palm (*Phoenix dactylifera*) is by far the most important cultivated fruit-producing tree of the Sahara. It furnishes the basic staple food of the people except at altitudes of above 1,500 m (4,500 ft) along the Atlantic coast and in the southern half of the desert. Its importance decreases progressively as one moves southwards, however, and dates become increasingly a luxury except along the Nile banks. The culture of palms began before the Arab invasions of the Sahara, and probably originates from pre-Roman times. Palm trees are fertilized artificially, and all male trees in excess of about 2 per cent of the total plantation are eliminated.

The products of palms are used for a number of purposes. The fruits are eaten or distilled to make alcoholic *aragi*, the stones are crushed and used to feed camels, the leaves are burned as fuel and the trunks are used for building houses. The fibres of the leaves can be twisted into ropes, or woven into a coarse cloth. This is used to cover the wooden frames in which agricultural produce is transported, and for many other purposes. Very large numbers of date palms are grown at some oases—at Oued Rhir, more than two million and, at Colomb-Béchar, one million, for example. The number of palms in an oasis is determined by the amount of water present. Underneath and between the trees are grown a variety of exotic plants, such as citrus and fig trees, olives, vines, apricots, pomegranates, guavas. Vegetables and fodder are also grown, as well as tomatoes, pimento and other aromatic spices.

Although oases are very important, the greatest agricultural potential of arid regions comes from irrigation schemes of one kind or another. These are discussed in Chapter 13. Nevertheless, oases are significant, not only on account of their own productivity, but because, to some extent, they reverse the world-wide tendency for deserts to increase, largely as a result of over-exploitation and mismanagement of the land.[38]

7

Animal Problems of Aridity

The terrestrial environment presents its inhabitants with two major problems of survival which are especially acute in arid regions: they must respire and excrete without losing too much water, and they cannot afford to cool their bodies by transpiration. The solution to these problems adopted by any particular species depends on the size of the animals concerned. No species exhibits all the possible adaptations outlined in the following paragraphs, but most of them combine a number of them in varying degrees.

Arthropods have such enormous surface areas in relation to their mass that life on land is only possible under two conditions. Either the integument is porous to water vapour, in which case they have to be nocturnal and spend most of the time in a moist micro-habitat—such animals include woodlice, centipedes and millipedes, which cannot usually exist under extreme desert conditions—or else they must possess an impervious cuticle, like most insects and Arachnida.[21, 22]

Only comparatively large desert mammals have a surface-to-volume relationship so small that they can afford to cool themselves by the evaporation of sweat. These include the camel, donkey, addax, oryx and dorcas gazelle. Because they have a greater reserve of water per unit area of surface, such large animals can suffer a given rate of water loss for longer than smaller ones before their water contents are reduced to a lethal minimum. For instance, a flea could tolerate a water loss of 5 mg/cm²/h for only 15 min before losing 10 per cent of its body weight of water. A man could tolerate 4,500 times this rate, or an equivalent rate for 3 months before experiencing an equivalent degree of desiccation.[50, 51]

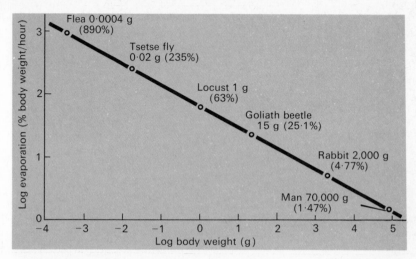

Fig. 7.1   The relation between body weight and the amount of water which must evaporate per hour from the body to preserve a constant temperature in desert conditions. Such a rate is tolerable for some hours by a large animal because it represents only a small percentage of total weight, but a small animal would have to lose several times its own weight per hour. Figures in parentheses show the amount of water, expressed as a percentage of total weight, to be evaporated each hour by animals whose weights are also shown.[51]

BEHAVIOURAL ADAPTATIONS: CIRCADIAN RHYTHMS

The survival of small animals in desert regions depends very much upon the selection of suitable environments. Because of this, the behavioural adaptations and the time of activity of desert animals are probably often more important than any physiological specializations. Most species are nocturnal in habit and pass the day in holes, burrows and other sheltered retreats. Consequently, the fauna of the desert at night is quite different from that during the day. Diurnal rhythms of activity are found in nearly all terrestrial habitats, for all living organisms appear to possess a 'biological clock' and most animals maintain a fairly inflexible routine of activity and rest. In the desert, where the climatic differences between day and night are more marked than in any other environment, such daily rhythms are especially conspicuous.[21]

Most desert arachnids and insects confine their activities to the hours of darkness when the temperature is low and the relative humidity of the air comparatively high. This generalization applies even to species with comparatively impervious integuments, whose relatives in temperate climates are normally active during the daytime. Scorpions and camel-spiders

(Solifugae) are markedly nocturnal, although they can withstand remarkably high temperatures and considerable desiccation. It is difficult, therefore, to ascribe any function, other than the avoidance of vertebrate
animals, to their strict rhythms of activity. Of course, it might be argued
that scorpions are protected by their poisonous stings. However, poison
is not always an effective deterrent to large and powerful enemies, which
might well trample a scorpion underfoot just as deer will stamp on a
snake. And it is well known that baboons and other monkeys become adept
at catching scorpions without themselves getting stung. On the other
hand, certain desert beetles can be seen wandering around in broad day-
light. These are distasteful to predators, however, and have extremely
hard integuments. Their black coloration has a warning function (Chapter
8) and they are not compelled to be nocturnal in order to avoid being eaten.
Day-active beetles are exceptional, however, and related species are often
strictly nocturnal. Animals with moist skins, such as worms and slugs, or
with porous outer coverings such as woodlice, centipedes, millipedes,
certain mites, soft-bodied insects and amphibians, are usually only active
at night, whatever part of the world they inhabit: desert forms, invariably
so.[21]

Day-active insects tend to leave the sand when its temperature reaches
about 50°C (112°F). Some climb grasses, some dive into holes, while
others fly about above the ground, making hurried landings to enter
their burrows. When confined and prevented from burying themselves,
or from flying away, they very soon die. There are only a few animals,
including some grasshoppers, beetles and spiders, that are active in the
desert during the hottest part of the day in summer. Many of these have
long legs which raise their bodies above the scorching sand. Long legs are
also found in some nocturnal or twilight-active animals such as the desert
woodlouse (*Hemilepistus reaumuri*) (p. 77), the large white dune spiders
(*Cerballus* spp.) and some darkling beetles of the Namib desert.[23, 31]

It would be hard to point to any significant physiological adaptation to
desert life among vertebrates that is not found in at least some non-desert
forms, but the importance of behavioral adaptations is very apparent.

Many skinks and iguanid lizards are day-active and most geckoes are
nocturnal. The scaly-tailed lizard (*Uromastix acanthinurus*) is active during
the late part of the night and at dawn in the Tibesti mountains, while a
skink (*Chalcides ocellatus*) and the gecko *Pachydactylus hasselquisti* are
diurnal in habit, although they shelter from the midday heat. Micro-
climatic measurements in the holes and retreats of these animals shed light
on such differences in behaviour. The scaly-tailed lizard burrows deeply
in the sand so that the temperature in its hole remains constant at about
35°C (95°F) in June. The skink shelters under fallen leaves at midday,
while the gecko, the most active of the three, avoids high temperatures by

resting in the shade of rocks.[113] Desert snakes tend to be nocturnal while tortoises are day-active. Nevertheless, they shelter themselves during the hottest part of the day.[34]

Small mammals such as kangaroo-rats, jerboas, gerbils and other rodents, fennec and kit foxes, only survive in the desert because they are nocturnal. Birds, except for owls and nightjars, and large mammals such as camels, antelopes and wild asses which cannot burrow, are day-active although, again, as far as possible, they seek the shade when the sun beats down most fiercely.

Although diurnal rhythms are clearly related to physical changes in the environment, they are seldom a direct response to them. Organisms are believed to possess an inherent physiological 'clock' having a frequency of approximately 24 hours. For this reason, daily rhythms are usually called 'circadian' (from the Latin *circa*, about, and *dies*, a day). Circadian rhythms are regularly synchronized by variations in the physical conditions of the environment. Fluctuations of light intensity are the most important of these, but changes in temperature, relative humidity and other factors may also be important. The rhythm of nocturnal species is usually synchronized by the dusk, that of day-active animals by dawn.[21]

By means of its circadian rhythms, the animal mirrors internally, or even pre-adapts to, diurnal changes in the external environment. At the same time, the daily rhythm is itself constantly modified both by an endogenous seasonal rhythm and by environmental changes in day length, ambient temperature, and so on. For example, day-active desert lizards, beetles, etc., often show two peaks of activity each day in summer, when the weather is very hot at noon. These peaks occur at dawn and dusk. In spring and autumn, the animals show a single peak around midday; the winter is spent in hibernation. Seasonal changes also occur in the preferred temperatures of poikilothermic animals. (Poikilothermic—with a variable body temperature which approximates to that of the surroundings.) In contrast, homoiothermic birds and mammals maintain a constant body temperature.

Whereas endotherms appear to regulate their body temperatures around a single set point, ectotherms have both high and low points, separated by several degrees Celsius (K). They commonly undergo fluctuations in body temperature, even though these are less, as we have seen, than the fluctuations that occur in the environment. In general, the preferred temperatures tend to lie in the upper regions of the normal range of activity. This can be explained by the fact that metabolic efficiency increases at higher temperatures, up to the point at which enzymic and other metabolic processes begin to suffer damage or disorganization from excessive heat.

The physiology of circadian rhythms is thus closely inter-related with temperature regulation and the avoidance of climatic extremes in the desert. The lives of desert animals are closely connected with the physical environment, through its influence on the vegetation which forms the bases of their food-chains. They are, moreover, affected directly by the environment. But the inter-relationships between animals and the desert environments in which they live are even more complex than this, for climatic changes affect such animals at different physiological levels, which then inter-act with one another to produce additional secondary effects.[23, 35, 40]

PHENOLOGY

Seasonal changes of the environment in hot, arid regions result from one or other of two factors which may, or may not, coincide. These are seasonal precipitation and a consequent outburst of plant growth, and seasonal periods of cooler weather even if rain does not fall. These changes are reflected in the numbers and stages of development of the fauna so that populations of adults reach their peak at the time of the rains. For example, adult *Adesmia bicarinata* begin to appear in small numbers in Egypt during late October. Their population then gradually increases, reaching a peak in March. By the end of May the beetles have disappeared completely and only dead bodies can be found. During the hot season, their life-cycle is continued by the larval and pupal stages of development.

In the case of life-cycles such as this, which are extremely common among desert insects and arachnids, aestivation may, or may not, occur in the developmental stages. (Aestivation—dormancy during the summer or dry season. It is often correlated with diapause, a state of suspended development or growth accompanied by greatly decreased metabolism.) Either way, a vernal rain fauna appears at the time of inflorescence, when the desert is transformed by an abundance of plant and animal life. Flowers are visited by butterflies and moths, bees, wasps, hover-flies, bee-flies and other Diptera. The droppings of camels and goats are rolled away by dung beetles, and grass seeds are harvested by ants. Termites extend their subterranean galleries to the soil surface and indulge in nuptial flights, while predators, such as scorpions, camel-spiders, spiders, ant-lions, bugs, wasps, robber-flies and predatory beetles, glut themselves on an abundance of food. With the rains, too, come swarms of desert locusts which breed in the damp sand. The ephemeral vegetation is devoured by hordes of caterpillars and crickets, and the air buzzes with an abundance of flies, wasps and bees, rarely seen at other times of the year. Moths and butterflies are plentiful, migratory birds appear and build their nests, and most of the resident reptiles, birds and mammals produce their young while the harshness of the desert is briefly alleviated.[19, 37, 41]

The circadian rhythms of nocturnal animals tend to be delayed by light, while those of day-active animals are accelerated. Darkness has a reverse effect. In temperate regions, the time of activity of an animal is adjusted in this way to keep pace with seasonal climatic changes, but this effect is not marked among the animals of tropical deserts where day-length is fairly constant throughout the year. Changes in the length of the day, measured by means of the circadian clock, are utilized by most animals to synchronize their breeding periods with the season.[21] Among the birds and other inhabitants of deserts, however, even where this occurs and the animals are physiologically ready to breed, reproduction often needs to be triggered by some immediate stimulus from the environment, such as rainfall or the appearance of green vegetation. Maturation of desert locusts (*Schistocerca gregaria*) occurs in response to terpenoids and other aromatic chemicals produced seasonally by certain desert shrubs at the time of the annual rains. These compounds are responsible for the characteristic scents of frankincense and myrrh.[20]

The importance of a limited season of plant growth in arid environments is clearly seen in its influence on the hereditary adaptation of the rutting and birth of various species of gazelle. There is a close correlation between the birth of these animals and the normal time of rainfall. Calving usually begins about one month after the onset of the rainy season when plenty of grazing is available. Again, the camel, in contrast to most domestic animals, has a pronounced rutting season at the time of rainfall and its pregnancy lasts for 12 months. The fertility of jerboas, voles and other rodents is greatly reduced or even interrupted during dry weather and, at such times, the population level drops considerably. The staple food of these animals consists of grain and roots, but they also nibble at green plants when these are available. Their sterility in times of drought is believed to be caused by the absence of some factor occurring in green vegetation.[13, 14]

SIMILARITIES BETWEEN PLANTS AND ANIMALS

Plants and animals of arid environments show many striking similarities in their responses to the rigours of drought and heat. Setae, hairs, scales etc., that create a boundary layer reducing transpiration and the flow of heat from the environment, are common to both; stomata and spiracles are similar in the possession of a complex passage way which resists the diffusion of water vapour; cuticular transpiration in plants and arthropods is reduced by the presence of waxes having high melting points; and both plants and animals may possess mechanisms for salt excretion, the uptake of moisture from unsaturated air, the retention of metabolic water, and so on.[58]

Surface-to-volume relationships are an important factor in determining transpiration and heat flux relationships between plants, as well as animals, and their environments. Large succulent cacti, and euphorbias, heat up

76

Insect integument

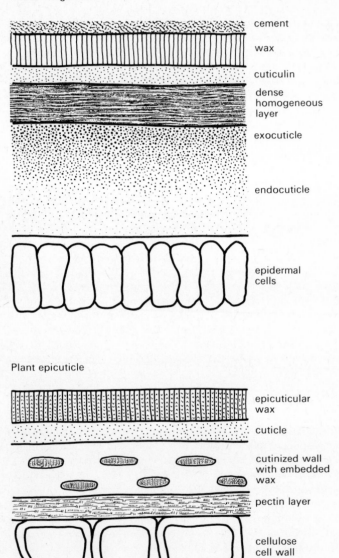

cement

wax

cuticulin

dense homogeneous layer

exocuticle

endocuticle

epidermal cells

Plant epicuticle

epicuticular wax

cuticle

cutinized wall with embedded wax

pectin layer

cellulose cell wall

Fig. 7.2 Diagrammatic structure of the insect integument compared with a diagrammatic representation of the plant epicuticle.[58]

more slowly than smaller-leaved desert shrubs. But, while they may eventually exhibit temperatures up to 15K above the ambient air, the temperatures of herbs and shrubs are maintained near to that of the surroundings because of the increased heat transfer from their small, narrow leaves. Convection is the dominant factor in the energy budget of leaves whose dimensions are less than one square centimetre, although transpiration contributes to their lower temperatures. Further examples of analogies between desert plants and animals will be given in subsequent sections of this, and in the next chapter.

REDUCTION IN TRANSPIRATION

The ratio of surface area to volume is so high in terrestrial arthropods that they must either inhabit very moist environments or be well adapted to resist water loss by transpiration. Indeed, it is probable that many insects and arachnids of temperate environments live under conditions which are physiologically as stringent as those that face desert vertebrates. Nevertheless, the insects and arachnids of arid regions are, as a rule, particularly resistant to water loss by transpiration through the cuticle.

Fig. 7.3 The desert woodlouse, *Hemilepistus reaumuri* (length, 2 cm).

Although woodlice are not found in extreme desert conditions, some species are able to exist in quite arid environments by exploiting moist microhabitats. Examples are afforded by *Hemilepistus reaumuri*, which is not uncommon in North Africa and the Middle East, *Buddelundia albinogriseus* of South Australia, and *Venezillo arizonicus* of the Sonoran desert in North America. These are all characterized by unusually low rates of transpiration and it has even been claimed that *V. arizonicus* may possess an epicuticular layer of wax. The point has often been made, however, that either one of two alternative courses was open to the ancestors of terrestrial arthropods: to evolve an impervious integument and all the physiological adjustments that must accompany it; or, like woodlice, to remain most of the time in relatively moist surroundings by means of behaviour responses, including nocturnal habits. That a desert isopod which has, presumably, followed the second of these to its furthest limits, should then have been able to evolve a discrete epicuticular wax layer *de novo* would be, therefore, a matter of considerable surprise.[40]

Millipedes are generally even less well adapted than are woodlice and centipedes to life in arid places, but transpiration from the North American desert millipede (*Orthoporus ornatus*) is less than one tenth that from allied species from the humid tropics.[44] Similar results have been obtained with centipedes from arid regions. Indian millipedes (*Cingalobolus* and *Aulacobolus* spp.) possess epicuticles of lipoprotein in the summer months. Although these lack an outer lipid layer, they restrict the permeability of the cuticle. At the commencement of the rainy season, however, when there is no need to restrict water loss, the new cuticle that is formed after moulting is without an epicuticle.[95]

The permeability of the insect cuticle has been the subject of extensive research and it is clear that the rate of transpiration is particularly low in desert species. There is evidence, moreover, that the epidermal cells of the migratory locust (*Locusta migratoria*) expend energy continuously in regulating the water balance of the cuticle which, to be in equilibrium with the blood, would contain 60 per cent more water than it actually does. This may result from active transport or from a cuticular water pump.[106]

Cuticular transpiration, although low in absolute rate, is a greater source of water loss from desert beetles than is respiratory transpiration, and an adaptive feature of long-lived Tenebrionidae is the ability to produce secondary sclerotization if the elytra are damaged. This is of particular importance since the main function of the sub-elytral cavity is to reduce water loss through the spiracles. Desert beetles lose water from four to ten times faster than desert scorpions when both are expressed as percentages of total weight per unit time. Ecologically significant though this criterion may be, it gives no indication about cuticle permeability. If a scorpion weighed 100 times more than a beetle, and both lost an equal percentage of weight in the same time, the rate of loss per unit area would be five times greater in the scorpion. In the comparison of a flea with a man cited above, the difference in rates was as much as 4,500 times because the decrease in surface-to-volume ratio was so enormous.[50, 51]

Cuticular permeability is exceptionally low in unfed desert ticks, and the transition temperatures of their epicuticular waxes extremely high—52°C for *Hyalomma dromedarii* and 63°C for *Ornithodorus savignyi*. Although the camel-spider *Galeodes granti* has a fairly high rate of water loss, compared with scorpions, it does not die until it has lost up to two-thirds of its total weight. Conflicting results have been obtained with regard to transpiration from the whip-scorpion *Mastigoproctus giganteus*. Although large specimens lost water in dry air at different temperatures in proportion to the saturation deficiency of the atmosphere, smaller individuals showed a marked increase at 37.5°C which results from a change in cuticular permeability. It is probable that the cuticles of the larger animals had been abraded by the desert soil.[45]

Amphibia require fresh water for breeding and, therefore, do not penetrate far into the desert, although a few species are able to exist on its fringe, provided that temporary or permanent water is available for reproduction. In some species the rate of evaporation through the skin is retarded. This adjustment occurs among Australian frogs of the genus *Neobatrachus*, while the Rhodesian *Chiromantis xerampelina* loses water very slowly, at a rate comparable with that of reptiles. Furthermore, it excretes uric acid rather than urea, a necessary concomitant of an impervious integument.[79] In contrast to that of most amphibians the reptilian skin is comparatively impermeable. The presence of a thick corneous stratum and small number of dermal glands ensures that water loss is minimal. Evaporation through the integument constitutes a major source of water loss from desert tortoises, lizards and snakes, but it is much less than in species from wetter regions.[85] Cutaneous water loss is far less significant in larger vertebrates such as birds and mammals. Small birds lose water by evaporation much more rapidly than do mammals of comparable size, but most of this is dissipated in panting rather than through skin transpiration. It is significant that sweat glands are absent from rodents and other small mammals (p. 91).

Plants and animals adapted to hot, dry environments often show an enhanced ability to survive desiccation. For example, ants inhabiting drier situations usually survive experimental drying better than other species of the same genus that normally inhabit more humid environments. Certain organisms, during diapause, are able to withstand almost complete dehydration; others can survive considerable desiccation even when not in a state of diapause. The Sudanese solifugid *Galeodes granti* can withstand a loss of two-thirds of its body weight and the camel as much as one-third. Most desert animals, however, are normally in a state of water balance, however arid their surroundings.

RESPIRATORY ADAPTATIONS

Membranes permeable to oxygen and carbon dioxide are also permeable to water vapour. The air leaving any respiratory surface is therefore normally saturated with water vapour and some loss of moisture through the respiratory membranes is probably inevitable. Land arthropods without occlusable spiracles or lung books are therefore at a grave disadvantage in comparison with those that have mechanisms for closing the respiratory apertures. The lung books of Arachnida, like the spiracles of arachnids and insects, are kept shut by special muscles until the amount of carbon dioxide in the respiratory system exceeds about 5 per cent: only then are they relaxed to permit ventilation.

Woodlice represent a group that probably invaded the land much later

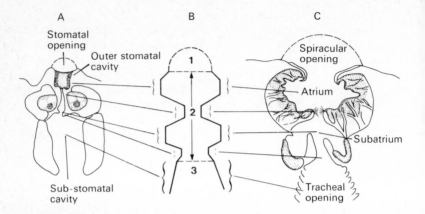

Fig. 7.4 Comparison of diffusion resistance within and outside a plant stoma and an insect spiracle. A, cross-section of stoma of *Yucca filamentosa*. B, schematic representation of relative resistance to diffusion through an aperture of varying diameters: (1) external resistance (boundary layer), (2) stomatal (spiracular) resistance, (3) sub-stomatal (tracheal) resistance. C, horizontal section through left spiracle of fourth abdominal segment of *Strategus julianus* (Scarabaeoidea).[58]

in geological history than did other terrestrial arthropods. Adaptation to terrestrial conditions has occurred mainly through modification of the respiratory organs with the development of pseudotracheae, the ability to roll into a ball, and so on. Conglobation, as this is called, reduces considerably the amount of water lost in transpiration because the respiratory organs, from which much of the loss takes place, are situated on the ventral side of the body. The spiracles of insects and ticks living in dry environments tend to be small and often sunken or hidden. It has long been known, too, that the spiracles of xerophilous buprestid beetles are covered with a basketwork of outgrowths which are believed to impede the diffusion of water molecules more than those of oxygen and carbon dioxide. A special case is found in desert Tenebrionidae with a sub-elytral cavity, a morphological adaptation to conditions of extreme aridity, whose major function is to reduce water loss by transpiration, for the spiracles open into it.[40]

Amphibia are apparently unable to control their respiratory water loss, but reptiles have some capacity to do so. The desert iguana (*Dipsosaurus dorsalis*) can to some extent cool the air it exhales, just as mammals and birds do (see below). In addition, fluid secreted from the nasal salt glands helps to cool and moisten the inhaled air. As water is evaporated, this fluid becomes even more concentrated, and encrustations of crystalline salt may be deposited around the openings of the nares. The tendency of

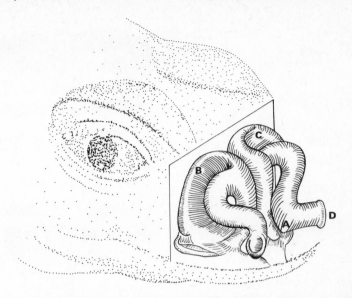

Fig. 7.5 The nasal passage of the desert iguana forms a slight depression (A) just inside the external nares (D). Fluid from the nasal salt-excreting glands, (located at B and C) accumulates in this depression and contributes moisture to the humidification of the respiratory air.[103]

tortoises to hold their breath for long periods, especially at high ambient temperatures, may also be concerned with the conservation of moisture.

Respiratory water loss is reduced in kangaroo-rats (*Dipodomys merriami*) and, presumably, in other small desert mammals, by means of a counter current heat exchange system in the nose. When the animal breathes saturated air, the temperature of the nose approaches that of the surroundings but, if dry air is inhaled, the temperature at the tip may be several K below the ambient air temperature. During inhalation, the walls of the nasal passage are cooled to about 28°C by the relatively cool air inside the kangaroo-rat's burrow. When air from the lungs, saturated with water vapour at 38°C, passes over those cool surfaces, condensation takes place and, if the heat exchange is complete, the exhaled air temperature will approach that of the environment. In fact, during inhalation, water evaporates from the moist nasal mucosa, which therefore becomes even cooler than the air in the burrow. Consequently, the temperature of the exhaled breath may actually be as low as 23°C when the kangaroo rat is breathing dry air. Cross sections of the nose of one of these animals show a very narrow passage with a large wall surface. This facilitates, to the utmost, the exchange of heat between the air and the nasal tissues.[103]

Fig. 7.6 Cross-sections of the nasal pathways of cactus wren and kangaroo-rat.
The passages are wider and the wall area smaller in the bird than in the mammal
of the same body size (about 35 g). In both animals the profiles were obtained at a
depth of 3 mm and 9 mm respectively, from the external openings.[103]

Similar mechanisms operate with varying degrees of efficiency in many
other mammals and, probably, in most birds too. In man and other large
mammals, however, the exchange of heat between the air and the walls of
the nasal passage is so incomplete that it is of only minor importance.

Birds do not have sweat glands but, when their body temperature rises,
evaporative cooling through the respiratory tract is increased by panting.
In some species, such as the desert poor-will (*Phalaenoptilus nuttallii*),
increased air movement is achieved by a rapid flapping of the loose, gular
skin on the ventral surface of the throat. Either one or both processes may
occur. The fact that birds show greater evaporative loss than mammals of
comparable size is quite possibly due to the fact that avian body temperature is normally higher than that of mammals. Consequently the expired
air is warmer and has a higher moisture content.[103] In large mammals that

cannot escape the desert's blast, sweating is reduced to a minimum by toleration of hyperthermy (Chapter 9).

EXCRETORY ADAPTATIONS

The excretory products of insects and arachnids—uric acid and guanine respectively—are extremely insoluble. Consequently nitrogenous waste matter can be eliminated from the body in a dry state and no water is lost in the process. In addition, water is reabsorbed from the faeces through the rectal gland, for rectum and Malpighian tubules function together as an osmotic and ionic regulatory system, whose capacity has been demonstrated in the desert locust (*Schistocerca gregaria*) and other insects.[106] In this respect, therefore, terrestrial arthropods are pre-adapted to life in arid regions.

That ammonium hydroxide is the main excretory product of woodlice, confers on these terrestrial crustaceans an especially acute problem when they inhabit arid regions. Furthermore, it is clear evidence of the fact that they cannot long have evolved from aquatic ancestors. Terrestrial animals must either concentrate a non-toxic substance, such as urea, or else eliminate an insoluble, harmless waste product, such as uric acid.[50, 51]

Amphibians that live in terrestrial habitats usually respond to dehydration by decreasing the rate of urinary water loss and increasing the rate at which water can be absorbed through the skin. This response is adaptive and is mediated by a neurohypophysial hormone, arginine vasotocin, similar to, but not the same as, the anti-diuretic hormones of mammals. Several desert species have been found in areas of high salinity, but only the Argentinian frog *Pleurodema nebulosa* has, so far, been found to produce hypotonic urine when immersed in a medium of relatively high salinity. Amphibians produce little urine and store urea in their bodies when water is restricted. They can tolerate high concentrations in their blood and tissues while they are aestivating or hibernating.

The urinary wastes of reptiles are eliminated as a pulpy or semi-solid mass, containing a high proportion of uric acid and accompanied by little water. The excretion of uric acid is highly advantageous to reptiles since they are unable to form urine that has a salinity greater than that of the blood-plasma. The cloaca, in fact, can reabsorb water only up to the point at which the urine has the same salinity as the blood. Lizards and snakes are not strictly uricotelic as was once thought, however, and the proportions of uric acid and urea may vary considerably. Tortoises show even greater variations than snakes and lizards in the ratio of urea to uric acid excreted. It has been suggested that urea may be absorbed through the cloaca, reduced to ammonia by the enzyme urease and then synthesized into uric acid.

Urea is the principal excretory compound of mammals, uric acid of birds, reptiles and insects. The excretion of uric acid is associated with the possession of cleidoic or enclosed eggs. If an embryo bird or insect were to produce ammonia, it would poison itself. Urea, on the other hand, might become so concentrated that it would upset the internal osmotic pressure of the egg and thus also kill the embryo. But uric acid can be left behind, inside the eggshell, when the young insect, reptile or bird hatches. So, it is assumed that the secretion of uric acid and guanine have been developed in relation to the evolution of terrestrial eggs—the aquatic eggs of fishes and amphibians produce ammonium hydroxide. Having once been evolved, however, uricotelic excretion has been retained by the adult animal; and very useful it has proved to be, especially in regions where water is scarce.[25]

Like mammals, but unlike reptiles and amphibians, birds are able to excrete a fairly concentrated urine: the ratio of water lost to that of nitrogen eliminated can be as high in the domestic fowl, under experimental conditions, as it is in desert rodents. Moreover, the fact that the ureters branch to join the kidney tubules directly, there being no renal pelvis as in mammals, is a key structural factor that enables birds to utilize uricotelism or the excretion of insoluble uric acid whilst simultaneously forming an osmotically concentrated urine. This thick urine is forced by peristalsis from the tubules directly through the branches of the ureters into the cloaca. There is, however, no good evidence for the re-absorption of water from the urine in the cloaca or rectum.

North American kangaroo-rats and other small rodents avoid the midday heat by burrowing (see earlier). Their physiological problems are therefore concerned with water shortage rather than with temperature stress. They can survive indefinitely on dry food without any water to drink. Indeed, on an exclusive diet of dry grain, some can even gain weight. No physiological water store is drawn upon, nor is there any increase in the concentration of the blood while living on a dry diet. This means that water is not conserved by the retention of waste metabolites, but the urine is almost twice as concentrated with respect to salts as is the urine excreted by the white rat, and 1.6 times as concentrated with respect to urea. Kangaroo-rats are even able to utilize sea-water for drinking, as they can excrete such large amounts of salt and yet maintain normal water balance. They can also eliminate an excess load of urea, about 23 per cent, which is nearly four times as much as in man.[104] Camels and other larger desert mammals are able to excrete concentrated urine but, in many of them, the urea content is low. This phenomenon is correlated with a diet containing little protein, and will be discussed further in Chapter 9.

The accumulation of salt in desert soils presents both xerophytic plants, the animals that feed on them and those that drink saline waters, with an additional problem of excretion. In some species, such as the desert salt-bush (*Atriplex* spp.), sodium chloride is eliminated through specialized groups of cells known as 'salt glands' which resemble stomatal pores. A hyperosmotic secretion is produced, thus minimizing water loss. Insects that feed on these halophytic plants, such as grasshoppers and lepidopterous larvae, are able to maintain osmotic equilibrium by excreting the surplus salt in their diet through their Malpighian tubules. Counterparts to the salt-excreting structures of plants can be found in the nasal salt glands, already mentioned, of some desert reptiles and birds, including the ostrich. Insect-eating lizards build up accumulations of potassium salts, because insects contain these in large quantities, but some vegetarian species such as the chuckwalla (*Sauromalus obesus*) also possess these glands. It has been suggested that extra-renal secretion of salts by these animals is related to the cloacal re-absorption of water, and thus results in improved economy[103]

Terrestrial birds usually have a low tolerance to saline waters, and the American mourning dove (*Zenaidura macroura*) and house finch (*Carpodacus mexicanus*) are no exception. The Australian zebra finch (*Taenioptygia castanotes*), however, can exist on a saline solution slightly stronger than seawater. So can the American savannah sparrow which normally lives and nests in salt marshes. Pallas's sand grouse (*Syrrhaptes paradoxus*) feeds only on salty, succulent, desert chenopodiaceous plants in Central Asia and other birds may be able, by virtue of their powerful kidneys, to take advantage of the water in salt-marsh plants. Desert birds, in general, appear to utilize physiological capacities which they share with non-desert species, minimizing cloacal water loss and concentrating salt in their urine.[10]

The kidneys of desert mammals need to be efficient to produce urine with high concentrations both of urea and of salt. Antelope ground squirrels (*Citellus leucurus*), for example, can profitably drink salt solutions that are more concentrated than sea water and maintain their water balance with an intake equal to only 2 per cent of their body weight per day. Camels, too, can tolerate drinking salt or bitter water that would be poisonous to man and many other animals, and their powerful kidneys can produce a concentrated urine.[100]

WATER UPTAKE

Just as plant roots are able to absorb moisture from damp soil, so some spiders, 'vinegaroons' (*Mastigoproctus giganteus*) and other arthropods may be able to imbibe capillary moisture from damp soil.[45] This is detected by means of hygroreceptors on the antenniform front legs of the vinegaroon. This ability has not yet been demonstrated in insects.

Some arthropods are capable of absorbing water vapour from unsaturated air either through the integument or the rectum. These include Thysanura, larvae and adult female sand roaches of the genus *Arenivaga*, flea prepupae and ticks.[50] At one time it seemed that the mechanism might be related to the properties of anomalous or polywater, but it now appears unlikely that this hypothesis can be tenable (NB. A proportion of the water in a fine capillary has been claimed to have an abnormally low vapour pressure, and other anomalous properties.) The process is certainly adaptive, but it is surprising that it should not be more widespread among desert arthropods. Even the millipede *Orthoporus ornatus* is unable to absorb moisture across the cuticle, although both oral and anal uptake has been demonstrated from moist surfaces.[44] Nor can tenebrionid beetles do so, although the cryptonephridial renal complex is associated with very efficient removal of water from the faeces.

Parasitic mites and ticks obtain ample water from their food but, when separated from their hosts, they may have to withstand long periods of starvation under extremely desiccating circumstances when a low rate of transpiration and the ability to take up moisture from unsaturated air may be of vital importance. The critical equilibrium humidity varies from 45 to 95 per cent in different species. In most arthropods the osmotic pressures of the haemolymphs are in equilibrium with air at approximately 99 per cent relative humidity.

A common physiological adaptation of both herbivorous and carnivorous desert invertebrates is the ability to live on moisture obtained with food. Insects tend to conserve the high moisture content of plants and their bodies may contain water greatly in excess of that found in their diet. Water absorbed hygroscopically at night from desiccated vegetation is also utilized. It is probable, too, that water produced by the metabolism of food is retained within the body, for certain species of beetles have been shown to eat more food at lower humidities to produce a given body weight; of course, some of this water may have been obtained by the dehydration of undigested food.[19]

It has been argued that, in order to oxidize more food, a higher respiration rate is necessary. Consequently, additional moisture must be lost in the process, and what is gained from metabolism may be lost in increased respiration. It has not yet been proved that the insect, by doing metabolic work, may be able to remove water vapour from the air before it is expired. In view of the fact that moisture can be absorbed from unsaturated atmospheres through the integument, however, it does seem highly probable that this may occur.[23]

Various species of reptile have been thought to absorb moisture through their skin in damp sand and to lose it in dry surroundings, the ability of a species to resist desiccation being correlated with the habitat normally selected. The permeability of reptile skin is variable, however, and depends upon external conditions—it is permeable when saturated with water but is almost completely impermeable in dry air. An apparent exception may be found in the curious spiny lizard (*Moloch horridus*) which inhabits the sandy districts of western and southern Australia where it feeds upon ants. The rough skin of this animal is hygroscopic and sucks up water like blotting paper. This water travels to the mouth by capillarity and is swallowed. Moisture is also absorbed through the mouth from damp sand. Like lizards, snakes possess a relatively impervious skin which is especially impermeable in desert species, and little water is used in excreting urinary waste matter. Their carnivorous diet is rich in moisture, and evaporation is greatly reduced by daily or seasonal quiescence in a relatively cool and humid burrow.[34, 35]

Although for larger birds, over about 60 gm in weight, the difference between metabolic water production and evaporative water loss is slight and can often be compensated by free water in the food, smaller birds can survive only by drinking or by eating very succulent food. For this reason the majority of species that inhabit desert and semi-arid scrub are insectivorous or carnivorous.

By remaining in their relatively cool and damp burrows throughout the day, kangaroo-rats and jerboas are able to maintain water balance on a diet of dry seeds without ever drinking. If they were to breathe the dry air outside their burrows during the day, the rate of evaporation from their lungs would exceed the rate of formation of metabolic water. Other desert mammals obtain sufficient moisture for their needs from preformed water in their food. These include the sand-rat (*Psammomys obesus*) of North Africa which lives and nests in places where the vegetation consists of succulent plants. These are usually extremely salty, but sand-rats eat them in great quantities and secrete a copious urine which may be up to four times the concentration of sea water. The American pack-rats (*Neotoma* spp.) and ground squirrels (*Citellus* spp.) which feed on juicy cholla fruits, do not possess the same ability to eliminate large quantities of salt but, nevertheless, excrete a concentrated urine.[105]

Other small American desert rodents are grasshopper mice (*Onychomys* spp.), so called on account of their insectivorous diet which provides them with all their water requirements. The desert hedgehog of North Africa also obtains water from its food, while the crest-tailed marsupial mouse or mulgara (*Dasycerus cristicauda*), which inhabits the most arid central parts of Australia, lives predominantly on insects, supplemented by occasional lizards and small rodents. Like the grasshopper mice, it is able to excrete in a relatively small volume of water the large amounts of urea which result from its carnivorous diet. In common with most other deserticolous mammals it is a pale sandy colour (p. 97).

Although many species of desert hares and rabbits excavate tunnels and burrows, the American jack rabbits remain above ground and have no underground retreat. They live in areas where no free water is available and depend upon the moisture obtained with their green food. It is not entirely clear how they can survive in the desert, but the suggestion has been made that their very large ears, with a network of blood vessels, may serve to radiate heat to the sky while the animals are resting in the shade. Large ears are a characteristic of many desert animals, and the Saharan hare has ears much larger than those of its relatives of temperate climates.

Little is known about the adaptations of desert carnivores but there is no doubt that they obtain considerable quantities of water from the body fluids of their prey. In addition, they tend to have a more varied diet than their relatives from more temperate regions. Carnivores include foxes, jackals, hyaenas, coyotes, small cats, badgers, skunks, ferrets, some carnivorous marsupials and the Australian dingo. Of these, only foxes are found in extremely arid regions and may be entirely independent of drinking water.[102]

The water requirements of camels, donkeys, antelope and gazelles, animals of direct economic importance to man, will be considered in Chapter 9.

8

Thermal Problems of Animals

In this chapter we shall consider the solutions evolved by animals to the second major problem of desert life—how to keep their body temperatures below lethal limits when they cannot afford to cool themselves by transpiration. The burrowing and nocturnal habits described in the last chapter not only help to conserve moisture, but they also enable small animals to avoid the extremes of the desert heat.

BEHAVIOURAL THERMOREGULATION

The physiological responses of animals to extremes of temperature have been the subject of a considerable amount of study. Behaviour reactions play a major part in the regulation of body temperature in poikilothermic animals, both invertebrate and vertebrate.

Since they do not transpire rapidly, insects and reptiles are not restricted to nocturnal habits, as are most small desert animals. But, of course, they would soon be killed if they became too hot. So they spend their time adjusting their temperatures by moving into the sun or shade, by orientating the axis of the body to the angle of the sun or to the direction of the prevailing wind, by increasing or decreasing contact with the soil, by perching on branches or by burrowing in the soil.

Thermoregulation by sun basking and the avoidance of excessive heat, supplemented by more subtle parameters of behaviour, is intimately associated with rhythmical activity. An endogenous periodicity resulting from operation of the 'biological clock' (p. 73) is responsible for emergence at dusk or dawn, independently of cyclical environmental changes in temperature or light intensity. But for this, ectothermal arthropods and

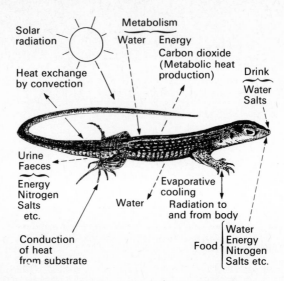

Fig. 8.1 Thermal and metabolic relationships in a desert lizard.

reptiles would be unable to make full use of their burrows and other retreats without losing valuable time at the commencement of their normal
periods of activity. Thermal control is achieved by the interaction of external factors, cyclical processes and behavioural responses.

It is commonly assumed that reptiles can withstand very high temperatures, probably on account of their habit of basking in the sun, but this is
not so. Most species seem to prefer temperatures at the higher end of the
normal activity range but are stricken with paralysis and soon die above
about 45°C (113°F). In the Sudan, neither day-active skinks (*Mabuya
quinquetaeniatus*) nor the nocturnal geckoes (*Tarentola annularis*) can
survive more than 40°C (104°F) for 24 hours, but the latter can withstand
a considerably higher degree of desiccation which may be correlated with its
comparative lack of mobility.

Although a certain amount of water is lost by evaporation through the
reptilian skin, perhaps ten times the amount formed by metabolism, it is
doubtful if this contributes much to cooling the body. Small reptiles have
a higher rate of water-loss per unit body weight than larger ones, the difference probably being related to the larger relative surface area in smaller
animals. At high temperatures an increase in respiration rate, or panting,
takes place. Evaporative water-loss is thus greater than in small mammals
so that, at high temperatures, the production of metabolic water becomes
inadequate for the maintenance of water balance. On the other hand, a

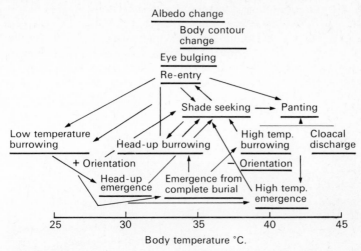

Fig. 8.2 The inter-relations of temperature regulating behaviour in *Phrynosoma coronatum*. The range of body temperature for each pattern is given[34] (after J. E. Heath).

considerable amount of water is obtained with an insectivorous diet which helps to redress the balance.[112]

Snakes are much less common in deserts than are lizards; nevertheless they comprise an important element of the fauna. They are the most highly specialized of the carnivorous reptiles and are exclusively meat-eaters. Although their tolerance of high temperatures in general is lower than that of lizards or tortoises—for example the lethal temperature of the desert rattlesnake (*Crotalus cerastes*) is 41.5°C, while that of lizards inhabiting the same area is 45°–47.5°C—snakes are even more adept at insinuating themselves into holes and crevices.[34, 35]

EMERGENCY MECHANISMS

Smaller animals cannot afford to expend water for evaporative cooling, but they do not need to do so because they can escape from the midday heat into cool burrows and retreats. Desert rodents do not sweat; indeed it seems likely that the general absence of sweat glands in small mammals results from the necessity to conserve water that is imposed by their relatively large surface area. In order to maintain a constant, normal body temperature when the air temperature is around 40°C (104°F), a kangaroo-rat would have to lose 20 per cent of its body weight per hour. Nevertheless despite this, emergency thermoregulatory mechanisms are sometimes found. For instance, jerboas (*Jaculus* and *Dipus* spp.)[68] and kangaroo-rats

(*Dipodomys* spp.) produce a copious flow of saliva in response to heat stress. This soaks the fur under the chin and throat, providing temporary defence when the body temperature approaches lethal limits.[102, 104] Similar responses occur in ground squirrels (*Citellus* spp.) and other small mammals whose water resources are insufficient to provide active temperature regulation for any length of time. An emergency reaction of this type may mean the difference between life and death if an animal is temporarily unable to retreat into its burrow.

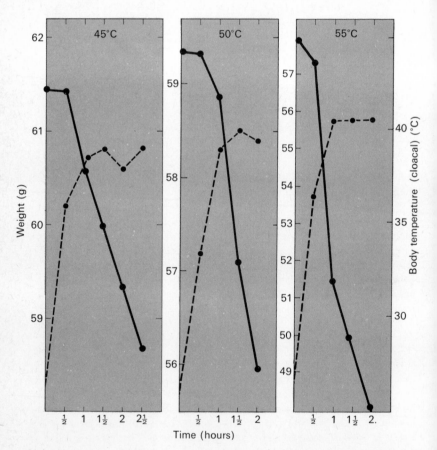

Fig. 8.3 Loss in weight and increase in body temperature during consecutive exposures of 30 min. in dry air at various high temperatures in *Testudo sulcata*, weight (————); body temperature (- - - - - -).[30] (Reproduced by permission of the Zoological Society of London.)

Thermoregulatory salivation is not restricted to small mammals: it also occurs in some reptiles, particularly tortoises, and again only under conditions of heat stress. Evaporative water-loss from the African desert tortoise (*Testudo sulcata*) increases greatly when the air temperature exceeds about 40.5°C (105°F)[30] because the temperature of the body is maintained at this level by the evaporation of urine which is discharged over the back legs, and of copious saliva which wets the head, neck and front legs. The function of the large bladders of desert tortoises has long puzzled naturalists. We now know the answer. Urine is stored, both as a defence against enemies, and for use in emergency cooling when the animals are unable to find a cool, shady hiding place.[34]

HYPERTHERMIA

Desert plants compensate to some extent for their lack of mobility, which prevents them from moving from an unfavourable microclimate, by having an extended range over which their metabolic activities function efficiently. Their resistance to heat is due, in some degree, to increased molecular stability, particularly of enzymatic proteins whose bonding is strengthened by reduction in the degree of hydration. This phenomenon makes it possible for lichens to grow on substrates whose temperature may exceed 70°C (158°F).[58, 114] In a comparable way the upper lethal temperatures of desert arthropods and reptiles are somewhat higher than those of species from other terrestrial biomes.[31]

The same principle is extended even to large mammals which experience hyperthermia under conditions of heat stress. For instance, the camel allows its body temperature to vary over a wide range and does not begin to sweat until it has risen to 40.7°C (105.3°F) (p. 102). In this way, heat is stored during the day and lost at night, when the environmental temperature drops, thus avoiding undue water loss. Moreover, when the camel's temperature rises, the difference between it and that of the ambient air is reduced so that less sweat is required to prevent a further increase in body temperature.[102] Other large desert animals, such as addax (*Addax nasomaculatus*), oryx (*Oryx* spp.),[111] dorcas gazelles (*Gazella dorcas*)[55] and ostrich (*Struthio camelus*)[78] also show hyperthermia, especially when somewhat desiccated. Although the body temperatures of gazelles and antelopes may reach 46°C (115°F), the blood that supplies the brain is cooled by means of heat exchange in the carotid rete, a network of small blood vessels in the cavernous sinus. This sinus is filled with venous blood that drains from the nasal passages where it has been cooled by evaporation from the moist mucous membranes. In a gazelle whose body temperature had been driven up by exercise, the brain temperature was found to be as much as 2.9 K lower than that of the blood in the central arteries.[111]

The fact that birds, in general, have a higher body temperature than mammals is also an advantage in that it allows them to rely to a greater extent upon the dissipation of heat by conduction and radiation but, since they are well insulated, this is of slight significance. In most species, the body temperature varies from 40–42°C (104–107.5°F) and the lethal temperature is about 47°C (116.5°F): desert birds are seldom more tolerant of increased body temperatures than are their non-desert relatives. The capacity of the American mourning dove (*Zenaidura macroura*) to endure elevated body temperature and extensive dehydration, combined with the ability to make up water deficit and fly long distances, allows it to meet the demands of a desert existence. Unlike most other species, the mourning dove is not confined to the immediate vicinity of water.[10, 48, 102]

Even more so than other birds, the ostrich (*Struthio camelus*) cannot escape to a favourable microclimate to avoid high temperatures. But it makes maximum use of radiant and convective cooling. Its head, neck, legs and belly are almost naked, while its feathers provide considerable insulation from the sun's heat. The feathers are erected while the wings are held away from the body to shade it and, at the same time, to allow the slightest breeze to cool the skin. Only as a last resort will the ostrich employ evaporative cooling by raising its respiration rate suddenly from about 4 to 40 breaths per minute. Finally, salt-excretory nasal glands enable it to drink brackish or even salty water.[78]

Although aestivation has been described in only one bird, the poor-will (*Phalaenoptilus nuttallii*), it occurs in a number of desert rodents such as ground squirrels which become torpid during the summer and early autumn. Deep in their cool burrows, their body temperatures drop to that of the surrounding air; their respiration rate is much reduced and other physiological processes are likewise slowed down. It would seem that this must be a mechanism that tides these animals through periods of food shortage when it would not benefit them to wander actively outside. Many invertebrates remain throughout the dry season in a state of diapause, as described in the previous chapter.

ADAPTATIONS FOR LIFE IN SAND

Many desert animals possess adaptations for living in sand. For instance, bristle-tails (Thysanura) form an important element of the desert fauna. They are extremely numerous in the Namib, for example, and take refuge at the base of tussocks of the grass *Aristida* spp., where they wriggle or almost swim with fish-like movements in the sand. At least one species of Hemiptera has the same habit, and several species of tenebrionid beetles have become flattened and plate-like in appearance, with short legs and the thorax and abdomen expanded into thin, wide plates with sharp edges.

They burrow rapidly into the sand with alternate sideways movements. Some of these flattened beetles, which feed on the leeward side of the dunes, orientate themselves horizontally so that the smallest digging movement of the legs starts a cascade of sand above which covers them very rapidly.[69, 73]

In the Sahara, too, many of the species associated with dunes and *ergs* show morphological adaptations for burrowing. Some are modified to swim through a loose substratum without making a hole, some excavate pits, and others, such as scorpions and Solifugae, mine tunnels in more cohesive sand. A number of insects and arachnids have enormous brushes of flattened hairs or bristles on the undersides of their legs which act like snowshoes and facilitate their movements through the sand.[23, 91]

The lizards of sand dunes and *ergs* also show adaptations to the environment according to whether they are 'sand-runners' or 'sand-swimmers'. The former have the toes of the fore and hind limbs fringed with elongated scales. These presumably widen the surface which presses on loose sand, in the manner of snow shoes.[19] A modification that serves the same function is found in the duck-like webbed feet of the nocturnal geckos (*Palmatogecko* spp.) which live among the sands of the Kalahari Desert. In this animal there is a complete webbing between the fingers and toes for support on loose sand. Lizards that live in sandy deserts are usually extremely rapid in their movements. When not running, they stand alert with their heads held high and the front part of the body raised on the forelimbs so that they clear the hot sand. In motion, the tail is held well above the ground as a counterpoise. Such adaptations are found in a number of unrelated families from different parts of the world.[19]

'Sand-swimmers' include the skinks as well as other lizards and snakes which exhibit several profound modifications for rapid burrowing in loose sand. The nose or rostrum is pointed or shovel-like and some species can dive head first into loose sand as though it were water. The nostrils tend to be directed upwards instead of forwards and thus are protected from the sand. In most snakes, they are shielded by complicated valves, or are reduced to small pin-holes. The eyes of the worm-like *Typhlops* spp. are overhung by large head shields. Lizards of the genus *Mabuya* may have the lower lid much enlarged with a transparent window in it so that the eye can be closed without impeding sight, an arrangement carried to an extreme in *Ablepharus* spp., where the lower lid is fused with the rim of the reduced upper lid.[41] The ear opening is also either small and protected by fringes of scales, or may even be abolished in certain reptiles.

Desert lizards and snakes often have widened bodies for burrowing by lateral and vertical movements instead of ploughing forward into sand. Helical side-winding in found in snakes such as the American side-winder (*Crotalus cerastes*) and horned vipers of the genus *Cerastes* in the

Fig. 8.4 Feet of desert lizards showing scales: 1–3 fore feet, 4–6 hind feet. 1 and 4, *Phrynocephalus* sp., 2 and 5, *Uma* sp., 3 and 6, *Stenodactylus* sp.[19]

Great Palaearctic Desert. These snakes progress by lateral loops of the body which cause them to move obliquely, leaving a ladder-like succession of furrows behind as they travel through the sand. No piles of sand are produced, so no effort can be lost in horizontal thrusts. Such helical side-winding causes the snakes to move obliquely in the direction to which the heads are pointing.

The adaptation is probably related primarily to life in wide open spaces as much as for locomotion in a shifting substratum, for it not only pro-duces a high speed, but it halves the area of the body in contact with the hot surface. It also prevents the snakes from sinking into soft sand, and has an additional function in that it enables the prey to be approached in a devious manner so that it is not alarmed until too late.

Mammals may also show adaptations for life in sandy places. The camel, having lost all except two of its toes in the course of evolution, is unable to recover them but has increased the surface area of its feet by developing fleshy pads which do not sink into the sand. Its eyes are protected by its long and abundant lashes and it can close its nostrils at will to prevent the entrance of sand. In the saiga antelope (*Saiga tatarica*) the nostrils face backwards so that sand is excluded during grazing (p. 106) The bipedal gait of jerboas and kangaroo-rats, like that of marsupial kangaroos and certain desert lizards, is an adaptation for speedy locomotion in open country.[66]

ADAPTIVE COLORATION

The colours of desert animals have long been a matter of interest and their functions of dispute. Most of the inhabitants of arid regions are either black or pale in colour, resembling their background. In many, the under-surface of the body is very pale or even white. Desert species and sub-species differ from their near relatives of other environments just as much in their pale ventral surface as in their buff or sandy backs. Moreover, the pale ventral area is often extended over the flanks in desert forms to a greater extent than it is in related species from other habitats. The same phenomenon occurs in spiders, centipedes, woodlice, insects, lizards, snakes, birds and mammals.

Desert dwellers are not coloured fawn, brown, cream or grey indiscriminately: there is often a close similarity between the animal and the soil of the particular desert in which it is living. Although the suggestion has been made that desert coloration must result from some unknown physiological influence of the environment, because it is found equally in nocturnal and day-active forms, there is now little controversy as to its function of concealment. In the desert, starlight renders nearby objects visible even to the human eye and the moon bathes the scene in a flood of silver light.[24] An apparent paradox is, however, presented by the black pigments of other desert animals, because black objects generally absorb more heat than paler ones.[59]

To some extent, this may be an evolutionary legacy but the proportion of species and individuals that are black, especially among insects and birds, is higher in deserts than elsewhere. Although melanin may render an integument especially impermeable, this cannot be its biological function, because evaporative cooling for purposes of thermoregulation cannot be employed by any animals of such small size, whatever their environment. Transparent insect wings reflect more infra-red solar energy than the black elytra of desert beetles so the function of the black pigment cannot be protection against radiation. In any case, infra-red radiation can hardly be responsible for visible colour differences.[50]

We are therefore reduced to one of two hypotheses: either the black colours of desert animals have a thermal significance, or else their function lies in advertisement. Colour is probably relatively unimportant thermally, because a high proportion of energy is transmitted at infra-red wave lengths. Moreover, if black cuticle, feathers or hair should become very much hotter than the environment, the excess heat would be removed by conduction, convection and, to some extent, by radiation unless the heat were conducted inwards. Various insulating devices, however, militate against such conduction. One must therefore conclude that the functions of the black pigments of desert animals are ecological rather than physiological.

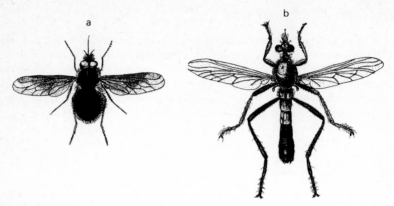

Fig. 8.5 Desert insects (a) Black bee-fly (*Bombylius* sp.); (b) Black and yellow robber-fly (*Lamyra* sp.).[41]

For a yellow wasp to become conspicuous it must acquire black markings. Similarly, on a yellow background of desert sand, black is by far the most conspicuous colour—reds, yellows and browns do not show up at all well. Consequently it would be natural to expect any desert animals that make themselves conspicuous to be black as, indeed, they nearly always are. The functions of such advertisement may be diverse—warning, social interactions, and so on. In the case of desert beetles, which are hard and distasteful, black coloration is probably aposematic, serving to deter potential predators (Aposematic—warning coloration.) It may also represent Müllerian mimicry, in which two distasteful species resemble one another, thereby reducing losses incurred in teaching predators to avoid them, although it would be difficult to imagine any advertising colour, other than black, that would be equally striking in the desert environment.[51]

In addition to the adaptations already discussed, desert animals may possess a number of other, somewhat less significant modifications which can be correlated with their open, hot and arid habitats. About 80 per cent of desert mammals, for example, show hypertrophy or enlargement of the bullae tympanicae. These are the bony projections of the skull that enclose the middle ear. Such hypertrophy is particularly evident among gerbils, cats and hedgehogs. The bullae probably function as resonators, facilitating the perception of soil vibrations and acting as amplifiers. This is but one of many specializations of the sensory system of desert animals. In their harsh environment, natural selection has resulted in enhanced efficiency; sight becomes more keen, hearing more acute, and so on. Similarly, speedy animals are said to be faster, and venomous species more poisonous than their counterparts of biomes less severe than the desert.[41]

In this chapter, I have outlined the main types of adaptation to environmental heat in animals of arid environments. They have not been discussed in detail, however, not only because it would take too long but because, with the exception of those in animals of direct concern to man, they are not strictly relevant to the theme of this book. Further information may, however, be obtained from the sources listed in the bibliography.

9

Adaptations and Exploitation of Larger Mammals

Larger desert animals, such as camels, asses, addax and oryx antelopes, gazelles, etc., are in a situation completely different from that of the creatures we have been discussing so far, because they are too big to be able to escape from the rigours of the desert by burrowing. Instead, they must employ physiological adaptations to reduce water-loss and avoid thermal stress during the daytime. At the same time, their surface-to-volume ratio is much reduced in consequence of their increased bulk. This means that they need not use so much energy for metabolic heating in cold weather and at night. At the same time, insulating hair not only keeps them warm at night, but it shields them from the heat of the sun.

CAMELS

The camel is one of the most typical and best adapted of the larger desert animals. There are two species of camel; the Arabian camel or dromedary (*Camelus dromedarius*) which possesses a single hump, and the two-humped, bactrian camel (*C. bactrianus*). The dromedary is widespread throughout the Middle East, India and North Africa: the bactrian camel inhabits the deserts of central Asia where the winters are very cold. Its winter coat is longer and darker, it has shorter legs, and it seldom measures more than 2.1 m (7 ft) from the ground to the top of the humps. This is about the height of the shoulder in the taller and more slender dromedary. The dromedary is known only in domestication, but the small humps and feet and short, brown hair of the bactrian camels of the Gobi desert indicate that they are genuinely wild and not merely feral (that is, descendants of domesticated stock that have escaped over the centuries).

As has been said earlier camels are well adapted for life in sandy places (see p. 96).

The dromedary had been domesticated on the borders of Arabia by 1800 B.C., a fact confirmed by the finding of Middle Bronze Age remains of camels at ancient urban sites in Israel. Dromedaries were subsequently introduced to North Africa, the Nile Valley and north-western India. They appeared in the Roman arenas about 29 B.C. and were later used in chariot races. In modern times, 20 of the animals were imported into Australia first as carriers for the ill-fated Burke-Wills expedition which crossed the Australian continent in 1860–61 and the descendants of these and other camels imported from Afghanistan during the last century still live there in a feral state. Dromedaries were also used in the United States after the Mexican War of the 1840's, on mail and express routes across the newly acquired arid regions, but they were later killed.

Less is known of the history of the bactrian camel. Remains found at Shah Tepe in Iran and at Anan in Turkestan, dating from about 3000 B.C., have been tentatively assigned to this species. It probably had a wide distribution as a wild animal in central and north-western Asia during prehistoric times. By the 6th century B.C., bactrian camels were being domesticated in Persia.

Camels are still of great importance in desert countries as beasts of burden. A pack dromedary can carry 270 kg (600 lbs) for 50 km (30 miles) in a day and a bactrian camel up to 450 kg (1,000 lbs). When moving fast, camels pace. Like the giraffe and brown bear, they raise both legs on the same side of the body and advance them simultaneously whilst the weight is supported by the legs of the opposite side. In this way a speed of up to 9.5 km/h (6 m.p.h.) may be achieved, but cannot be maintained for more than a few hours. The normal walking speed of a racing camel is only 5.5 km/h (3½ m.p.h.), almost double that of a pack animal, and its maximum speed is approximately 10 m.p.h. A camel cannot gallop for more than a few yards. In order to keep a racing camel at its fastest pace, the long trot, the rider must cultivate a rankling sore on its neck and prick this continuously. Camel hair is used for making clothes, tents and carpets. The milk is nutritious, the flesh tastes somewhat like beef, and the liver is considered a delicacy.

Although they chew the cud, camels differ from true ruminants in that the adults retain two incisor teeth in the upper jaw. Furthermore, they lack an *omasum* or third section to their stomachs. The smooth-walled rumen or anterior section has small sacs or diverticula leading from it. These were formerly called 'water sacs' because of an erroneous hypothesis, dating from Pliny's *Historia Naturalis*, that they served the function of water storage. These glandular rumen sacs contain a fluid having the same salt content as the rest of the body. It is like green pea soup in appearance and is quite

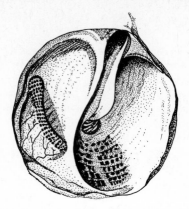

Fig. 9.1 Rumen of the camel showing so-called 'water sacs'.[102]

repulsive to drink. To the desert traveller who has no water, however, any fluid is attractive. The many tales of people who have saved their lives by killing their camels to drink the fluid in the rumen sacs may therefore well be true.[102]

Equally erroneous is the idea that the camel stores water in its hump, or that the fat composing the hump is essentially a water-store itself. On oxidation, this fat produces metabolic water, but the extra oxygen that must be used in the process involves, in turn an extra loss of water through the lungs which just about cancels any gain from oxidation of the fat. The camel's hump is actually a food store which, by being concentrated in one large depot and not distributed as a subcutaneous layer of fat, allows the rest of the body to act as a radiator for cooling purposes.

The rate of urine flow is low in camels and little water is lost with the faeces. Instead of eliminating all the urea produced in metabolism the camel, like ruminants, can utilize it for microbial synthesis of protein. In this way the amount of water excreted is reduced and greater use made of the food.

The coarse hair on the camel's back acts as a barrier to solar radiation and slows the conduction of heat from the environment. It is well ventilated, so that evaporation of sweat occurs on the skin where it provides maximum cooling. At the same time the camel avoids undue water-loss by allowing its temperature to vary over a range greater than that of other mammals as we have already seen (p. 93), heat being stored during the day and lost at night when the environmental temperature is lower. Moreover, when the camel's temperature rises, the difference between it and that of the air is reduced so that less sweat is required to prevent a further increase in body temperature.

The dromedary can tolerate a much greater depletion in body water

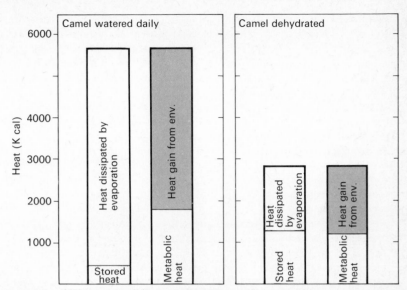

Fig. 9.2 Environmental heat gain of the camel. The total heat load is determined as the sum of stored heat and heat dissipated by evaporation (unshaded columns at left). The metabolic heat (unshaded portion of columns at right) can be subtracted from the total, leaving a fair estimate of the environmental heat gain (dotted area). In a dehydrated animal (right) the environmental heat gain was much smaller than in the same camel when watered daily (left).[102]

than most other mammals and may, without ill effects, lose about 30 per cent of its body weight (100 kg out of 450 kg) as compared with about 12 per cent in man. It also has an unusual drinking capacity and can assimilate 115 litre (25 gallons) or more in a very short space of time. The blood and tissue fluids become rapidly diluted to an extent that would cause other mammals to die from water intoxication. This ability is related to the physiology of the blood, whose red corpuscles or erythrocytes are unusually resistant to dilution and can swell to twice their initial volume without rupturing.[100, 102]

With most mammals subjected to high temperatures in dry air, desiccation proceeds steadily while the body temperature remains constant. As water is lost through evaporative cooling, however, the blood gradually becomes more viscous until it cannot circulate quickly enough to carry away metabolic heat to the skin. At this point, the temperature suddenly rises and 'explosive heat death' results. In camels, however, this misfortune is avoided by a physiological mechanism which ensures that water is lost from the tissues only, while the blood volume remains fairly constant.[102]

Thus the adaptations of the camel to its desert environment do not involve independence of drinking water but the ability to economize the water available and to tolerate wide variations in body temperature and water content. In winter, when the temperature is comparatively low and water is not needed for heat regulation, camels become independent of drinking water for several months. In summer the length of time between drinks depends on the environmental temperature and the amount of work that the animal is called on to perform. Police camels require water every third day in summer in the northern Sudan, if they are to maintain their strength (cf p. 110–11).

In contrast to most other domesticated animals, the dromedary has a pronounced rutting season at the time of the rains and its pregnancy is prolonged for nearly a year until the following rainfall. The bactrian camel has an even longer gestation period of 370–440 days. The young are born singly and are suckled for three or four months. They are full-grown at 16–17 years. The interval between births is two years, and longevity about 25 years. Droves of wild bactrian camels in the Gobi desert usually consist of one or two males and three to five females. They sleep at night in open spaces and graze during the day on grasses, brushwood and shrubs. They migrate to the northern part of the range in spring and return southward in the autumn. Mating takes place in January and February. In hot weather dromedaries orient their bodies so that a minimal area is exposed to the rays of the sun.[28]

ANTELOPES AND ASSES

The larger mammals of the desert of the Old World include antelopes, gazelles and wild asses. In the arid regions of North America their ecological niche is occupied by the pronghorn (*Antilocapra americana*), formerly very common in the prairies but now extremely rare, and the mule-deer (*Odocoileus hemionus*). The larger herbivores of the Australian deserts are kangaroos and wallabies. None of these animals is able to escape the rigours of the desert climate by burrowing but, to a lesser degree, they show many of the physiological adaptations of the camel and have low water requirements. Their mobility enables them to travel long distances to obtain drinking water if required.

Oryx antelopes are found throughout the deserts and plains of Africa south of the Sahara, Arabia and Iraq. The Arabian oryx (*Oryx leucoryx*) is the smallest, with a shoulder height of 90 cm (35 in). It is mostly a dirty white colour with a tail-tuft and a few blackish-brown marks on the head and legs. The white oryx (*O. algazel*) differs from other species in its scimitar-like horns whose length may exceed 1.1 m (45 in); its shoulder height is up to 1 m (40 in). It is whitish in colour with chestnut markings and its range extends from Senegal to Dongola and Kordofan in the Sudan.

The gemsbok (*O. gazella*) of the deserts of South-West Africa is found in less arid country. Its shoulder height is 1.2 m (48 in) and, like the related beisa of East Africa and Ethiopia, its coloration is more striking than that of the Arabian and white oryx.

Oryx, whose numbers have been greatly reduced in recent years, are formidable creatures when attacked. Charging with head down, thrusting their horns to either side with a scythe-like movement, they emit through their nostrils a curious vocal challenge. The smaller addax antelope (*Addax nasomaculatus*) lacks the speed and stamina of the larger oryx—its shoulder height is about 1 m (40 in)—but is even more independent of water and consequently is able to exist in more remote regions of the Sahara.

The dorcas gazelle (*Gazella dorcas*), one of the smallest of the gazelles with a shoulder height of up to 60 cm (24 in), is widely distributed throughout the Sahara desert. The back and sides are sandy reddish-brown, the belly white, the two colours being separated by an indistinct dark stripe. The horns of the male are stouter and more curved than those of the female. In Morocco, Palestine and other desert regions of the Mediterranean basin, dorcas gazelles do not require water and can obtain sufficient moisture for their needs from succulent roots and plant material, but in the Sudan they lose weight steadily on dry food when deprived of water. After five days' desiccation a maximum of 1.5 litres of fresh water can be ingested and smaller quantities of saline water are taken. With increasing dehydration, body temperature tends to fluctuate and there is some degree of hyperthermia or increased temperature; the urine becomes concentrated, faecal pellets smaller and drier, and food intake is reduced. Feeding ceases when 14–17 per cent of normal body weight has been lost, the animals then appearing weak and emaciated. This may take up to 12 days in winter but, in summer, gazelles cannot survive for more than five days without drinking.[55] It seems that, whereas camels are able to survive on a low water intake, the physiological adaptations of the dorcas gazelles are not so well marked and their survival depends upon speed and mobility which enable them, when necessary, to travel great distances to water. Gazelles can run at 80 km/h (50 m.p.h.). They migrate from the western Sudan to the Nile during the dry season. During the rains herds of two dozen or more can be seen but in dry weather they are more solitary. In very hot weather they have been seen to cool themselves in the Red Sea, but they do not drink salt water. A dwarf subspecies of the Arabian gazelle, one third of the normal weight, is said to inhabit islands in the Red Sea where no fresh water is available for drinking.

The odd-looking saiga antelope (*Saiga tatarica*), which roams the arid plains of western Asia, is about the size of a fallow deer (shoulder height 76 cm, 30 in). Its coat is dirty yellowish in summer, longer, thicker and paler in winter. The most peculiar feature is a greatly elongated and swollen nose with very wide nostrils widely separated and facing backwards so that as mentioned earlier, sand is excluded while the animal is grazing. In common with other animals of steppe and desert, where concealment is scarce and sources of water infrequent, it has great swiftness and can cover long distances. Once almost exterminated, the saiga is now under government protection and harvested annually (p. 156–7).

Among the most interesting of the ungulates of the African and Asian deserts and steppes are the wild asses. Several species are known, including the onager (*Equus onager*), of which different subspecies occur from Central Asia to North-West India, Baluchistan, Iran and Syria. This is the 'wild ass' of the Bible; it is white with a large yellowish area on each flank and a black dorsal stripe, mane and tail. It is gregarious, the herd being led by an old stallion. The kiang (*E. kiang*) is a deep reddish-brown colour and is more solitary. It inhabits the high desert plateaux of Tibet, Ladak and Sikkim. The kulan or chigetai (*E. hemionus*) is smaller 1.5 m (4 ft 3 in) at the withers. It is sand-yellow with a black dorsal stripe, mane and tuft on the end of the tail. Its range extends from the steppes of Transcaspia, Transbaikal and Mongolia into the Gobi desert. African wild asses (*E. asinus*) are represented by the Nubian and Somali subspecies. It seems probable that none of the wild asses of today are pure descendants of the original, true wild ass and there has been much interbreeding with domestic asses.[39]

Asses are sure-footed, long-eared animals that resemble the camel in their ability to tolerate a considerable degree of dehydration and to withstand a water loss of 30 per cent of the body weight. Their drinking capacity is also impressive; within a few minutes they can ingest more than a quarter of their body weight. Donkeys appear to lose water more rapidly than camels, however, because the fluctuations in their body temperature are smaller. Their fur coats are thinner and provide less effective insulation and their behavioural adaptations, which reduce heat gain from the environment, are less extreme. Nevertheless their importance as beasts of burden in desert regions is second only to that of the camel.

CATTLE, SHEEP AND GOATS

Zebu cattle, sheep and goats, like camels, are able to continue eating during the heat of the day despite acute water shortage, and to store fat when there is surplus food. They can extract maximal amounts of metabolites from dry vegetation and conserve nitrogen. In contrast to asses, they have a low rate of excretion of urea, which is retained and the nitrogen recycled. Addition of urea to their diet increases the amount of protein synthesized. During growth, lactation, or low protein intake, these animals have a powerful renal urea reabsorption mechanism. The ability to retain urea, which diffuses into saliva and tissue fluids, permits rumen bacteria to re-use nitrogen.[83]

MARSUPIALS

The Australian red kangaroo (*Megaleia rufa*) and other species range widely throughout the inland desert regions of the continent. They can exist on the water content of their vegetarian diet, supplemented by infrequent drinking. Their bipedal, leaping gait, in which the body is carried well forward and counter-balanced by the massive tail, enables them to travel long distances at 20 m.p.h. In short bursts a speed of 30 m.p.h. can be achieved with leaps of over 7.6 m (25 ft). Both the red kangaroo and the euro (*Macropus robustus*) have low basic metabolic rates compared with those of eutherians of similar size. Consequently, comparatively little water is required for temperature regulation, and the major avenue of evaporative heat loss is by panting. The red kangaroo, an animal of the open plains, is exposed to considerably more solar radiation than the euro, which inhabits rocky hill country where it makes use of small caves to escape the heat. The fur of the red kangaroo is almost twice as reflective as that of the euro. Red kangaroos have panting rates much below those of the euro, and they sweat more readily.[47]

The quokka (*Setonix brachyurus*) is a medium-sized marsupial, about the size of a rabbit, which inhabits the offshore islands and coastal regions of south-west Australia where no fresh water is available and moisture obtained from the vegetation is supplemented by sea water. In hot weather, the body is cooled by sweating, supplemented by copious salivation, licking the feet, tail and belly, a trait also found amongst kangaroos.[9] These animals are fully discussed in another book in this series.[115]

EVAPORATIVE COOLING

A comparison of the camel's performance with that of man and dog, provides an interesting illustration of the different ways in which various mammalian species react to high temperatures. Both man and dog begin to transpire as soon as the body temperature rises above normal. Man sweats and cools himself by evaporation from the skin; the dog pants and evaporates from his respiratory surface. In this respect, they are at a disadvantage as compared with the camel which, as we have seen, allows its body temperature to rise so that heat is stored during the day and lost at night.

In man, sweating increases as the heat load gets larger until it may reach a maximum of about 1.5 litres (2.6 pints) an hour. This high rate of water loss persists, in spite of desiccation, until dehydration has reached an advanced stage. The urine cannot be concentrated very much and is not reduced much below 0.5 litres per day. This is insignificant, however, compared with the amount of water lost in sweating.

When supplied with unlimited water, man's capacity for physical work in the desert is far greater than that of the dog which can only cool its body by panting. Total evaporation from the dog may be 2.6 per cent of body weight per hour, compared with 1.74 per cent from that of man, but, if measured in terms of surface area, evaporation from the dog is lower —0.65 litres per hour per square millimetre compared with 0.7 litres from man. The dog is therefore less able to cool itself by evaporation.[102]

Since dogs transpire only through the lungs, they do not lose any salt in the process. Human sweat, on the other hand, is saline and the salt that is lost through sweating in hot climates needs to be replaced. Visitors to hot desert regions are well advised to take plenty of salt in their food or they will feel sick and listless, unable to exert themselves and enjoy the novelty of their surroundings. One of the characters of adaptation to hot climates is a reduction in the salinity of human sweat.

Because the dog does not sweat, its skin becomes much hotter than that of a transpiring man. It may reach 45°C (113°F), so that heat may even be lost by conduction to the air whereas, in man, heat flow will be in the reverse direction. In this situation, by not sweating through the skin and having a high skin temperature, the dog has a distinct advantage over man as far as water economy is concerned. Indeed it would be true to say that greater efficiency is achieved by cooling the lungs through panting than by cooling the skin through sweating. Why, then, has sweating evolved?

Only comparatively large mammals can afford to cool their bodies by sweating. Possibly our ancestors lost their covering of hair and developed their extraordinarily effective sweating mechanism about the time that they left the rain-forest and became hunting animals of the savanna, when there would have been a strong selective pressure to reduce over-heating during the chase. Alternatively, they may have lived at the edge of the forest, where the temperature is pleasantly warm at night, before it had been degraded into savanna. When they came out into the open during the day, they would have benefited from the absence of hair.

Sweat from the horse evaporates outside the animal's coat, unlike that from the camel. Its effect is therefore rather wasted, and horses normally sweat only when driven by man or chased by predators. For them, sweating is an emergency procedure, not normally evoked. The same is true of asses, antelope and other large herbivores of the desert. Sweating is an uneconomical method of cooling the body where water is scarce, and it is employed only in special circumstances (see further discussion on p. 115).

In conclusion one might say that desert mammals conform to expectation. Small ones avoid extreme conditions and large ones resist them by sweating. Large mammals without efficient powers of transpiration would be unable to exist in hot climates. Perhaps the most salient feature of the mammalian fauna of deserts is the wide array of adaptive patterns exhibited. These can be correlated with the many different ecological niches that mammals occupy.

CARNIVORES

The large desert animals that we are discussing are all herbivorous. The largest desert carnivores are lynxes, hyaenas, foxes, coyotes, dingoes and so on—animals far too small to prey on the herbivores. Yet natural food chains are normally headed by a large carnivore, and one might well wonder why there does not appear to be any large carnivore in the deserts of the world. The explanation is that man has removed all large carnivores from the fringes of the desert, and has altered the environment, making it quite unsuitable for them. The desert is not a particularly unfavourable habitat for large carnivores, if there is enough shade for them to lie in during the day. They have a low surface-to-volume ratio, and the blood of their prey provides them with an adequate intake of fluid. Pumas (*Felis cougar*) still manage to exist in the American deserts and formerly ranged throughout North and South America from Patagonia to southern Canada. In Australia, the marsupial wolf (*Thylacinus cynocephalus*), now almost extinct, reached a good 1.5 m (5 ft) in length (of which one-third was tail). It formerly wrought havoc in Tasmania among the sheep and fowls of the colonists. In 1888, a Government bounty was introduced: from then to 1914, 2,268 animals are known to have been killed, and the total figure was probably much higher. It seems probable that thylacines were exterminated much earlier in Australia, as a result of competition with dingoes introduced by the original aborigines.

Lions (*Felis leo*) are distributed throughout the Kalahari and were formerly common in the Sahara. The ancient Egyptians worshipped lions at Leontopolis, and at Heliopolis where the sacred lion lived in the Temple of Ammon Ra. His food was most carefully selected and sacred melodies were played to him during his meals. The Egyptians not only tamed, but trained for the chase, lions, cheetahs, leopards, wild cats, hyaenas and wild dogs, all of which were plentiful within their frontiers and throughout the arid regions of Asia and the Middle East. Lions were common in Algeria until the time of the French occupation of that country. By the middle of the last century, however, their numbers had greatly diminished. Cheetahs (*Acinonyx jubatus*) were plentiful too, but are now probably extinct in North Africa except possibly for a few in the Tripolitanian desert of northwestern Libya.

In the absence of large predators, one might logically expect an increase in the numbers of herbivores, until over-grazing and the resulting shortage of food limited their increase. This does not occur, however, because man has proved to be a far more efficient predator than any wild carnivore in reducing the numbers of wild grazing animals. In their place, he has introduced domesticated stock—cattle, goats and sheep, which are far more harmful than any wild game. The reason why domesticated sheep and goats are so much more destructive is that they are less mobile. In contrast to gazelles which only nibble at grasses and the leaves of thorn bushes, goats climb trees to reach the upper branches and eat shrubs and smaller plants to the ground so that they do not recover.

EXPLOITATION OF DESERT MAMMALS

Man has harvested plants by utilizing domestic animals since pastoralism first began, but in arid regions the herds need larger areas in which to graze than in more fertile parts of the world. Controlled grazing has become the specialized occupation of many nomadic people. In the Gobi desert, pastoral Tartars were the first people to domesticate the horse, and trading caravans became a way of life in central Asia. The domestication of camels enabled caravans, by way of oases, to cross immense tracts of desert. This opened up even greater areas for trade.

The goat has a wider geographical distribution than any other domestic herd animal. Recent archaeological finds suggest that it is among the oldest, having been domesticated in South East Asia at least 10,000 years ago, almost certainly from progeny of the bezoor (*Capra hircus*). There is good reason to believe that the markhor (*C. falconeri*) of north-west India and the Abyssinian ibex (*C. ibex*) have entered into the provenance of certain breeds in Asia and Africa respectively.[61] The dwarf beduin goats of Sinai are especially well adapted to desert conditions and can lose up to 30 per cent of their body weight without loss of appetite.[108]

Wild game animals are not harmful to the desert ecosystem, because they are very mobile and their numbers are low. True nomads, with their few camels and small flocks, likewise seldom remain in the same area for long enough to cause serious overgrazing. Severe damage, however, is caused by the large herds of sedentary people who live in villages for at least part of the year near wells and oases and in the valleys of the rivers. In such places, overgrazing and soil erosion assume extreme proportions, even when the herds are dispersed over wider areas at the time of the rains.

It has been argued that greater productivity could be achieved, with less overgrazing, if sheep and goats were to be replaced by camels. These are more mobile, require water less frequently and, consequently, can exploit larger areas of vegetation. Unlike sheep and goats, camels continue to feed even when they are desiccated. In the Northern Province of Sudan, they

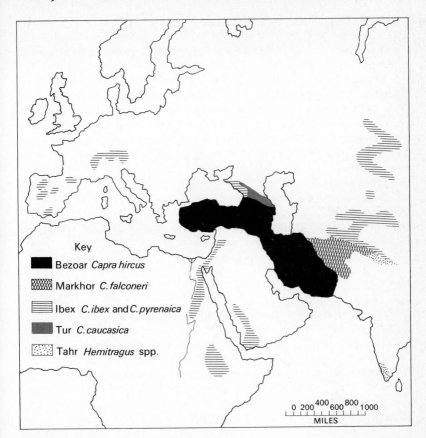

Fig. 9.3 Distribution of the wild goats.[61]

usually drink once per week during the dry weather but, to be in the best condition they should be watered twice weekly even when not working. During and after the rains, when they are grazing on green grass, they can go for 2–3 months without drinking. As a source of food, however, camels have little significance in the Sudan. They are a means of transport and provide some milk, but their meat is not popular. Tens of thousands are exported annually, on the hoof, to markets in Upper Egypt and it is clear that any development plan aimed at increasing animal production must take into account the preferences of the people it is intended to benefit.

Another way to utilize available resources more effectively might be to employ the principles of game ranching (p. 156), the value of which has been effectively demonstrated in other parts of Africa. Dorcas gazelles, oryx and addax antelope, gerenuk (*Lithocranius walleri*), and so on provide excellent meat and are well adapted to life in arid regions. They are so extraordinarily mobile, however, that they would probably be unsuitable for ranching.

Certain East African species, such as buffalo (*Syncerus caffer*) and black rhinoceros (*Diceros bicornis*), show a degree of thermolability and their body temperature varies almost as much as that of the non-dehydrated camel (p. 93). Similarly, the eland (*Taurotragus oryx*) can endure comparatively large variations in body temperature without sweating, thus conserving moisture. Its faeces are dry, and high food consumption enables it to take in a considerable quantity of moisture when it browses on succulent acacia leaves.[53, 111] Similar considerations apply to the ostrich, which could well be farmed extensively in desert regions where it is now regarded merely as an animal for hunting. Unlike domesticated species, game animals feed at night when the moisture content of vegetation is at its highest, and this increases their independence of drinking water.

IO

Biology of Man in the Desert

The human species inhabits desert country at many different levels of civilization. The utilization of plants by food gathering cultures is described in Chapter 6, their use of indigenous animals is outlined below. At the opposite extreme are the mining engineers and petroleum workers who may live for three weeks in the desert and spend the rest of the month at home in a temperate zone. Even during their brief tours of duty, they sleep in air-conditioned buildings, drink bottled mineral waters and eat fresh food that is flown in daily. In fact, they scarcely experience true desert conditions at all! It may well be better, in the long run, to get accustomed to the heat and then forget about it. I have often thought that the most important adaptation to heat is to the feeling of sweat trickling down one's face and body. At first this feels like a thousand tickling flies but, once one has become used to it, it ceases to be a problem. The one factor to which the human body does not become adapted is shortage of drinking water.

INDIGENOUS ANIMALS AS HUMAN FOOD

There are few living animals that come amiss to the aborigines of the Australian desert or to the Bushmen of the Kalahari. The same is true to a lesser degree of the inhabitants of other desert regions—Arabs, Berbers, Mongols, American Indians and so on.

Desert snails do not reach the size of tropical *Achatina* spp., but they all have high nutritive value and several kinds are eaten to some extent in Algeria, Morocco and other countries of North Africa. These species include the indigenous *Levantina guttata*, *Otala lactea* (a Mediterranean non-desert species) and *Helix aspersa* and *H. pomatia* which have been introduced from Europe. In contrast to the people of West Africa and China, who are greatly addicted to snail meat, North American Indians, many Arab tribes and most other desert peoples eat them very little, if at all. Indeed, it has been argued that snails are an acquired taste and that they are seldom eaten by the inhabitants of deserts, except for aborigines and Bushmen, who have little choice in the matter of diet.[80]

Insects and arachnids, raw or cooked, appear to be generally popular in all arid regions and, in contrast to molluscs, are an important article of food among sedentary and nomadic peoples throughout the deserts of the world. It is, perhaps, not surprising that the insects richest in proteins, fat and carbohydrates, such as grasshoppers, locusts, termites and witchetty grubs, should be eaten in the largest quantities.

Grasshoppers, and especially the migratory locusts, have always been eaten by man, and they provide an important source of animal protein in many arid regions of the world. Nor are they gastronomically unpleasant. Grasshopper sandwiches in Mexico used to cost twice as much as chicken sandwiches, and it was considered that they tasted twice as good! For centuries, the Indians of California have chased grasshoppers into pits containing hot stones which serve both to kill and roast the catch simultaneously.

The Bushmen of the Kalahari are practically omnivorous, ignoring nothing that is edible—mammals of all kinds, birds, snakes, lizards, fish, spiders and insects. When a swarm of locusts or grasshoppers alights they kill as many as possible and dry them in the sun. Termites, butterfly and beetle larvae, bee grubs and wild honey are eagerly devoured. One of the most important insect foods of the Arunta aborigines of central Australia are the witchetty grubs. They are probably the caterpillars of ghost moths (Hepialidae), goat moths (Cossidae) and other large larvae that live on desert shrubs. The honeypots of sugar ants (*Melophorus* spp.) are a favourite article of consumption whenever they can be obtained and, as in the case of the witchetty grubs, special ceremonies are conducted to promote their supply. The abdomens of these ants, distended with food, are also bitten off and swallowed by the Arunta tribe of Australia.

Sweets are the delight and culinary joy of the desert nomads. It is not surprising that the sweet-tasting manna of Sinai provoked excitement among the Children of Israel (*Exodus*, XVI; *Numbers*, XI). Manna is the dried excretion of two related species of scale insects (*Trabutina mannipara* and *Najacoccus serpentius*) that feed on tamarisk bushes in mountains and lowlands respectively.[12]

In the harsh environment of the desert, few items of food come amiss unless specifically proscribed by customs or religion. In contrast to the Australian Bindibu, who will eat almost any species of animals, the American Papago have a highly selective list of animals that are regarded as acceptable. The difference between the two may be related to the fact that the Bindibu live in an area where the average rainfall is only 0–12.5 cm (0–5 in), while the Papago inhabit a region with 18–28 cm (7–11 in) of average yearly rainfall, which produces one of the most luxuriant desert vegetations in the world. Large mammals such as kangaroos, gazelles and antelope are an obvious source of food. The Bushmen, Bindibu and Arab nomads, however, find each day sustaining food sources of the kind mentioned the existence of which the European does not suspect, and could not find even if he did. For survival in the desert, such knowledge is of paramount importance.[80]

WATER AND ELECTROLYTES

Man seems most nearly adapted for life in a warm, wet climate where shade is easily obtainable. The insulating value of human hair is negligible, so that the critical temperature below which metabolism increases at rest is 27–29°C (80.5–84°F). The human capacity to sweat is probably greater than that of any other mammal. Consequently, although the expenditure of water is extremely high, hot dry conditions are withstood comparatively easily provided that adequate supplies of water are available for drinking. Not only water is lost, however. One litre of sweat drains the sodium from 150–600 ml of extracellular fluid. This is because the sodium chloride concentration of human sweat varies from 0.5–5.0 g/l while the main range is 1.0–3.0 g/l.[82] The low values are mainly associated with salt deficiency or acclimatization to heat (see below). The fact that desert water is often somewhat saline may, therefore, benefit the local people that drink it. Dogs, foxes, and other animals that evaporate water mostly through the mouth and respiratory passages, are at an advantage in that they do not lose much salt in the process, as mentioned above (p. 108).

In a hot, dry environment, evaporation increases by insensible perspiration from the skin and by loss from the mucous membranes of the mouth and respiratory passages. If this does not provide sufficient cooling to maintain thermal equilibrium, sweating begins. As a method of cooling the body, sweating involves the extravagant use of water and is only found in comparatively large animals. By cooling the surface of the body, the thermal gradient between the skin and the ambient air is increased. In consequence the tendency for heat to flow from the environment into the body is increased. This is not the case when evaporative cooling takes place via the mouth and respiratory passages. As already mentioned (p. 108), however, when supplied with unlimited water, man's capacity for physical work in desert conditions is very much greater than that of the dog. His rate of sweating is so great that, in comparison, the amount of water lost in his urine is almost negligible.

If there is acute exposure to heat, or if dehydration occurs, significant changes take place in the renal circulation which may embarrass the excretory function of the kidneys. A low protein intake over a moderate period of time reduces the amount of urea that needs to be excreted but it also affects adversely the homeostatic conservation of water. There is, however, some adaptation to habitual levels of salt intake. The kidney operates on a 'surplus budget' and homeostasis of the volume of body fluids and tonicity is possible only when there is a surplus of water and salt intake over loss.

When a horse sweats, liquid percolates through the animal's hair and evaporates on the surface of its coat. This is extremely inefficient and, as already mentioned (p. 108), would probably be evoked normally only in emergency situations, such as escaping from a predator. In the case of the camel (p. 102) and of man, evaporation does at least take place on the surface of the skin. The hair of the camel is both sparse and coarse: the relative hairlessness of man is related to the development of eccrine sweat glands at high density over most of the body surface. These are far more efficient than the apocrine glands of horses, apes, monkeys and most other mammals, which produce a relatively scanty secretion and are by no means as resistant to fatigue. Some physiologists regard the eccrine as a transformed apocrine gland. It is equally plausible, however, to regard the eccrine glands as merely replacing the apocrine by an extension from the areas where they are found in other mammals—that is, the pad of the foot and hand and the adjoining regions of the wrist and ankle. In monkeys and apes, eccrine glands are distributed sparsely over the body surface: in man, they may reach a total of about 2,000,000.[122]

CIRCULATORY ADJUSTMENTS

People living in arid regions are generally able to cope adequately with the stresses imposed upon their circulation. Warming of the body causes peripheral vasodilation due to a diminution in the frequency of sympathetic vasoconstrictor impulses. This is most marked in regions which have the richest blood supply to the skin—that is, the limbs, fingers and toes. When heating ceases, it is in these areas that vasoconstriction first occurs. In this way, heat generated internally is either transported to the surface layers of the body where it is dissipated, or else is retained in the deeper tissues. It follows, therefore, that variations in temperature are greatest at the tips of the extremities and smallest in the deep tissues of the body. The distribution of blood is governed primarily by the need to avoid excessive fluctuations of temperature in the brain and other important organs.[56]

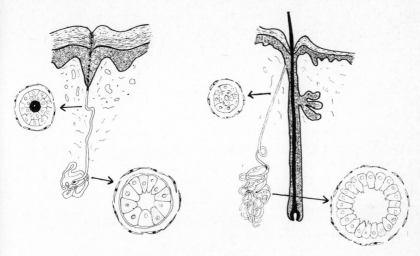

Fig. 10.1 Eccrine and apocrine sweat glands.[122]

Thermostatic control of the human body is characterized by (a) the large number and wide distribution of its heat-sensitive elements, (b) the degree of integration which allows varying sensitivities of thermal control according to the greater or lower resistance to changes in temperature of some parts of the body than of others, (c) the ability of its controlling mechanisms to modify their responses in the light of previous experience to appropriate stimuli, and (d) the means to change the properties of the controlled system so that the body can cope more effectively with thermal situations to which it has been frequently and recently exposed.[70, 71]

The efficiency of the circulation can be maintained over only a limited range of blood volumes. Loss of water from the human body, unlike that of the camel, in the first instance, is a loss of extracellular fluid of which the blood plasma is a part. Consequently loss of body water will always cause a diminution of blood volume. The cells, however, only begin to lose significant amounts of water after a total loss amounting to nearly 5 per cent of body weight. Small losses of water are not serious but, if much water is lost, the ratio of blood corpuscles to plasma (haematocrit ratio) becomes too great and the viscosity of the blood increases. In extreme cases, this may lead to 'explosive heat death' (p. 103).[2]

PHYSIOLOGICAL ADAPTATIONS

Man can survive almost anywhere on the surface of the earth and is probably one of the most adaptable of all animals. This adaptability is

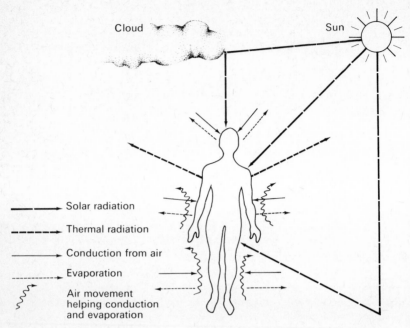

Fig. 10.2   Paths of heat exchange between man and desert surroundings.[75]

brought about by conscious and unconscious physiological processes, and by conscious processes of learning·and reasoning. It is well known that the inhabitants of hot countries are better able to adapt to further heat stress than are people unaccustomed to heat, probably as a result of behavioural as well as physiological adaptation.

The immediate responses by which the human body compensates for an increase in heat load include (a) dilation of the peripheral blood vessels, which increases the transfer of heat from the interior to the surface and facilitates the loss of heat by conduction; (b) sweating, which produces evaporative cooling from the skin; (c) reducing activity and consequent reduction of metabolic heat production; and (d) increasing surface area by adopting a relaxed posture.[75]

There is very little difference in the reactions to heat of quite dissimilar ethnic groups. For example, Australian Caucasians and aborigines in hot, humid tropics, or Arabs and Caucasians in the desert, show very similar heart rates and rectal temperatures. Similarly, the fundamental water requirements of a Tuareg nomad do not differ from those of an acclimatized European. This suggests that climate must play a much greater part in acclimatization than do differences in anthropometry: rectal temperatures and heart rates do not appear to be genetic factors in adaptation.

ACCLIMATIZATION

Acclimatization to high temperatures results in both short-term and long-term changes. The former include an increase of 10–20 per cent in the rate of sweating brought about by an increase both in the number of sweat glands active at any moment and in the rate of secretion by each gland. There is, however, no evidence of any increase in the number of glands. The volume of circulating blood may be increased by up to 15 per cent, also that of the extracellular fluid, accompanied by the retention of urinary sodium and chloride. This increase in the amount of circulating fluid maintains the transport of oxygen and nutrients to the tissues despite the demands of sweating. The concentration of chloride ions in the sweat also falls progressively, so that the normal dietary intake may be nearly sufficient to replenish the salt lost in perspiration and little supplementation is necessary.[82]

Other adaptations are an increased tone in the walls of the veins which helps to return the blood to the heart from the regions of arterioles and capillary dilation. The pulse rate is reduced and the rectal temperature tends to become more stable. Although the basic mechanism of such acclimatization is not yet clear, long-term changes are even less well understood. They include a reduction in the extent of short-term acclimatization mechanisms, possibly as a result of psychological rather than physiological adaptation. The attitude of a person to heat and drought seems to play an extremely important role. Some Europeans adapt quickly and well to desert life, others never seem to adjust to changing conditions of life. In an emergency, the European, anxious to do something, is active, gets hotter and uses up his limited supply of water. In contrast, the nomad, secure in the will of Allah, tends to relax and behave more calmly.[75]

The cerebral cortex plays an extremely important part in adaptation to heat. In most cases, tropical fatigue or neurasthenia appears without any physiological causes and it must be concluded that mental mechanisms are responsible for the form of inadaptation.[72] Although there does not appear to be any unusual intensity or frequency of neurasthenia in tropical countries, heat, and especially humid heat, does provoke definite psychological disturbances. These appear as impairment of mental initiative, inability to concentrate, inaccuracy and so on.[99]

PIGMENTATION

The inhabitants of deserts are usually dark skinned, but the significance of this feature is by no means universally agreed. There is also some dispute as to whether a light or a dark skin is primitive in man. It is difficult to see why pigmentation should have been evolved in our hominid ancestors before the loss of hair, or how the complex intra-specific signal system of flushing and blushing could have evolved in an animal whose pigmentation renders it invisible. On the other hand, the correlation of hairlessness with black coloration, especially among tropical animals, suggests that man's hairless black skin may be an adaptation to tropical conditions. It has been suggested that a hairless black belly may have evolved as an adjunct to sunbathing, for captive gibbons and other apes often hang for considerable periods with the ventral surface towards the sun.[59]

We shall probably never know what was the skin colour of the first hominids, nor its range of variability. Perhaps it was intermediate between white and black. The absence of pigmentation among peoples of cloudy, temperate regions may be correlated with the synthesis of vitamin D (calciferol). This requires ultra-violet radiation whose penetration into the epidermis is facilitated by the absence of melanin. Conversely, the pigment melanin protects the skin against the carcinogenic action of ultra-violet light and, presumably, has an adaptive function in this respect, for geographical variations in human skin colour are related to the intensity of ultra-violet light.[122] At the same time, however, it has been shown experimentally that black pigment enhances the absorption of solar radiation and therefore increases the heat load of people living in the tropics.

The suggestion has been made that the adaptive significance of black skin may lie in the camouflage it provides at night, and that it results from the selective influences of tribal warfare and effective hunting in a tropical forest environment. Another hypothesis has been advanced, that dark coloration in man may be a social signal—the degree of pigmentation indicating the level of threat. According to a third, a dark skin may be an adaptation to enhance the absorption of radiant solar energy as mentioned above and, associated with sunbathing, thus economize on the calorific expenditure of maintaining a homeothermic body temperature. It would almost certainly be incorrect to ascribe the degree of skin pigmentation to any single environmental factor. Colour probably represents a compromise between adaptations to a number of conflicting selective influences. In deserts, protection from ultra-violet radiation may well have been particularly important.

TECHNOLOGICAL ADAPTATIONS

Opinion is somewhat divided as to the exact nature of the relationships between man and his environment. Some writers stress the importance of biological adaptation, others emphasize the role of artificial microclimates.

CHAP. 10 TECHNOLOGICAL ADAPTATIONS 121

The design of houses often leaves much to be desired. The nakedness of the Australian aborigines who, even during cold winter nights, never think of covering themselves, has given rise to many hypotheses. While some observers regard this as being due to lack of imagination, others claim that it is a logical choice in a difficult situation. The aborigines have no beasts of burden. Compelled by a hostile environment to lead nomadic lives, they cannot afford to weigh themselves down with heavy skin blankets. Instead they have become adapted physiologically to extreme heat and cold: they are able to sleep in frosty weather with only a fire, their dogs and a screen of brushwood to shield them from the bitter cold.

In the worst climates man has been able to create satisfactory micro-climates. But he also accepts highly imperfect solutions, either through lack of means or by his willingness to accept routine. The Bushmen's civilization is little more advanced than the Australian. His hut provides a fairly useful shelter, but it is only temporary and he does not sleep in it. Bushmen sleep in a circle in the open air, with their feet towards the fire, but they cover themselves with skins. In this way they create conditions which render physiological adaptation to the cold unnecessary. Other nomadic civilizations are incomparably more advanced. The problem of heat, of course, is not fully solved, but tents and warm clothing provide protection against the cold at night.[105]

Suitable clothing can also do much to reduce the thermal stress of the desert's heat. The traditional loose garments of the Arabs and Tuareg, for example, protect the body from solar radiation and, at the same time, permit sufficient circulation of air for the evaporation of sweat to cool the surface of the skin. It is significant that, when compelled to undertake strenuous physical activity during the heat of the day, these people remove their outer wrappings so that evaporative cooling is facilitated. Less efficient is modern European tropical dress but it is, nevertheless, a great improvement on the idiotic spine pads and topees of the last century. Heatstroke is a well testified phenomenon: sunstroke, of which the Victorians were so terrified, does not exist as such.[99]

The criterion of modern man's adaptations to living conditions in hot arid zones is his ability to satisfy his needs in regard to comfort. Now the concept of comfort is purely subjective. It is the product of the interplay between the various elements of the physical environment—heat, cold, humidity, air movements etc. Discomfort results in inefficiency, loss of sleep and a deterioration in bodily functions. In addition to the physiological factors of thermal comfort, there are psychological, sociological and cultural factors which may sometimes become of primary importance because the cost of providing them may be incompatible with the economic level of the regions under consideration.

Of the various factors causing fatigue, loss of sleep is the most important.

The accumulation of sleep deficit, combined with the effects of heat on work and behaviour, leads to disorders in physiological and psychological adaptation, the seriousness of which, both individually and collectively, justify measures to secure adequate comfort. The reality of this harmful influence is illustrated by the fact that the frequency of industrial accidents characteristically follows temperature changes. The extent of behavioural disturbances has long been noted in hot climates and especially in the humid tropics where acute fits sometimes end in murder or suicide.[72]

Technological adaptations to life in hot, dry zones include the design of suitable housing conditions, installation of electric fans, evaporative coolers, air conditioners and heat pump systems which employ the reverse cycle refrigeration system. By suitable valves, the flow of the refrigerant can be reversed in winter so that heat is then taken from the cooler air outdoors and transferred to warm the interior of a building. My personal experience suggests that it may be better to make do with a large sweep fan, than to indulge in costly air conditioning. The more one forgets the heat and discomfort of the desert climate, the less does it impinge on everyday life!

Part of Western man's problem of adjusting to life in the tropics is that many of the techniques of his civilization are inappropriate to an environment in which he needs to lose heat, not to conserve it. Adjustment to life in desert conditions, therefore, requires a change in his way of life to suit the peculiarities of the climate—and some individuals are more adaptable than others in this respect.

11

Agricultural Pests

The necessity to feed an ever increasing human population in a limited world, compels man to seek sources of food in arid zones where they did not exist previously, and to increase production in semi-arid areas not already fully exploited. The irrigation and land reclamation involved have caused many changes, some of them conducive to increases in the numbers of pests and parasites. The ecological implications of such developments will be discussed here and in the next chapter. In these, an account is given of the biology of some of the economically more important agricultural, medical and veterinary pests of arid lands.

LOCUSTS AND GRASSHOPPERS

Both solitary grasshoppers and the comparatively few species, known as locusts, which periodically swarm gregariously, in vast numbers, share in common the fact that their populations fluctuate greatly from one year to another. In hot deserts, especially where irrigation takes place, insect numbers may increase very suddenly. Every year, vast swarms of desert locusts (*Schistocerca gregaria*) emerge from their scattered breeding grounds and ravage the crops of Africa and Asia. A single medium-sized swarm may contain 1,000,000,000 insects, each eating its own weight every day, and range over 48,000 km (3,000 miles) from its starting point.

The area subject to invasions by swarms of the desert locust covers about 30 million km^2 in northern and eastern Africa and in south-western Asia. At any one time, however, only a fraction of this area is infested, even at the height of a plague, and breeding occurs only in certain localities where conditions are suitable. In summer (July–September) the area of

Fig. 11.1 Desert locust swarm, west of Omdurman.

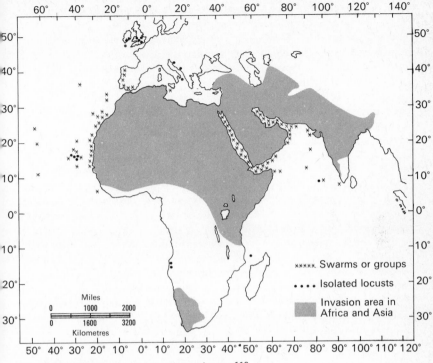

Fig. 11.2 Distribution of the desert locust.[119]

breeding is centred on a belt around 15°N, south of the Sahara, in Somalia and south-western Arabia, and in the deserts of Rajasthan (Thar) and Sind. In winter (October–March) breeding occurs in East Africa, northern Arabia and around the Red Sea. In spring (April–June) it lies over north-west Africa, East Africa and much of the Near East. Migration of swarms between these seasonal breeding areas often covers hundreds, and some-times thousands, of kilometres.

The positions of the breeding sites vary from year to year because they are dependent upon rainfall that is erratic in distribution and amount. The direction of movement of desert swarms is down-wind, so that most swarms are carried into regions of low pressure where rain has either fallen recently or is about to fall. The soil is damp so that the eggs have sufficient moisture for development and, by the time they hatch, a mass of tender shoots will have sprung up to provide food for the emerging hoppers. Moreover, displacement by down-wind drift, from one area where seasonal rains are ending to another where they are about to begin, seems to be essential for the maintenance of locust swarms when food supplies at the breeding sites decrease as drought sets in.[94]

The life-cycle of *Schistocerca gregaria* consists of three phases: egg, nymph or hopper (of which there are five instars) and adult. The female locust lays about 50–100 eggs at a time. These are packed like peas in a pod. Each pod is deposited in a hole 5–7.5 cm deep, which the locust makes by thrusting the hardened tip of her abdomen into the damp soil. During six months of life, an average female lays three or four batches of eggs at intervals of one to two weeks, giving a total of about 300 eggs. Hatching takes place after 10–20 days. When the hatchlings have adequate living space, they remain in the solitary phase, developing breeding and dying in their original home in exactly the same way as normal grass-hoppers. If living conditions are crowded, however, either by the hatching of very large numbers or by the contraction of the breeding grounds through climatic action, the hoppers become gregarious. They develop a dark colour, quite different from the cryptic, inconspicuous green of solitary individuals, and march together in bands often numbering many millions. The insects thus exhibit phase polymorphism, for solitary and gregarious individuals differ in morphological characters as well as in coloration (Polymorphism—having several different forms in the same species, occurring within a freely interbreeding population). Marching and feeding continue for about a month after hatching, by which time the hoppers have passed through all five developmental instars and moult to become adult, winged locusts. Sexual maturation occurs during the next few weeks, and is stimulated by the presence of aromatic chemicals in various desert shrubs at the season of the monsoon-type rains (p. 64).[20]

For a few days after the individuals have become adult, the locust swarm takes short daily flights. These become increasingly longer until true migratory flights finally develop. Such flights may be long or short: they usually continue until flying conditions become unfavourable or the locusts are exhausted. Some of the swarms resulting from summer breed-ing in the Sudan in 1968, for instance, moved north-westward to Morocco during October and November covering, in a few weeks, a distance of about 4,000 km (2,500 miles) downwind. Locusts usually settle during the high temperatures of midday, and at night as the temperature falls, but night flying has often been recorded.

Since 1910 there have been five widespread plagues of the desert locust and five major recessions. Declines of desert locust plagues do not occur simultaneously throughout the affected area, but take place in a series of stages, first in one place, then in another. The end of a plague and the onset of a recession occur at a break in the succession of swarming periods which, up to then, have formed a direct lineage with the swarming generations that occurred during the plague. During recessions, the area in which swarming and non-swarming insects previously occurred is reduced by at least a half. The area of recession coincides approximately with the arid belt running through the middle of the invasion area and leaves free many countries with higher rainfall which are invaded during plagues. Within the recession area, local populations of solitary or swarming individuals reflect their continued mobility and changes with the seasons.[119]

The most recent plague began as a result of breeding in the Thar desert of India during the monsoon of 1964. In 1966, breeding occurred in southern Libya, Algeria, Tchad, Niger and north-eastern Mali. The following year, despite ground control operations, there was widespread and prolonged breeding in southern Algeria and, later, in the Sahel savanna zone. Population increases occurred independently around the Red Sea and in south-eastern Arabia during late 1966 and in 1967. These may have been influenced by a tropical cyclone which struck the region in November, 1966 and gave rise to favourable breeding conditions over a wide area. It was followed by unusually heavy rains in 1967.

The last plague of the African migratory locust (*Locusta migratoria migratorioides*) lasted from 1928–41. Unlike the desert locust, this species has a permanent outbreak area—in the flood plains of the River Niger in Mali. For this reason, it is very much easier to control. Provided that populations are kept low on the breeding grounds, so that the gregarious phase does not develop, swarms do not form. During the 13 years following 1928, however, swarms of migratory locusts invaded most of Africa south of the Sahara, covering an area of about 17,200,000 km² (6,650,000 sq. miles). Most of this was infested within four years from the initial outbreak in the Niger floodplains. Control of locust populations here was necessary in 16 of the 23 years from 1942 to 1964 and, during six of these, the infestations were serious.[116]

Different subspecies of migratory locust (*L. migratoria capito* and *L. m. migratoria*) are pests of arid regions in Madagascar and western Asia respectively, *L. m. rossica* in U.S.S.R. and *L. m. manilensis* in eastern China and the Pacific Island from Japan and Taiwan to the Philippines, Borneo and Celebes. *L. m. gallica* occurs in south-west France but has only been known to swarm once, in 1944–47.

The red locust (*Nomadacris septemfasciata*), the third most important plague species of Africa, has outbreak areas in two or three restricted regions of Malawi and Tanzania. It is not a primarily desert species although, before it was brought under control, swarms used to range throughout the southern half of Africa, also with disastrous consequences. The last plague of this species began in 1927 and ended in 1944. The brown locust (*Locustana pardalina*) has been observed in South Africa only where mosaic vegetation is available. Local plant sociologists are of the opinion that this type of vegetation is comparatively recent and due to overgrazing.

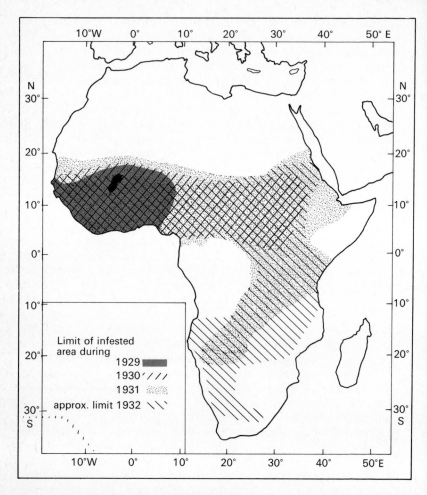

Fig. 11.3 Distribution of the African migratory locust (after A. Batten). The solid black spot indicates the outbreak area.

Similarly, numbers of the Moroccan locust (*Dociostaurus moroccanus*) have increased because of deforestation and overgrazing of the hill slopes.[97]

Intensive and wide-ranging studies have been carried out on the Australian plague locust (*Chortoicetes terminifera*) in order to provide a basis for forecasting outbreaks at the invasion of cultivated areas. It is believed that the movement of solitary locusts from the outbreak areas in central and north-western New South Wales and south-eastern Queensland to western regions of these provinces, play an important role in providing populations which, if they breed successfully, lead to the production of swarms that eventually invade cultivated areas further south. In this species, egg diapause, induced by photoperiod conditions experienced by the parents, provides a means of surviving the more inclement seasons. In the United States, the Rocky Mountain locust (*Melanoplus spretus*) occasionally swarms, its depredations costing hundreds of millions of dollars; other species are pests in arid and semi-arid regions throughout the world.

Not only locusts, but non-gregarious grasshoppers and crickets, may be important insect pests of arid regions. The small plague grasshopper (*Austroicetes cruciata*), a pest of pastures and crops in southern Australia, sometimes invades the central desert region. *Gastrimargus musicus* occasionally swarms in Queensland, and the black field cricket (*Gryllulus servillei*) is, likewise, sometimes a pest. Crickets are active chiefly at night, hiding by day in the soil. When they are present in swarming numbers, however, they may travel in bands by day or emerge from their shelters to sun themselves and feed. The mole cricket (*Gryllotalpa gryllotalpa*) at times reaches economically important population levels throughout the Middle East.

TERMITES

Termites are an important element of the invertebrate fauna of all the warmer countries of the world, and some species thrive in arid and desert regions. Since their food consists mainly of wood and the woody tissues of plants, they are a threat to structural timber, to manufactured goods, wood, paper, cloth or certain plastics, and to trees and growing crops. Termites of arid zones include dry wood termites (Kalotermitidae), harvester termites (Hodotermitidae) (*Anacanthotermes* spp. are found throughout the Great Palaearctic desert), Rhinotermitidae (*Psammotermes hybostoma* occurs right round the edges of the Sahara and on either coast of the Red Sea) and various Termitidae. The mound-building genus *Amitermes* has a special ability to survive in arid areas—*A. desertorum* is found in Algeria, *A. wheeleri* in south-western U.S.A. and Mexico, *A. vilis* in Iran and Arabia, and *A. messinae* in deciduous woodland and *Acacia* scrub from Aden south to the Limpopo River.[62]

Generally speaking, the number of different kinds of termites present in any locality is greatest in tropical rain-forests, but their activity is highest in savanna and deciduous woodland where mound-building species are dominant. Termites are not very important agricultural pests in desert regions, but dates and citrus trees are damaged by *Microcerotermes diversus* in southern Arabia, and citrus trees by *Reticulitermes lucifugus* in

Palestine and by *Paraneotermes simplicicornis* in Texas. The trees wither when their taproots are destroyed. Termite damage to cotton has been reported in many parts of Africa, often by species of *Microtermes*, while subterranean termites have been recorded as pests of groundnuts and pastures throughout the drier parts of the world.

Termite damage to building and timber is extensive throughout the tropics. Any unprotected woodwork will be attacked unless it has been rendered unpalatable or is naturally resistant to termites. The wood need not be in contact with the ground since subterranean species build tubular runways from the soil, often for considerable distances, to reach roof-beams or ceiling boards. Dry-wood termites will fly direct into the roof of a building and start their colonies in timber far removed from the ground. They have been found in isolated plugs of wood set up high in concrete walls to support electric fittings. The traditional adobe or mud brick houses of arid regions have thick walls and a minimum of timber so they are not vulnerable to termite attack as are the modern style buildings that are replacing them.[62]

OTHER AGRICULTURAL PESTS

Because of their harsh climates, desert regions are remarkably free from agricultural pests, with the exception of locusts and termites. Even oases, with abundant water and generally favourable conditions, are often comparatively free from crop pests because the surrounding desert acts as a barrier to their introduction. When they do become established, however, usually as a result of human activity, both pests and human diseases tend to flourish. For example, the scale insect *Parlatoria blanchardi*, an important pest of date palms, was probably introduced into the Sahara long before the Arab invasion. It is now distributed widely throughout North Africa, but has not yet reached Tchad or the western oases of the Sahara. It was, however, accidentally taken to Colomb-Béchar in 1920, to certain oases of Tourat in 1912, and to Tata in Morocco as recently as 1945. This distribution supports the theory of the eastern origin of the date palm, whose progress from east to west has been followed by that of its parasite. This scale insect and another, *Phoenicoccus marlatti*, were also accidentally introduced along with their host plant into Arizona and California. Subsequently, over 30 years were required to eradicate them by defoliation and torching, showing how important it is to preserve the isolation of desert oases.[38, 39]

Another example is afforded by the pink bollworm (*Platyedra gossypiella*). This moth has been established in Egypt for almost half a century but did not cross the Sahara and infest the cotton fields of West Africa, although it spread rapidly there after it had been introduced with infested seed samples sent by post. Canals, however, may serve as routes for the infestation of irrigated areas. Thus the cucumber beetle (*Diabrotica balteata*) has spread widely through California along the irrigation canals. Some pests travel from one oasis to the next—for example, the beet leafhopper (*Circulifer tenellus*) which carries the curly-top virus disease.[4]

Although many plant-eating insects are unable to cross the intervening desert, unless inadvertently transmitted by man, a few, including locusts, may be carried long distances by wind. Examples are afforded by Lepidoptera, such as the pale western cutworm (*Porosagrotis orthogonia*), whose larvae attack crops in Colorado and New Mexico, aphids and other plant bugs, fruit-flies and beetles.[93]

Crops of arid lands are not only subject to the onslaught of indigenous insects; as already mentioned, they also suffer from attack by a large number that have been inadvertently introduced, especially in irrigated areas. These include *P. blanchardi* and the Australian citrus scale (*Icerya purchasi*), introduced into California and controlled in 1888 by the ladybird beetle *Roadlia cardinalis*, its natural predator. This is a classic example of successful biological control—another is the control of mealy bugs in California by the parasite *Cryptolaemus montrouzieri*.

After its introduction to Australia, possibly for domestic decoration or with the idea of cultivating cochineal, the prickly-pear cactus (*Opuntia inermis*) spread rapidly throughout Queensland, and much of the rest of the continent was overrun. The cost of clearing the country was greater than the capital value of the land itself until the most successful of all attempts at biological control was embarked on. Larvae of a Mexican moth, *Cactoblastis cactorum*, associated with a fungus which also attacked and rotted the cactus, achieved spectacular success within two or three years.

HUMAN INFLUENCE ON THE ECOLOGY OF PESTS

The activities of mankind throughout the world can be beneficial or harmful with regard to the encouragement of pests. The introduction of water into arid land, for instance, creates new ecosystems that may encourage the breeding of locusts and mosquitoes, and inhibit the reproduction of thrips (Thysanoptera) and leaf hoppers (Jassidae). Irrigation of fields may also interfere with the development of subterranean insects, including beetle larvae and pupae. Overgrazing may create conditions favourable for locust development while the improvement of pasture encourages lepidopterous pests such as the swift moth *Oncopera fasciculata* (Hepialidae) and scarabaeid beetle larvae.

No living organism exists by itself. Each is part of a biotic community which, taken in combination with the physical components of the environment, forms an ecosystem whose functioning depends on the inflow of energy from sunlight. A stable ecosystem is characterized by a constant balanced turnover of materials. Most human activities tend to simplify and degrade the ecosystems of the world. Of course, without such simplification and channelling of solar energy into pathways of man's choosing, there would be no civilization on earth today. At the same time, however, the alteration of ecosystems can be dangerous. Soils may not be able to withstand ploughing and planting with agricultural crops, the turnover of minerals may be prevented and fertility reduced.

Insects, both harmful and beneficial, are affected in countless different ways. Ploughing the soil, for example, exposes moister layers and buries drier earth. Insect stages that are immobile, such as eggs, pupae, and larvae in diapause, may be killed by such drastic changes in soil conditions. The introduction of new crops invites infestation with insect pests. Thus, a field of safflower in the arid northern Negev, which had never previously been planted there, was destroyed by the bollworm (*Heliothis armigera*). Larvae of *Prodenia litura* (Noctuidae) became a major pest of ground nuts when these were first cultivated into Israel, while newly introduced cotton became heavily infested with Egyptian cotton bollworm (*Earias insulana*). In order to avoid dense populations of this species in the Sudan, the planting of okra, an alternative host plant, is prohibited after the beginning of August when the cotton has been harvested.[97]

Not only does the abundance and quality of their food play an important role in the increase of insect pests, but so also does the continuity of the crops. With irrigation, several crops can be grown each year in the arid tropics. Rain crops, in contrast are limited to short seasons between which the land is dry and fallow. Pest control measures must be employed with caution. Elimination of one pest may encourage another. Destruction of its predators and parasites may cause more harm than the beneficial effects of killing a pest. Any disturbance of the balance within an ecosystem may be dangerous unless backed by pilot experiments. In an effort to control particular pests, the entire environment should be considered. Insecticides may be essential, but should be used only when necessary and in such a way as to harm beneficial species as little as possible. With these principles in mind we will now turn to some specific examples.

LOCUST CONTROL

During recent years, many new ideas have been proposed for the control of desert locusts (*Schistocerca gregaria*) and other pests of arid regions. Present methods of survey for potential breeding sites of non-swarming locusts, or for the earliest swarms of an upsurge, consist of reconnaissance by aircraft or ground vehicles within areas chosen because of the seasonal incidence of rain. These methods are slow, restricted and expensive.

Survey on a larger scale is based on looking for areas of rainfall on daily synoptic weather maps. Since rains often fall from large cloud systems, analysis of climatic conditions, aided by information from meteorological satellites, may indicate the localities of potential breeding areas rapidly and relatively inexpensively. Contrasts in tone and colour could also be used to locate potential breeding sites on a smaller scale. More precisely, changes caused by recent rains or renewed growth of vegetation would have to be detected. Such changes are best emphasized by the computer, using digitized data from successive pairs of images in a time sequence. Regions of semi-permanent contrast, due to differences in soil and rock or the presence of irrigated areas, would thus be eliminated.

Radar is already used to study the flight activity of *Chortoicetes terminifera* and other plague locusts and, with the use of pilot balloons, to monitor low level winds during the day and at night.

Because of their swarming behaviour, locusts are well suited to control by insecticides. Swarms in flight can be attacked in isolation and in such a manner that the fall-out of insecticide on the ground is negligible unless persistent materials are used. When hopper bands are treated, this can be done in such a way that only a small fraction of the ground surface is actually covered with insecticide, and the effect on other insects is comparatively small. Locusts vary considerably in their susceptibility to insecticides, and there is always a risk of the development of resistant strains. Resistance to a specific insecticide would not be particularly important but for the fact that the phenomenon is often associated with cross-resistance between or within groups of insecticides.

Numerous new methods of insect control are being developed, some of which may find a place in locust control. The addition of phagostimulants (phagostimulants—substances that stimulate eating) could cause the insects to prefer to feed on poisoned bait and thus reduce the amount of insecticide needed for control against hoppers. Neem seed extract can be used as a deterrent to protect individual crops, but this is of little general value as the locusts will simply move to untreated areas. Liberation of sterile males, effective in the control of screw-worm flies (*Callitroga americana*) in America, is unlikely to be practical in the case of locust swarms in view of the vast number of insects that would have to be liberated.[81]

In recent years, numerous studies on the growth hormones of insects have shown that certain related substances or 'mimics' have similar hormonal properties and might possibly be used as pesticides. Synthetic 'mimics' of plant growth hormones are effective weed killers because they upset growth and development. Similarly, the application of substances like ecdysterone, juvenile hormone and synthetic analogues may prove to be useful in locust control. Fortunately, these substances pass through the insect cuticle when dissolved in acetone. There is increasing evidence that the various 'mimics' are not equally effective on all insects, which opens up the possibility of specific pesticides being created for particular pests. Formidable problems have still to be overcome, before any of the known 'mimics' can be used as a pesticide. The problem of persistence has not yet been answered, and the possible adverse effects of these substances on non-pest species still cannot be evaluated from the present evidence.[81]

PREVENTION OF TERMITE DAMAGE

Dry-wood termites eat out galleries in timber and these provide accommodation for the colony. Eventually these galleries coalesce to form large cavities. From time to time the worker nymphs make tiny holes to the exterior through which they eject faecal pellets. Small heaps of this accumulate beneath infested wood and these provide the first indications of termite attack. If they are ignored, the termites will weaken the entire structure to such an extent that eventually it may collapse.

Unlike dry-wood termites, whose colonies consist of only a few hundred individuals, which are usually built up from a single pair, subterranean termites have fixed nests from which many thousands of workers may travel distances of one hundred metres or more to gather food. Infestation is indicated by the presence of covered ways between the soil and the timber that is being eaten. If the timber is in contact with the ground, however, the termites will approach it from below through tunnels in the soil, leaving no trace of their entrance.

Termite damage can be avoided by design and siting of buildings, the provision of facilities for inspection and the use of mechanical barriers such as concrete slabs and metal caps or 'ant guards' which prevent the insects from working up through wooden pillars. Chemical barriers, consisting of insecticides or repellents in the soil, are a useful method of protecting temporary or low-cost structures. Insecticides and repellents are also employed against attacks by termites on agricultural crops. Biological control methods have not been employed.[62]

ALTERNATIVE METHODS OF PEST CONTROL

In addition to the methods already mentioned, insect control in arid lands with an over-abundance of labour can be achieved by hand collecting and destruction, e.g. for the control of *Prodenia* spp. caterpillars on cotton. Light, sound and chemical traps are also used. Cultural control and the use of resistant crops are important. In addition to insecticides, antifeedants which inhibit feeding can be applied to crops so that their insect pests die of starvation. Microorganisms can be used in the biological control of certain pests in addition to chemosterilants and sex-attractants which lure insects to their death. Diapausing insects may be adversely affected by artificial alteration of photoperiod, ultra-sounds can act as deterrents, pests of stored products can be controlled by electro-magnetic energy, infra-red heating, ionized radiation and so on. None of these methods is an answer in itself. All methods of pest control must be considered and integrated within ecologically balanced schemes, adapted to particular situations.[4]

The fundamental premise on which integrated control is based, is that complete eradication of pests is neither necessary nor even desirable. They should merely be kept below an economic threshold. Knowledge of this threshold for each pest is essential to success of the system. At present, the only practical alternative to large-scale chemical control measures of one form or another, is integrated control based on a thorough knowledge of the ecology, life history and behaviour of the pest. For this reason, biological researches must spearhead the development of all methods of pest control.[25]

12

Pathogenic and Venomous Organisms

All living organisms are vulnerable to the attacks of pathogens, parasites, and animals that feed on them. To a considerable extent, desert plants and animals are protected and isolated by their environment, but this is not invariably so. The problems of infecting new hosts are certainly increased, both by the harsh climate and by the dispersal of the vegetation and fauna. At the same time, the concentration of plants and animals in oases and other favourable localities engenders the transmission of diseases once they have been introduced. In this chapter, we shall consider a number of topics, related only in that they are of economic or medical importance to man.

PLANT PATHOGENS

Pathogenic fungi that are well adapted to survive the drought of arid climates are not usually economically important. They include species of *Alternaria* and powdery mildews. Strong pathogens such as rusts, downy mildews and *Phytophthora* spp. are adversely affected by climatic influences and are thus easily susceptible to cultural control methods. For instance, *Puccinia sorghi* and *Ustilago zea* attack maize in Israel only when it is grown near the coast or under overhead irrigation. In general, root and stem diseases are more prevalent in arid regions than are diseases of foliage, for the latter usually require rainfall or high atmospheric humidity in order to spread. An exception is the black rust of wheat (*Puccinia graminis*) whose uredospores are normally destroyed by low winter temperatures. Warm arid regions, in which native grasses grow throughout the winter, are therefore potent sources of infestation, not only for the arid regions themselves, but, also, for adjacent steppe lands where wheat is grown.[4]

Irrigation tends to favour the incidence and spread of many crop diseases, such as downy mildews, which require a moist atmosphere. The relationships between climate, type of irrigation, cultural methods, and the biology of the various pathogens may be extremely complex. Moreover, virus diseases are often influenced indirectly through their vectors.

Plant diseases can often be avoided or checked by suitable agronomic practices, but a basic problem is created by the fact that the environmental requirements of the pathogens are often very similar to those of their hosts. Control methods include the eradication of alternative hosts, suitable seeding methods and achieving a favourable balance of nutrients for the host crop. Crop rotation, antibiosis and the breeding of resistant varieties are also important. By antibiosis is meant the use of non-susceptible crops whose residual effect on soil pathogens is so great that subsequent susceptible crops are not harmed. Antibiosis may be achieved by the secretion of organic compounds that exert toxic effects on the pathogens. In the case of legumes, all available soil nitrogen is fixed so that the take-all fungus (*Ophiobolus graminis*) of wheat is thereby starved.

EPIZOOTICS AMONG MAMMALS

Apart from food shortage and predators, which normally exact their toll from every community of animals, population sizes are usually regulated by mortality resulting from parasites and disease. These, naturally, are especially effective among sedentary species. Nevertheless, even nomadic desert mammals are sometimes affected by epidemic diseases or epizootics which sometimes have important connections with human health and welfare. Diseases of animals which also affect man, are known as 'zoonoses'. Examples include plague, turalemia, and leishmaniasis.

A well-known example, bubonic plague, produced by the bacterium *Pasteurella pestis*, is naturally an epizootic of rodent populations. It is transmitted by the bites of fleas. Human plague is merely a blind alley of the normal cycle among the rodents, especially gerbils in arid and semi-arid regions. Sylvatic, or free-living plague, is transmitted from these gerbils to domestic rats and thence to man. In Africa, *Xenopsylla cheopis* and *X. brasiliensis* are the species of fleas mainly serving as vectors among rats and man. In South Africa, *X. philoxera* and *X. pirei* are not only vectors among gerbils (*Tatera* spp.) but also harbour *Pasteurella pestis*.

Mastomys spp. carry fleas from both groups and thus transmit plague from gerbils to domestic rats and man. In the steppes of Mongolia and Manchuria, plague is endemic among marmots and the bobak (*Marmota* spp.), and its main vector is the tarbagan flea (*Ceratophyllus silanteri*). In

North America, sylvatic plague is found in hares, ground squirrels and other lagomorphs and rodents. A somewhat similar disease is turalemia, discussed below (p. 139). Epizootics of ungulates that may be passed to domestic stock include rinderpest and trypanosomiases. Wild game are often resistant to diseases fatal to exotic domesticated animals such as cattle, sheep and goats. Conversely, they may be exceptionally susceptible. Rinderpest, a virus disease native to central Asia, was inadvertently introduced to the horn of Africa towards the end of the last century. Within a few years an epidemic spread throughout East and southern Africa killing most of the cattle, many large antelopes and almost all the buffalo. The disease is now endemic throughout most of Africa but the game has acquired some resistance and numbers have recovered. The mammals that suffered most from rinderpest were buffalo, hartebeest, camel, gazelle, waterbuck, springbok, gemsbok and many other antelopes. Horses, asses, zebras and other perissodactyls, carnivores and rodents are naturally immune.[26] In arid regions the impact of the disease is mainly upon gazelles, antelope and cattle.

The Indian wild ass (*Equus hemionus khur*) once inhabited expansive arid steppe land from northwest India into Iran. Man's demands on its environment, however, long ago reduced the population to less than 500 individuals. Then, between 1958 and 1960, epidemics of surra, caused by *Trypanosoma evansi*, eliminated most of these. In 1961, the much feared South African horse sickness, a virus infection transmitted by biting midges (*Culicoides* spp.), claimed many more victims. It seems now that the species can only be saved by a programme of effective health control measures, including the immunization of domestic horses and donkeys in the region.

Trypanosomiases which are transmitted by tsetse flies (*Glossina* spp.) are excluded from desert regions where tsetse does not occur. Yet, by driving pastoral peoples and their cattle into a more arid, tsetse-free country, overgrazing is much increased indirectly by trypanosomiasis. The main agents of cattle disease, *nagana*, in domestic stock are *Trypanosoma brucei*, *T. congolense* and *T. vivax*, for which wild game act as a reservoir. Some people believe that *nagana* is a blessing in disguise, protecting, as it does, much of Central Africa from the scourge of overgrazing. *T. evansi*, which parasitizes camels as well as horses, is passed directly and mechanically from one animal to another by biting flies such as horse-flies (Tabanidae) and stable-flies (*Stomoxys* spp.); dourine (*T. equiperdum*), a disease of horses in Algeria, is venereal and transmitted during copulation.

At the end of the dry season, the saiga antelope (*Saiga tatarica*) in the Gobi are occasionally infested by warble flies (Oestridae) which, in cases of strong infestation, sometimes kill the emaciated animals. The same thing happens to reedbuck (*Redunca redunca*) in the Dinder region of the Sudan.

DISEASES OF MAN

The desert climate is a healthy one. While there are, of course, many diseases to be found among the human inhabitants of desert regions, there are few that can truly be said to be of desert origin. Trachoma, for instance, is essentially a disease of poor hygiene, which the dust and flies of many desert regions may help to spread; but they do not create it. Nevertheless, in much of North Africa, up to 70 or 80 per cent of the people are affected, and many are left partially or completely blind as a result. The disease is particularly common in oases where flies are such a pest and transmit this and other human eye diseases mechanically. Desert sore and other skin ulcerations caused by bacteria may also be transmitted by flies to abrasions of the skin.

Sandfly and oroya fevers, and leishmaniasis, are spread by sandflies (*Phlebotomus* spp.). Sandfly fever, or pappataci fever, is caused by a small, filterable virus. Usually mild, with a duration of three days, it is endemic throughout the Sahara and Sind deserts. Oroya fever (Carron's disease) is caused by a small bacterium (*Bartonella bacciliformus*) and is characterized by high fever, often resulting in death. It is an important disease in the Peruvian sector of the Atacama desert above 760 m (2,500 ft).

Leishmaniasis, in fact, is not one but a group of tropical infectious diseases caused by species of flagellate Protozoa (*Leishmania* spp.). Some of these occur on the arid fringes of subtropical deserts, such as the borders of the Sahara and in the Gran Chaco of Argentina—others are found in true desert. Visceral leishmaniasis or kala-azar is characterized by enlargement of the liver and spleen, fever, anaemia and other symptoms. The mortality rate is high. Cutaneous leishmaniases takes the form of Oriental sore and allied complaints. It may be spread by contact with skin ulcers, although, like kala-azar, it is usually transmitted by sandflies. One of the most serious forms, espundia or uta, is widespread in Mexico, Central and South America. This produces an ulcerating infection of the mouth and nose. Jerboas, gerbils and other rodents, jackals, monkeys and so on act as reservoirs for leishmaniasis.

Another zoonosis of arid regions is turalemia, a plague-like disease of rodents etc. Widespread in the Middle East, Russia and the North American deserts, it is sometimes contracted mechanically by handling rabbits, but the agents by which it is normally transmitted are horse-flies (Tabanidae) and ticks (e.g. *Dermacentor* spp.). The causative agent, *Pasteurella turalensis*, can be passed directly from the infested mother tick to her offspring.

Coccidiomycosis, or San Joaquin Valley fever, is a disease of the pulmonary system caused by inhalation of the spores of the fungal parasite *Coccidioides immitis*. The symptoms vary in intensity from a mild discomfort to an acute bronchitis or bronchopneumonia of a few days to several weeks duration. Primary cutaneous infections have also been reported, but secondary lesions can occur in almost any organ of the body. Meningitis is the most significant coccidioidal lesion of the central nervous system and the most likely cause of death in man from coccidiomycosis. Nevertheless, fatalities are rare, for the disease is almost invariably benign. Arthritis is an allergic response that frequently accompanies infection, giving rise to the popular name 'desert rheumatism'.

Although limited to arid regions of the south-western United States and Western Argentina, it is doubtful if dry conditions are essential for the transmission of coccidiomycosis. Nevertheless, *C. immitis* appears to be concentrated in arid and semi arid areas of North and South America. A facultative parasite of man and many other mammals, the fungus flourishes in desert soils, especially the surface layers that have been sterilized by the sun's heat, after the onset of rain. Perhaps drying of the mucous membranes of the eye and nose may open the way to allergens and infective agents such as this.[80]

Rheumatism, diseases of the respiratory system including infective tuberculosis, and venereal complaints are common in many Old World oases, while digestive disturbances—often traceable to bad water, a defective diet or parasitic worms—are widespread. Amoebae (*Entamoeba histolytica*) and bacteria are responsible for different types of dysentery which are frequent causes of infantile mortality. By no means all these diseases are found in every oasis, of course, but travellers moving from one oasis to another tend to spread them. Unfortunately, as contact with the outside world increases it is almost certain that other diseases will also become prevalent.[38]

Because populations are dense there, human diseases are widespread among oasis dwellers and, with the exception of venereal disease, are correspondingly scarcer among the nomads of the desert until they visit the oases. Malaria is endemic throughout much of the Great Palaearctic desert except in very arid regions. Epidemics are irregular, however, as is the distribution of the various species of the malarial parasite (*Plasmodium* spp.) and of the mosquitoes that transmit them. Of more than 200 known species of the genus *Anopheles*, over 60 are incriminated as vectors of malaria and several of these occur in arid regions. Indeed one or more species are found in every major desert of the world. Nevertheless, malaria is far more prevalent in humid than in arid regions, like most of the other diseases discussed above. The same is true of West Nile infection, an arborvirus disease of children throughout the Great Palaearctic desert. (Arborvirus—a small group of arthropod-borne viruses.) It also has a wide distribution beyond the desert in East Africa, central and southern India. It is a zoonosis of birds and is transmitted by mosquitoes of the genus *Culex*.

Each year, at the time of the rains (July–September), there is an outbreak of malaria among the people who inhabit the semi-arid belt of Sahel savanna south of the Sahara. It is transmitted by the mosquito *Anopheles gambiae*, of which a few females are able to survive through the long dry season. They take frequent, but incomplete, blood meals, which result in a failure of ovarian development. This partial diapause is engendered by the onset of cool weather accompanied by low humidity. The ovaries undergo only one gonotropic cycle during the dry season and develop extremely slowly so that, when the rains come, the gravid females are ready to lay their eggs. Along the Nile valley, and in places where there is permanent water, *A. gambiae* and malaria rage together throughout the year. Clearly this information will be important in the planning of mosquito control measures.[32]

Until the discovery of residual insecticides, malaria control was directed mainly against mosquito larvae, by draining swamps and removing potential breeding sites and by treating stagnant waters with oil residues. When DDT became available, however, it was possible to spray the interiors of human dwellings so that adult mosquitoes were poisoned when they settled on the walls after feeding. The efforts of the WHO malaria eradication campaign have been to eliminate the malarial parasite from its reservoirs in the human population before the vector mosquitoes become too resistant to the chlorinated hydrocarbon insecticides. Unfortunately, the widespread use of these and of organophosphates has endangered ecosystems throughout the world (p. 170). In addition, the reduction in the infantile mortality rates of underdeveloped countries that they have engendered has been largely responsible for the present population explosion. This subject is beyond the scope of the present book, but it should nevertheless be remembered that family planning programmes ought always to accompany campaigns to control disease.

Biological control methods have not been much used against insect pests of desert regions, and the ecological problems involved are formidable. Fish (*Gambusia* spp.) introduced from Texas in 1926 were subsequently transplanted to all the permanent waters of Algeria and proved to be very successful predators of mosquito larvae. Indeed, they actually eradicated the insects from several oases. Nevertheless, there is always the danger of large populations of mosquitoes when irrigation results in surface waters. For example, Beni Ounif was very unhealthy until malaria was eradicated from there in 1924. The disease did not reappear until an epidemic during the years 1944–49 struck down one third of the population. Obviously there must be constant surveillance.[38]

MEDICAL PROBLEMS OF DEVELOPMENT PROJECTS

Irrigation schemes soon become focal points of infection. Another very important health problem of tropical countries is the increasing incidence of bilharziasis caused by trematode flukes (*Schistosoma* spp.). The disease is carried by freshwater snails (*Limnea* spp.) and is extremely difficult to control. People become infected by the cercaria larvae when paddling, washing or drinking. Whole populations may become greatly debilitated and their work output is consequently lowered. Although the disease is clearly spread by the absence of sanitation and lack of education, it is almost impossible to prevent small children from bathing when the weather is hot, and newly infected people themselves excrete many more eggs and miracidium larvae than do older people who have suffered the parasites for many years.

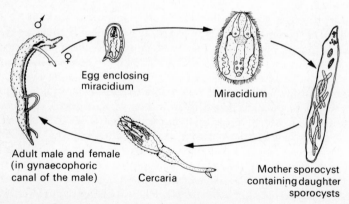

IN MAN   IN SNAIL

Egg enclosing miracidium

Miracidium

Adult male and female (in gynaecophoric canal of the male)

Cercaria

Mother sporocyst containing daughter sporocysts

Fig. 12.1   Stages in the life cycle of *Schistosoma mansoni*, one of the blood flukes that cause bilharzia in man (not to scale).

Irrigation of the Coachella Valley in the Sonoran desert of south-eastern California has resulted in considerable increases in eye gnats (*Hippelates collusor*) at certain seasons of the year. These irritating pests are responsible for catarrhal conjunctivitis; allied species are carriers of trachoma in other parts of the world.[38]

The development of man-made lakes and canals in tropical regions creates many other problems of medical entomology. For example, the

Sennar and Aswan dams on the Nile have created lake-like conditions favourable, in the dry season, for the multiplication of chironomid midges of the genus *Tanytarsus*. These can cause intense annoyance, asthma and other allergic symptoms. Other dams have encouraged blackflies (*Simulium damnosum*) which transmit onchocerciasis or tropical river blindness.

ARTHROPODS POISONOUS TO MAN

Arid regions are often thought of as being populated by hordes of biting and stinging animals. Although this reputation is not entirely deserved, poisons to kill prey and repel enemies have a special advantage in the desert environment where food is short and competition severe. Centipedes are not particularly well represented in deserts, but most of those that do occur belong to the genus *Scolopendra* and are large enough to give a painful bite with their poison claws. Millipedes are even fewer but, again, those that are found are particularly large. Their repugnatorial secretions contain benzoquinones and phenolic derivatives that can cause blistering of the skin and violent conjunctivitis if discharged into the eye.[27, 86]

Venomous and toxic insects

Painful stings are given by Hymenoptera (wasps, bees and ants). Bloodsucking insects, with poisonous salivary secretions used for subjugation of prey and for defense, include assassin or kissing bugs (Reduviidae) which are not uncommon in deserts. They inflict painful bites when handled. An East African species, *Platymeris rhadomanthus*, can eject its venom for a distance of 30 cm. On the mucous membranes and eyes it causes intense pain, oedema and vasodilation. These flying bloodsuckers normally feed on rats, ground squirrels and other mammals.

Blister beetles (Meloidae) are very numerous at the time of rain. When crushed they produce a toxin, containing cantharidin, which induces large blisters on the human skin. Blisters even appear if one of these insects merely walks across the body of a sleeping person. Cantharidin is extremely irritating to the urinary tract and can cause severe kidney damage. Its use, even in small quantities, as an aphrodisiac ('Spanish fly') is therefore extremely dangerous. Darkling beetles (Tenebrionidae) also produce a repellent secretion that may cause blistering. This contains benzoquinones, and is far less powerful than cantharidin. Some species are able to spray their repugnatorial secretions from the tip of the abdomen (p. 149); in South America, they are known as 'finacotes'.

Venomous arachnids

The terminal segment of the tail of scorpions is elongated to form a curved sting whose form and size varies. It is usually large in the Buthidae and small in most Scorpionidae. About 700 species are known and, of these, nearly all the dangerously poisonous ones belong to the family Buthidae. At least two types of scorpion poison exist. One of these is local in effect and comparatively harmless to man. The other is neurotoxic, resembling some kinds of snake venom. It also has an haemolytic action, destroying red blood corpuscles, and can be dangerous. The venoms of *Centruroides* spp. of the American deserts, and of the fat tailed scorpion (*Androctonus australis*) in North Africa, are as toxic as that of a cobra, although the amount injected is much less. Nevertheless, they can kill a man, and the death rate in parts of Mexico from scorpion stings is said to exceed one per thousand of the inhabitants.

The symptoms caused by scorpion venom of the less virulent type consist of a sudden sharp pain followed by numbness and local swelling which pass away within an hour or two. The neurotoxic poison causes intense local pain, a feeling of tightness in the throat, restlessness and involuntary twitching of the muscles. This may be followed by sneezing spasms, a copious frothing from the nose and mouth, followed by convulsions and death. This complex pattern of reactions may last from about 45 min to 10 or 12 hours. Much research has been devoted to producing antidotes from the blood serum of horses that have been injected with gradually increasing doses of venom. In several cases anti-venoms show cross-protection between different species of scorpion.[27]

Like scorpions, all spiders are venomous, but the poison apparatus is associated with the chelicerae or jaws. These consist of a large based segment and a terminal fang in which lies the duct of the venom gland. In few spiders are the fangs sufficiently powerful to pierce the human skin, and even fewer are harmful or dangerous to man. Those that are include species of the genera *Latrodectus* (the American black widows and South African shoe-button spiders), *Loxosceles* (the brown recluse spiders), and a few Mygalomorpha such as the Australian funnel-web spider (*Atrax robustus*).

Black widows and their allies are widely distributed in tropical and temperate regions including deserts. Their venoms are extremely toxic to mammals and occasionally cause death in man. Symptoms include local pain at the site of the bite, general manifestations of toxemia including sweating, salivation, congestion of the face and eyes, severe muscle cramps and hyperaesthesia of the skin. The blood pressure becomes abnormally high, as does the pressure of the spinal fluid, and the heart rate is profoundly affected.

The bite of the brown recluse spider and its relatives causes local stinging, followed by a haemorrhagic blister which gradually increases in size and becomes gangrenous, having an ulcer that heals only slowly. Soon after being bitten, some people develop severe intravascular haemolysis with high fever and shock, the urine becomes very dark as a result of the excreted haemoglobin and death not unfrequently follows. These spiders are widely distributed in the semi-desert regions of South America and the United States.[86]

The funnel-web spider (*Atrax robustus*) produces a venom containing a neurotoxin, a substance with activity like that of acetylcholine, another that resembles histamine, and a spreading factor. Although less widespread in Australia than the red-back spider (*Latrodectus hasselti*), the funnel-web is the more greatly feared and probably even more poisonous. It is responsible for a number of deaths annually, especially among children in arid districts.

Ticks occur in deserts wherever conditions are suitable for their vertebrate hosts. When they bite man they may cause pain followed by local haemorrhage or ulceration. A toxin present in the saliva has been known to cause paralysis in man and some other mammals—it inhibits the release of acetylcholine at motor nerve endings. Ticks also transmit various pathogenic organisms causing diseases such as turalemia and relapsing fever.

VENOMOUS REPTILES

The only known venomous lizards are the Gila monster (*Heloderma suspectum*) and Mexican bearded lizard (*H. horridum*) of the Sonaran desert. Their venom glands lie in the lower jaw and consist of 3–4 lobes, each with a duct opening at the base of one of the large mandibular teeth. These have deep grooves flanked by sharp flanges down which the poison flows. Its effects on man include severe local pain and swelling, and systemic symptoms of varying severity, occasionally resulting in death.

Venomous land snakes are found in all major deserts except those on the western coast of South America. They fall into four groups as follows:

(a) Back-fanged Colubridae

These are usually regarded as being only mildly poisonous to man Typical desert snakes of this group include the hissing sand-snakes (*Psammophis* spp.) of Asia and Africa, cat snakes (*Telescopus* spp.) of North Africa and the Middle East, skaapstekers (*Trimerorhinus* spp.) of South Africa and lyre snakes (*Trimorphodon* spp.) of the south-western United States and Mexico. Their venom has haemorrhagic activity in mammals.

(b) Elapidae

The only American representative of this family is the Sonoran coral snake (*Micruroides euryxanthus*), a small, unobtrusive species. Old World elapids—cobras, kraits and their relatives—show great diversity in all respects. The Egyptian cobra (*Naja haje*) is widely distributed throughout Africa but seems to prefer hot, dry and sandy places where its dull, lustreless scales are in keeping with its dusty surroundings. The 'asp' which Cleopatra applied to her breast, after having 'pursued conclusions infinite of easy ways to die' was either this species or else the horned viper (*Cerastes cerastes*) to both of which the name 'asp' has been applied.

(c) *Old World vipers (Viperinae)*

Represented by several specialized desert species, such as the saw-scaled viper (*Echis carinatis*) and the horned viper.

(d) *Pit vipers (Crotalinae)*

The common name of this group of snakes is derived from sensory depressions between the eyes and the nostrils. These are provided with an elaborate supply of sensory nerves and blood-vessels and act as directional infra-red receptors which make it possible for a snake to strike at warm prey, even in complete darkness, at distances up to 45 cm or more. The victim rarely dies immediately, however, and the snake may need to follow the stricken creature for some distance before it drops. Rattlesnakes (*Crotalus* spp.) trail their victims by means of a specialized sense organ known as Jacobson's organ. This comprises a pair of internal cavities at each side of the snout with ducts leading to an opening in the roof of the mouth. Odorous particles, picked up from the air or ground by the forked tongue, are transferred to these openings.[86]

Rattlesnakes have many representatives in the deserts of America, but Asian pit-vipers have evolved no specialized desert forms, although *Agkistrodon halys* is found throughout the arid regions of central Asia.

Snake venoms are usually pale yellowish, slightly viscid fluids consisting of toxins, enzymes and other components. The toxins are proteins, with molecular weights of 3,000–30,000 containing high proportions of sulphur and zinc. They lack enzymatic activity, but some of the associated enzymes may act synergistically with them.[17]

It is questionable whether viperine or elaphid venom is the more lethal, for the physiological effects of the two are quite different. The former causes collapse and heart failure, depending on the amount injected; the latter is neurotoxic and induces paralysis. Snake poison contains a large number of toxic compounds and varies from one species to another. Viperine poison usually includes an ingredient that causes clotting of the blood, while elaphid venom often contains an anti-coagulant and, at the same time, causes haemolysis or breakdown of the red blood corpuscles. Cobra venom acts rapidly and, if death from respiratory failure does not occur within about twelve hours, the patient usually recovers quickly. In the case of viperine snakebites, death is usually less rapid; but it may be several days before the patient is out of danger, because late complications, such as haemorrhage and septicaemia, are not infrequent. This suggests that Cleopatra's 'asp' was more likely to have been a cobra than a viper.[37]

In most cases, a snake strikes rapidly in the darkness, and disappears before it can be identified. The characteristic punctures made by the fangs, however, often enable diagnosis to be made, and this may be important in deciding what kind of treatment should be given. Only one snake in three is likely to be venomous, and only when two bleeding fang marks are present is the bite that of a dangerously poisonous species.

In cobras and other elaphid snakes, the poison fangs are situated at the front end of the upper jaw bone. Instead of being merely grooved, like those of back-fanged snakes, they are tubular like the fangs of vipers. Consequently, the venom can escape only from a minute hole near the tip. These fangs are permanently erected, though covered by fleshy folds, whereas, in vipers and rattlesnakes, the fangs are normally folded back, concealed in fleshy tissue and erected only in the act of biting. Non-poisonous snakes and the usually mildly poisonous back-fanged snakes have no large fangs, and their bite leaves double rows of tooth marks. In order to test whether fangs are present, a needle or similar instrument should be inserted in the angle of the jaw and passed forcibly forwards along the upper jaw of the snake from behind. This will reveal the presence of the erected fangs in cobras and, in the case of rattlesnakes and vipers, force the fangs into an erect position. They may then surprise the observer by their large size and prominence even though, previously they were invisible.[17, 29]

Reptile teeth are replaced throughout the lives of the animals, and each fang has a successor behind it, ready to take its place in due course. The jaws of snakes are only loosely attached to the skull and can usually be disarticulated. At the same time, the two sides of the lower jaw are united in

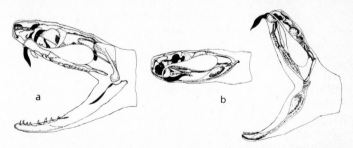

Fig. 12.2   The venom of a poisonous snake is stored in a sac with a tube leading to the hollow fangs. (a) The two large poison fangs in the top jaw of a cobra are permanently erect. (b) In vipers they are erected only in the act of biting. At other times viper fangs are folded back, concealed in fleshy tissue.[37]

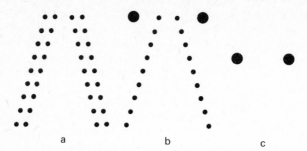

Fig. 12.3   Tooth and fang marks left by (a) Non-poisonous or mildly poisonous back-fanged snake; (b) Cobra or mamba; (c) Viper.[29]

front only by elastic ligaments so that they can be moved separately as the prey is forced down the throat of the snake. Ingestion is aided by a copious flow of lubricating liquid from the salivary glands. The skin of the neck can be stretched to accommodate large objects, and the windpipe or glottis can be protruded from the throat so that breathing is not obstructed while large prey is being swallowed. The rattle of a rattlesnake is composed of a number of interlocking horny pieces of cast skin which, when rapidly vibrated, produce an angry buzz. The function of this, like the hiss of an adder, is to warn potential enemies to avoid its dangerous possessor. No doubt it often allows the snake to save its venom for more profitable use than self defence.[17]

Although venomous animals have been discussed in some detail in this chapter, they do not significantly affect the life of man in the desert. With reasonable care, stings and bites can be avoided almost completely, and, in any case, only a minute proportion of these has serious effects. Scorpion stings cause nearly 2,000 deaths annually in Mexico, but these are mostly in the Pacific states which, although dry, are not genuinely desert areas. Stings are more frequent during periods of rain or high humidity here as in other desert regions of the world.

CHEMICAL DEFENCE

Biological interest in pathogenic and venomous organisms is by no means entirely concerned with their economic and medical importance. The main fascination of the study of parasitology lies in the wonderful examples it affords of the ways in which parasitic organisms may become adapted to their hosts.[25]

The great reduction of plant cover in desert regions makes activity hazardous except for the speedy and well armed. The presence of a poisonous sting or an unpleasant flavour may then be decisive for survival. The final defence of a prey animal when encountered by a predator is often to retaliate with physical or chemical weapons. The former include spines, teeth, and claws, while chemical weapons are usually glandular secretions which may originally have had some other function, such as the capture or digestion of food. There are no true salivary glands in reptiles, but the mucous labial glands of the mouth may be well developed. In the lizards *Heloderma suspectum* and *H. horridum* (p. 145) and in many snakes, they are modified to form the poison glands.

The 'vinegaroon' (*Mastigoproctus giganteus*) (p. 85) moves the tip of its abdomen and ejects a repugnatorial fluid from its anal gland. This contains acetic acid, which makes the animal distasteful to potential predators.[27] Nearctic tenebrionid beetles of the genus *Eleodes* practically stand on their heads to aim the tip of the abdomen at a predator, and spray it with a quinonoid secretion as mentioned above (p. 143). Some predators are able to overcome such defences. Grasshopper mice (*Onychomys* spp.) (p. 87), for example, are able to grab *Eleodes* beetles by the head and thus avoid being sprayed: they can also capture and eat 'vinegaroons' with immunity, because they are so quick.

Chemical defence glands are found in many arthropods. Their number, structure, and mode of operations, is extremely diverse, and they have arisen many times independently in the course of evolution. In some cases, the secretions merely ooze out, in others they are projected as a jet-like spray. In general, they are extremely effective against a large array of enemies, both invertebrate and vertebrate. Sometimes they have a direct mechanical effect, particularly on small arthropods. This has been demonstrated for the ephalic exudate of nasute termites and the droplets of blood released at the limb joints of coccinellid beetles.

Many poisonous animals react to predators by adopting a characteristic posture that serves to intimidate the enemy. This is often associated with the possession of aposematic (warning) coloration (p. 98). Such displays have been described in scorpions, which assume a warning posture when disturbed, and this may be associated with stridulation—that is, sound production by the mechanical friction of one part of the body against another; usually by means of a number of file-like ridges which rub against another set of ridges or a cluster of chitinous granules or pegs.[27] Stridulation occurs in many well-armed or poisonous desert arthropods, such as Solifugae and mutillid wasps; as well as in locusts, grasshoppers, crickets, cicadas and other harmless insects, in which its function is intra-specific and social. Although scolopendromorph centipedes are protected to some extent by their poison (p. 143), they will readily autotomize an anal leg when disturbed. This lies, stridulating on the ground, and thereby attract a predator's attention while its former possessor makes its escape.[27]

Many reptiles, as well as some mammals make explosive snorts or hisses when encountered by a predator; but this is only bluff. The hiss of a poisonous snake or the rattle of a rattlesnake, on the other hand, have a genuine warning function. African porcupines (Hystricidae) make warning sounds by rattling their quills before charging backwards and impaling aggressors with their sharp spines. New World species, which belong to a different family (Erethizontidae), hiss, erect their spines and turn their backs towards the enemy. Since the quills are barbed and easily detached, they provide a formidable deterrent. It is possible that many mammalian predators may instinctively avoid hissing and rustling noises as these are so often associated with poison and the other weapons of defence that are particularly well developed in desert animals.

13

The Desert Complex and its Rational Exploitation

The central problem of sustained land-use in arid regions is to find and maintain a balance between human requirements and the sustainable productivity of the land. Throughout his history, as we have seen, man has consistently reduced the productive capability of the land. This he has done through over-exploitation. Yet, by multiple land use, considerably greater returns could have been achieved without damage to the environment. Therefore, rational exploitation of the desert complex must be based, not on single, large-scale projects, but on a multiplicity of smaller schemes, each complementing the others. In this chapter are given examples of some of the various ways in which the desert complex can thus be exploited. To obtain maximum yields and, concurrently, to improve the potentialities of arid environments, no one form of land use can be employed to the exclusion of others. A balance must be struck between several different types of land use, so that the ecosystem is used to the best advantage possible.

PASTORALISM

Semi-arid and arid regions are readily degraded into desert; the reclamation of their climax vegetation is far less easy to achieve. Nor is this normally attempted. Historically man has merely changed his methods of land use to suit the changed conditions. From agriculture, he has switched to pastoralism, herding cattle and sheep until the vegetation and soil have become so impoverished that only camels and goats can survive.

Of all pastoral animals, the goat is chiefly responsible for enlarging the deserts of Asia and northern Africa. It has largely replaced the migrant gazelle, which only nibbles at thorn bushes, and either climbs trees to reach the upper branches, or eats them to the ground. Two contrary opinions are commonly expressed about goats. According to the first, these animals are a living testimony to the wisdom of Allah who has created such a wonderful machine that it can transform even waste paper and other refuse into wholesome milk. The second point of view stresses the fact that goats are a menace and that there is little hope for the re-habilitation of the Sahara and other deserts unless they can be eliminated. Personally, I subscribe to the first view in that I do not believe that the desert can be rehabilitated without irrigation, whether goats are present or not. On the other hand, by causing even further degradation of the land, the goat is encouraging the desert to advance. Thus, the future of land that has not yet been reduced to desert is being mortgaged for milk and meat today. There is nowhere in the world where goats and sheep may safely overgraze, but the dangers are greatest in arid lands.[36]

The combination of overstocking with a variable rainfall may lead to considerable fluctuations in the numbers of animals. The recent drought in the Sahelian belt of Africa has caused a crash in the numbers of live-stock from which they will take several years to recover. Again, during a succession of good years a population of 8 million head was built up in Algeria. After a few years of drought, however, it was reduced in 1945 to 2 million. In the Kajiondo district of Kenya the number of cattle increased from 350,000 to nearly 700,000 during the period 1942–60, but it was then reduced by two-thirds because of drought followed by floods which, in Botswana during the early 1960's, after some years of drought, half the national herd perished.

Adding to the number of places at which livestock can secure water widens the area of grazing and helps to reduce the pressure around the original sources of water. It can be achieved by boring new wells and by constructing *hafirs* or artificial ponds in which seasonal rain water may be stored. Such methods are effective, however, only so long as the herds are not permitted to increase. If they do so, the situation becomes worse, not better. By 1970 the Sahelian zone of Africa was supporting some 24 million people and about the same number of animals—roughly a third more people and twice as many animals as 40 years ago. The effect of recently drilled bore holes had been simply to make pasture instead of water the factor limiting numbers of cattle so that, when the inevitable population collapse took place, it was all the more ferocious. Thousands of starving cows clustered around the Sahelian wells: indescribably emaciated, they would stagger away with bloated bellies to struggle from the churned mud at the water's edge, so that each bore hole quickly be-came the centre of its own little desert of about forty or fifty kilometres square.[116] Pastoralism is clearly a major cause of desert expansion and

Fig. 13.1 Rain water stored in a *hafir*.

cannot, therefore, be advocated as a form of land use in desert regions except under strict control and supervision.

NOMADISM

True pastoral nomadism is found in the Sahara, the deserts of the Middle East and in Central Asia. It differs from the economy of the primitive independent hunter, the food gathering nomadism of the aborigines of north-western Australia, the Patagonians, and the Bushmen of South Africa, in that its practitioners traditionally do not depend exclusively upon their livestock, but obtain certain commodities from the settled populations of oases. The life style of pastoral nomads is a remarkably efficient adaptation to the vagaries of the desert environment. There is nothing random about their migrations in the Sahel savanna zone, for example. The dry season finds them as far southward as they can go without entering the range of the tsetse fly. There is then almost a symbiosis between the nomads and the sedentary farmers: the nomads' cattle graze the stubble of the crops and, at the same time, they manure the fields. In return, the nomads receive millet (*dura*) from the farmers. With the first rains, the grass springs up and the herds then move northwards. The rains also move north, and the cattle follow behind them in search of new grass. The migration continues until the northern edge of the Sahelian rain belt is reached and then the return to the south begins. This time the cattle are grazing the grass that grew up behind them on their northward journey, and are drinking the standing water that remains from the rainy season. Back in their dry season range, they find a crop of grass and stubble that will last them through eight or nine months of drought until the rains come again.[117]

The traditional migration routes and the amount of time a herd may spend at any particular well are governed by rules worked out by the tribal chiefs. In this way, overgrazing is avoided. Furthermore, the timing of the movements of the animals provides food and water with the least danger from disease or conflict with other tribal groups. This method of land use is efficient because the cattle do not remain long enough in one place to cause serious overgrazing, as occurs with semi-sedentary pastoral herds concentrated round wells and bore holes. Another example is afforded by areas of winter rainfall such as eastern Syria, Jordan and the northern parts of Arabia, where farmers begin to cultivate in autumn when the Bedouin move out into the desert, only to re-enter the cultivated areas to graze their animals on the stubble from July to October.[120]

In desert regions where the climate is more extreme than in the Sahel savanna, nomadism is the only way of life by which man can survive at all, except in oases. Like the larger wild mammals of desert regions, man and his domestic animals can only take advantage of the variable desert rainfall by wandering over large areas. The more extreme the desert and the more erratic its rain, the greater the areas that have to be scoured for pasture. An extreme example is afforded by the indigenous Tibu people of the Libyan desert who, until recently, wandered in small groups with a few sheep or goats across hundreds of kilometres of almost lifeless country where effective rain falls on the average only once between 30 and 50 years except on a few isolated patches of higher ground where the figure is reduced to about 4 to 10 years. Wild nomadic animals, such as addax antelope, roam over the same area.

Nomadic tribes are to be found all over the Sahara, but they differ greatly from one another in many respects. Some are small, and primitive, with little cultural organization. Desperately poor and owning little except the barest necessities of life, they sleep in the open and dress in skins and rags. Other tribes number several thousand people each and, sub-divided into clans, live in comfortable tents, are rich in livestock and have elaborate political, social and economic systems.[15]

The Nemadi are non-pastoral nomads. They live a solitary life, avoiding the settlements and camps of others. Their tents are made of antelope skins and their clothing is extremely simple. They live by hunting addax, oryx, ostriches and bustards with the aid of dogs which distract their prey until they can hamstring it. The Tuareg and Teda, in contrast, are huge tribes of pastoral nomads who, in the past, ranged over large areas of the Sahara—the Tuareg from Libya to Timbuktu, the Teda in the south-eastern Sahara. There are also numbers of Arab tribes such as the Cha'-amba of the north-western central Sahara, who once had a tremendous reputation as bandits. Experts in desert warfare, they eagerly joined the French Saharan Camel Corps to fight their traditional enemies the Tuareg and Moors. It was one of their patrols that broke for ever the military power of the Ahaggar Tuareg at the Battle of Tit in southern Algeria, in May 1902.

Unlike food gathering, nomadism is not isolated from other forms of land use in arid regions. Nomadic pastoralists exchange their produce—milk, meat and hides—with that of the cultivators who engage in dry farming or oasis agriculture. Some of the Bedouin of Libya, some Teda and the Gherib of Tunisia are semi-nomads who own plantations without actually cultivating them. In the old days they used slaves to carry out the work of agriculture and the cultivation of the dates: today these tasks are performed by former slaves and their dependents who are still linked economically and socially with their former masters.

In addition to hunting and pastoral nomadism, commercial nomadism in the Old World has long been an important and lucrative form of employment, to which the opportunities for pillage were an added inducement. With the advent of mechanical transport, however, it has declined and the 15,000 camels which formed the caravans between Timbuktu and Taoudeni, for example, are no longer required. 'Trans-humance' is the name for small-scale seasonal movements, as from low to high pastures in the Carpathians. These are responses to seasonal rainfall in a semi-arid rather than an arid climate.[120]

Although the nomadic way of life is probably the only one which will ever produce much in the way of food from arid desert regions, governmental policies towards nomadism are usually unimaginative and unenlightened. They appear to be directed chiefly towards the settlement of the nomads and the restriction of their migration routes. If traditional nomadism were to disappear, however, vast areas that are now productive would become permanently useless to mankind. It might be better, in the long run, therefore, to encourage and modernize the nomadic way of life. The hardships that nomadic people have to endure could be ameliorated by a flying doctor service, mobile markets and practical educational facilities. Grazing could be controlled and even improved, news of distant rainfall transmitted by radio, and so on. In this way, the desert cores might continue to contribute usefully to the economy of man, provided of course, that they were not exploited.

PRESERVATION OF WILD LIFE

Wildlife problems are acute in nearly all arid regions of the world. In the United States, for instance, overgrazing, soil erosion, river dams and channelization, and the development of cities have greatly affected the wild life of the desert. These changes have threatened the existence of some species and caused the extinction of others. The pronghorn (*Antilocapra americana*) and Yuma clapper rail (*Rallus longirostris*) are seriously endangered, the otter (*Lutra canadensis*) has not been seen along the Lower Colorado River for 50 years and prairie dogs (*Cynomys ludovicianus*) have vanished from southern Arizona. Certain fish have disappeared from the altered watersheds of the Colorado, Gila and Rio Grande, and bighorn sheep will quickly disappear if their environment is not protected.

This gloomy picture is to some extent offset by the establishment of wildlife refuges and game management areas, but the increase in human population poses problems. Introduction of the starling (*Sturnus vulgaris*) and new food habits developed by native blackbirds necessitate some bird control, while rabies and bubonic plague have become important problems locally. Faunal conservation is a way of land management and development. If natural predators are scarce or absent, herbivores must be controlled to prevent overgrazing. The relationships of an ecosystem are so complex that destruction of a single species may upset the whole pattern of a region.

With the spread of ecological knowledge, the fact is gradually becoming generally understood that man cannot create and maintain a purely artificial biocoenose with nothing but cultivated plants and domesticated animals. The importance of the natural flora and fauna is no longer in doubt. Nevertheless, the deserts of the world are not afforded the degree of nature conservation they require, either to maintain them as reservoirs of plant and animal species or to increase their tourist attraction. The destruction of wild game throughout the Sahara during the last century has been spectacular. Game reserves and national parks are few and poorly cared for, and it will require extensive expenditure and research before their potential can ever be restored.

GAME RANCHING

The indigenous fauna of any region is naturally better adapted and more productive than any exotic, domesticated species. For this reason, game ranching is frequently advocated as a form of land use in the wilderness regions of the world.[26, 46] The first large-scale management of a non-domesticated herd animal was that of the Asian saiga antelope (*Saiga tatarica*) which had been almost exterminated during the 19th century in response to demand for its meat and horns. Accorded complete protection by the Russian government in 1919, the population increased from about 1,000 animals in 1930 to over 2,500,000 in 1960. Since 1950 the animals have been cropped. Today, about 350,000 are killed annually, thereby providing 6,700 tonnes of meat and 20,000 m^2 of leather, as well as large amounts of fats and other raw materials for the chemical industry.

Apart from this, and ostrich farming in southern Africa, there have been few attempts at game ranching in the arid regions of the world. Yet wild game is more resistant to heat and drought than are domestic animals. Game animals are also less susceptible to disease, they include a multitude of widely differentiated forms that are able to utilize the natural vegetation more fully and evenly than can domestic herds, and they are better adapted to the natural environment, in which they have evolved, than are exotic domesticated forms. For these reasons, game ranching is, potentially, one of the most practical and efficient forms of land use available for desert regions (p. 168).[46]

In addition to true desert animals, many East African species are well adapted to heat and drought. These include black rhinoceros (*Diceros bicornis*), wild ass (*Equus asinus*), eland (*Taurotragus oryx*) and ostrich (*Struthio camelus*), which might profitably be re-introduced into the savanna belts on the desert's fringe. When their populations increased, they could be culled to provide food for the people without detriment to the environment.[32]

The problem of this type of land use is that the great mobility of game animals makes them difficult to control, or to protect from poachers. Large-scale game ranching in the desert would require a strong and mobile corps of wardens equipped with efficient ground transport and aircraft. If it became firmly established as a method of land use, however, it might well repay the initial capital investment. The ultimate object is to provide meat so cheaply that poachers and smugglers do not find it worth their while to compete with the products of the official government game ranching schemes.

DRYLAND FARMING

The utilization of the natural desert vegetation by food gathering peoples has been discussed in Chapter 6. Until recently, land in the Sahelian zone of Africa had been left fallow for 15 or 20 years before recropping. The people had developed a great variety of their staple crops, millet and sorghum, each adapted to different growing seasons and situations, and the land was not over-exploited. With the introduction of cash crops to earn foreign exchange, however, all this has changed. With the best land given up to the cultivation of cotton and groundnuts, the increasing population had to bring the more marginal areas into use to grow their own food crops and these ecologically fragile regions could not take the strain of intensive agriculture. Fertility declined, slowly at first, and then in a vicious spiral. Poor crops left the soil exposed to the wind and sun so that it lost its structure, while the rain, when it fell, was not absorbed but ran off uselessly, causing gulley erosion. Desertification took place.[117] The plight of the Sahel savanna furnishes a sombre warning against over exploitation of the desert's edge. The land can be productive up to a point, but no more. Dryland farming can be tolerated only up to a certain limit. It should be supervised and managed scientifically.

Productivity can, of course, be improved by scientific land management. Run-off during rainstorms can be reduced by keeping the soil surface as open as possible and by reducing the velocity with which the surplus water runs off the soil. The harmful effects of drought can be lessened by selecting crops whose water demands fit as closely as possible with the rains, and by adapting the crop to the growing season by plant breeding methods. Soil fertility can be raised by the use of fertilizers, crop-rotation and so on. During the last twenty years crop-husbandry in the semi-arid regions of the world has achieved better use of the available resources and the production of crops best suited to the climates in which they are to be planted.[98]

AGRICULTURAL CROPS

The principal crops of desert regions may be summarized as follows:[5]
Grain cereals   These are of two kinds, temperate or small grain cereals (of which wheat and barley can be grown in dry regions) and tropical cereals, such as maize, sorghum, millets (*Pennisetum* and *Paspalum* spp.) and rice. All of these can be cultivated in arid lands without irrigation. The progenitors of wheat (*Triticum* spp.) and barley (*Hordeum vulgare*) arose in the Middle East about 10,000–15,000 years ago. Sorghum originated in tropical Africa, from which it spread to the Near and Far East about 2,700 B.P., or its cultivation may have been initiated quite independently in India. Maize (*Zea mays*) is the basic food of much of the New World: there are many theories as to its origin. Wild rice is found in Asia and Africa. Cultivated varieties probably arose in S.E. Asia (*Oryza sativa*) and West Africa (*O. glaberrima*), over 5,000 years ago. *Pulses or grain legumes.* Peas (*Pisum arvense* and *P. sativum*) originated either in Ethiopia or in the Mediterranean region. They require cool, moist conditions, and are not well adapted to desert. Broad beans (*Vicia faba*), on the other hand, were cultivated in ancient Egypt and Palestine. Although they require considerable soil moisture, they show good drought resistance. Chick peas (*Cicer arientinum*), which originated in the Himalayas, and

lentils (*Lens culinaris*)—the small-seeded variety from S.E. Asia, the large-seeded from the Mediterranean—are widely cultivated in arid regions of the world. *Lathyrus sativum* is a drought resistant, cool weather legume from India: *Lupinus* spp. have been cultivated in the Middle East since earliest antiquity. Field beans (*Phaseolus vulgaris*) originated in tropical South America and were introduced into the Old World soon after the discovery of the Americas. They are widely grown under irrigation and as rain-fed crops.

Lima beans (*Phaseolus lunatus*) originated in Central or South America. They are usually sown in arid coastal regions because they require a long period of growth, moderate temperatures and high humidity. Mung beans (*Vigna mungo*) are widely grown in Brazil and S.E. Asia, pigeon-peas (*Cajanus cajan*) in tropical Asia and Africa. These thrive on poor soils, and, of all legumes, are the most resistant to heat and drought. The most important pulse crop in Africa is the cowpea (*Vigna unguiculata*), originally from Ethiopia or India. This was introduced into America with the slave trade and thrives in regions with low rainfall.

Sugar crops   Sugar beet (*Beta vulgaris*) is not suitable for cultivation in hot, dry countries, but it is an important crop of temperate climates. Sugar cane (*Saccharum officinarum*) on the other hand, originated in the islands of the Pacific Ocean and is grown in tropical desert lands. It is one of the oldest cultivated crops.

Oil crops   Ground nuts (*Arachis hypogaea*) originated in Gran Chaco and were brought to Africa by slave traders. Safflower (*Carthamus tinctorius*) is extremely resistant to drought and makes effective use of the available soil moisture. It is one of the Compositae of Asian origin. Sesame (*Sesamum indicum*) originated in Africa and Asia; it requires a great deal of heat and light, has a long tap root, and is very resistant to drought. Castor beans (*Ricinus communis*) originated in tropical Africa and are likewise drought resistant, as is linseed (*Linum usitatissimum*) of Mediterranean and S.E. Asian origin. Sunflowers (*Helianthus annuus*), originally from Peru or Mexico, are fairly drought-resistant as are soy beans (*Glycine max*), which are of Chinese origin.

Forage   In hot, dry regions with advanced agriculture, dairy cattle are frequently stabled for most months of the year. Forage is harvested daily and fed as silage. Seasonal fluctuation in quality is smoothed out by adding hay or silage stored at the time of optimum growth. Forage crops include lucerne or alfalfa (*Medicago sativa*), a desert species from Iraq, berseem clover (*Trifolium alexandrinum*) of levantine origin, vetches (*Vicia* spp.), elephant grass (*Pennisetum purpureum*), Sudan grass (*Sorghum sudanense*), and stock beets (*Beta vulgaris*).[5]

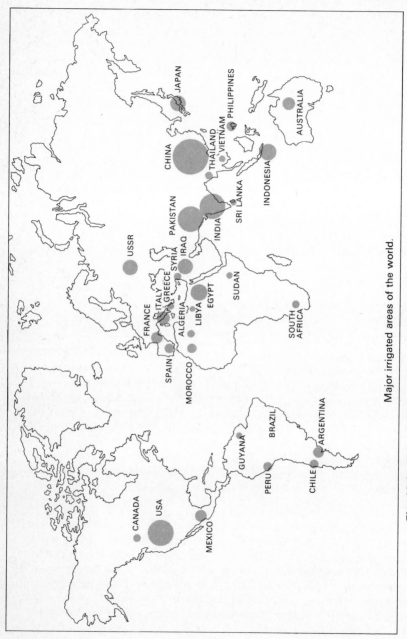

Fig. 13.2 Major irrigated regions of the world. The sizes of the circles are proportional to the areas irrigated.

IRRIGATION

Irrigation schemes are an effective form of land use in deserts where water is obtainable in quantity from regions beyond the desert's fringe. The Egyptian civilization has persisted for millennia because the Nile floods bring water and silt from Ethiopia so that the flood plains are invigorated annually by water and soil rich in minerals essential to plant growth. Irrigation may be effective even with quite saline water provided that the soil is permeable drainage adequate and irrigation water applied in considerable excess (50 per cent) to provide sufficient for leaching. Under such conditions, alfalfa and barley can be grown with water of a salinity above 3,000 p.p.m.

The desert climate is conducive to rapid plant growth when water supplies are unlimited. Many crops can be taken annually—indeed as many as 14 crops of alfalfa (lucerne) are harvested each year in certain Libyan irrigation schemes. Where artesian zones exist, water can be obtained relatively cheaply. Declining oases in Algeria have been preserved and new ones created for the establishment of modern palm groves by means of arterial borings. But, where pumping is necessary, the cost may be prohibitive unless, as in oil-rich Libya, fuel and cash are unrestricted. The Kufra scheme, to irrigate 50,000 hectares with the most modern concepts of sprinkler irrigation, coupled with a year-round growing season, is producing phenomenally high yields of alfalfa and grain. Nevertheless, the water is a fossil resource which is not being recharged. It has been in the ground for about 28,000 years and has been calculated to sink at a rate of 35 m (115 ft) in 40 years. When plentiful resources of ground water are found in the sedimentary basins of deserts, it may not be necessary to bother too much whether or not they are being recharged. It is difficult to be certain that fossil water, stored during pluvial cycles of the Quaternary period, is not being renewed. For example, the reservoir that underlies much of the central Sahara may be replenished by the rain that falls on the Atlas mountains. The use of artesian wells and intensive date farming have, however, had a dramatic effect on water balance in many parts of North Africa, as mentioned above (p. 42). It is clearly important, with the development of new irrigation schemes, to ensure that ground water is not exploited faster than it can be replenished. Many of the deep wells being bored today in deserts around the world, like those at Kufra, are tapping water that can never be replaced. In parts of Baja California, for instance, short-term farming projects are based on wells with an expectancy of 10–15 years at most. Exploitation of irreplaceable resources at this rate can scarcely be regarded as agricultural progress.

It may not be inopportune here to consider the effect of dams, for irrigation purposes, on the river systems in which they are situated. Let us take,

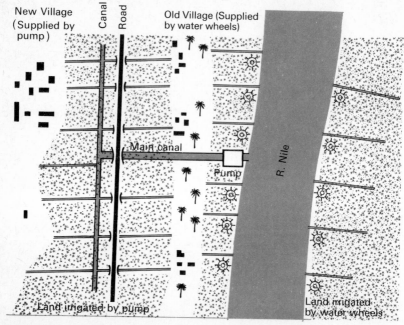

Fig. 13.3 Irrigation in the northern Sudan. Old villages obtain water from the river by means of the water-wheel (saggia) turned by oxen, or with small diesel pumps. Larger modern pumps feed water into irrigation canals which supply a broad strip of land, formerly uncultivated, behind the old villages; and new settlements have grown up inland at the edge of the desert.

for example, the high dam across the Nile at Aswan. This is merely the largest of a series of dams and barrages which, during the present century, have increasingly brought the flow of the Nile under control. It has produced a great deal of hydroelectric power and water for irrigation. Egypt's potential arable land has been increased from 283,000,000 to over 365,000,000 hectares (7-9 million acres) and the country has been made self-sufficient in wheat and an exporter of rice. The hydro-electrical capacity of the dam is 10 billion kilowatt hours per annum.[60]

Various ecological repercussions have, however, to be offset against these obvious benefits. Since the deposition of Nile sediment has ceased, the shoreline of the delta has retreated, endangering land reclamation projects further inland. Furthermore, salt water is penetrating the delta margin with consequent loss of cultivable land. The rich fishing industry off the Nile delta has been destroyed by the halt of nutrient flow into the Mediterranean. Before 1964, 18,000 tons of sardines were harvested

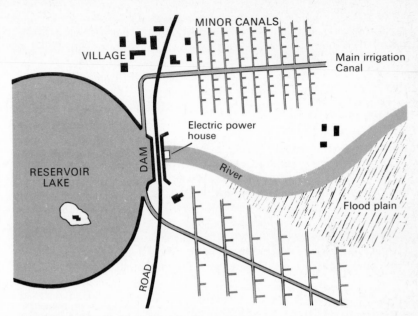

Fig. 13.4 Irrigation by means of a dam. Some of the stored water is used to generate electricity. Irrigation canals and field channels are potent sources of infection with bilharzia and malaria.

annually; in 1969 the catch was only 500 tons. Fisheries in Lake Nubia (Lake Nasser) are yielding 5,000 tons annually, but this will probably decline, as has occurred in Lake Kariba. The deposition in the lake of all Nile silt (50–100 million tonnes per annum) has led to the need for a large fertilizer industry to compensate for the loss of nutrients in the irrigation water, while the age-old industry of making bricks from Nile mud will have to find alternative raw material. The chief drawback to the Aswan dam, however, is none of these. It is the increased incidence of schisto-somiasis that has been engendered.[60] (p. 142)

WATER DESALINATION

The water which percolates underground inevitably dissolves minerals from rocks and sediments on its way. Consequently, when it emerges at springs and artesian wells, or is pumped from boreholes, it is often highly mineralized. Whereas man and animals can tolerate sodium chloride, they cannot live on water with a high content of sodium or magnesium sulphate, and plants are killed by chlorates, sodium carbonate and bicarbonate, in solution. Control of the ground-water table is the basis for irrigation farming and the reclamation of salt-affected ground. Many plants can tolerate a degree of sodium chloride and even grow when watered with sea-water if they are rooted in well-drained sand.[120]

Although desalination is still too expensive for the production of water for agricultural purposes, it has reached a stage of technological development at which the price per litre is not much greater than that obtained through a water board undertaking in humid countries. It involves high capital expenditure, however, large amounts of energy and a skilled labour force. It may be achieved by multiple flash-stage distillation, electrodialysis, freezing and reverse osmosis. Desalination processes clearly have a future in arid regions that are endowed with oil and natural gas. Elsewhere, atomic energy or solar energy may eventually be used. Indeed, 75,000 tonnes of distilled water for livestock are already being produced in the Kara Kum by means of cylindrical mirrors which focus the sun's rays on glass tubes which act as boilers. Nevertheless, at the present time, the prospects are poor in the major desert regions of the world for producing desalinized water in quantity sufficiently cheaply for it to be used for agriculture.[1]

HYDROPONICS

Economy of water is vital for efficient agriculture in desert regions, and the traditional agricultural methods of oasis dwellers have been developed over a long period of time and are by no means inefficient. Banks and palm trees provide shelter from the desiccating winds of the desert, and thus help to reduce evaporation. Transpiration from the palms themselves is, however, responsible for considerable loss of water which could only be conserved by growing other more economic cash crops. More efficient use of existing water can also be made through hydroponic cultivation. Nutrient solutions, pumped once or twice daily through plastic pipes perforated by small holes, will irrigate plant roots growing in silicious *erg* sand without wetting the surface of the soil, so that little water is wasted through evaporation. In this way, for example, one tonne of tomatoes can be produced from 40–50 cubic metres of water instead of 80–150 cubic metres required by plants grown with surface irrigation.[39]

DUNE STABILIZATION

In areas where the rainfall exceeds 150 mm a year, sand dunes are capable of supporting permanent vegetation provided that the surface has been stabilized. This can be achieved by spraying the dunes with a mixture of oil and synthetic rubber before planting seedlings of *Acacia* and *Eucalyptus* When these have become established their roots exploit the moisture stored below the surface of the dunes from one wet season to the next. As they grow, they provide a natural windbreak and dead foliage becomes incorporated into the soil, thus increasing its cohesiveness. Stabilization of dunes in this way is an important method of counteracting the expansion of the desert.

Considerable progress has been made in the stabilization of active sand dunes in the semi-arid Argentine pampas by another method, as follows. First, the sandy crests are smoothed with a beam drawn by a tractor. Forage mixtures are then sown with a common grain drill. The field is afterwards covered with a thin layer of straw which is anchored to the surface of the sand by passing over it a disc harrow with a short angle of penetration. This herbaceous covering can be replaced by an asphalt sheet, 1–2 tonnes per hectare according to the season and dune.[39]

Conversion to grassland can be achieved within three months, but it is a complicated procedure and requires a mass of men, machines and effort. Planting with cuttings of poplar (*Populus* spp.), on the other hand, fixes a dune in a couple of years. It is extremely simple and can be carried out by one man with the aid of a soil auger. No prior preparation is necessary and the cuttings are planted directly into the active sand dunes.

CHANGING THE CLIMATE

The fundamental cause of deserts is the pattern of circulation of winds in the world, and this will not change of its own accord. Various suggestions have been made, however, for changing the climate of the world's deserts in various ways. Most of these, including the idea that gigantic mirrors might be launched into orbit around the earth to focus the rays of the sun to melt mountain ice caps, are still in the realms of speculation. Nevertheless, on a smaller scale, rain may be produced by cloud-seeding. In France, experiments have been performed with a meteotron—an arrangement of oil burners which use over a tonne of fuel per minute but which, if lit at the right moment, may produce a growing rain cloud within six minutes.[109]

LAND RECLAMATION

Soil erosion may be checked in a number of ways, including mechanical and chemical control of trees and bushes, so that grass grows in their place, furrowing and contouring the soil to slow the rate of run off from disturbed and overgrazed areas, and the construction of dams in large and active gulleys. In California, large areas of Mediterranean macchia or chaparral are being converted into grassland for better fire control, to develop new forage for livestock or deer, and to increase the yield of water. Mature brush or excess tree cover is removed by hand or bulldozer, pushed into piles and afterwards burned. Perennial grasses are then sown by discing or other mechanical means, and the recovery of the natural vegetation inhibited by herbicidal sprays.

The effects of such drastic action will no doubt remain for centuries. Whether our descendants will bless us for such light-hearted opportunism is another matter. Ecologists are well aware that the results of habitat destruction are often very different from what was originally intended. A very minor climatic change of the kind that is to be expected over the centuries may wreak havoc in the artificial flora that has replaced the original brush vegetation. Moreover, preliminary findings suggest that the conversion of pinyon-juniper (*Pinus edulis, P. monophylla* and *Juniperus* spp.) woodland environments to seeded grassland have not necessarily increased infiltration rates, nor have they always reduced sediment yields from such lands.

The addition of irrigation water to the arid Colorado desert allowed the development of a vast agricultural area. Because of the salinity of this water, however, there is need for continuous leaching of the soil profile. This is most economically achieved by sprinkler irrigation which is much more effective than furrow irrigation for reducing soil surface temperatures. Sprinkling also maintains clay soil in a better structural condition. It should find wide application in the arid regions of the world because it uses water so efficiently, modifies the microclimate more favourably for plant growth and results in better tilth.

Scientific management of grasslands by regulated grazing and the maintenance of a nutritious combination of grass and legumes is essential for improving the productivity of cattle and sheep. The semi-arid Banni grasslands of Kutch in India, for example, are renowned for their wealth of cattle. The yield of milk is increased, however, when forage grasses like *Cenchrus ciliaris, C. setigerus, Panicum antidotale* and *Chrysopogon fulvus* are judiciously mixed with legume species of *Alysicarpus, Desmodium* and *Indigofers*. In addition, species of *Saccharum* and *Themeda* are effective in stabilizing the soil while *Spirobolus, Chloris* and *Cenchrus* spp. can be encouraged to reclaim saline tracts.

MINERAL RESOURCES

The most obvious and coveted riches of arid lands are the deposits of oil and minerals that lie underground. Many of the world's greatest sources of petroleum are located in desert countries—Arabia, Iraq, Algeria and south western U.S.A. The world's largest deposit of borax lies beneath the Mojave desert, silver is mined in northern Mexico and Mongolia, copper in Nevada and Chile, gold in Australia, diamonds in

South Africa, iron ore in Mauretania and uranium in Utah, New Mexico and at the foot of the Aïr in Niger.

The deserts of the world are far from having yielded all the secrets of their mineral deposits. With the exception of salt, the exploitation of minerals in arid lands has, until recently, been limited to the discovery of precious metals, because the cost and difficulty of transport precluded the removal of other deposits. Furthermore, water is required for the extraction of many minerals. Nevertheless, with modern techniques these problems can be overcome and some of the poorer countries of the world are now becoming rich. Apart from underground sources of energy, the desert possesses an inexhaustible supply of solar energy. This can already be harnessed for domestic and research purposes and may one day provide unlimited power for industrial development.

INDUSTRY AND TOURISM

Industrial economy uses very much less water per head of population than does agriculture or stock rearing. Indeed, where water is scarce, it may be more efficient land use to establish industrial townships where, even with watering of gardens, 454 litres (100 gallons) per head per day would be less demanding of water than would stock rearing or, even more so, agriculture. For this reason, the standard of living of desert dwellers in under-developed countries could be raised more simply by industrialization and the expansion of tourism than by over-exploitation of limited water resources. But it might take many years for these people to acquire the necessary technological skills, and innumerable sociological problems would be created for them. Other practical problems also remain. These include the disposal of sewerage and industrial waste which demands vast quantities of water unless expensive chemical conversion plants are installed.[119]

These problems have already made themselves felt in America where neighbouring towns compete with one another for the available water. Compared with their arid hinterlands, many towns in North Africa and the Middle East provide an irresistible attraction to country dwellers nearby. Consequently, there is a constant drift from the land to cities on the coast. Shanty slums, inhabited by landless labourers, spring up between and around modern office blocks and skyscraper flats; and the migration from the country accelerates in years of drought. In many of the smaller oases in the Fezzan the population now has an unbalanced age and sex structure. The young men have moved away, leaving the women and the aged to carry on the traditional agricultural activities.

In the rat-race of modern capitalist society, man often tires of crowded cities and longs for the wide open spaces. Air transport places the world at his doorstep and it is little wonder that desert tourism is already a healthy and expanding industry. Hotels are being built along the North African coast and hinterland, holiday resorts have transformed the deserts of America.

MULTIPLE LAND USE

The problems of arid lands are complex, and there is no single solution to any of them. The advantages and disadvantages of the various forms of land use that are available have been outlined in the present chapter. It is not to be expected either that they could all be applied to one desert region, or that any one of them should be universally applicable. But the more ways in which a region can be rationally exploited concurrently the less heavily will this exploitation harm the environment. If some of their new wealth results in improved standards of living, the peoples of arid lands will become less dependent upon their domestic stock, and the desert may then, at last, finally cease to expand.

14

Epilogue

It is, perhaps, idle to speculate as to what the African savanna and desert might have been like had they developed free from the influence of man, for the two have been evolving together since the Pleistocene period. To restore what might have been their climax vegetation is, of course, not possible, because the changes wrought by mankind are irreversible. One of the difficulties in reconstructing the chemical processes by which life may have arisen lies in the fact that subsequent evolutionary developments have produced irreversible effects. For instance, if, as seems probable, the primeval atmosphere was without oxygen, the formation of this gas by photosynthesis must have resulted in irrevocable changes. Much of the sun's ultra-violet radiation today is absorbed by ozone which is derived from oxygen. Before life began, therefore, very much more radiation would have reached the ground than can do so today or at any future time. Were life to disappear from the world, it could never start again exactly as it did previously, because the conditions under which it appeared in the first instance have been altered for always. Similarly, once desert conditions are firmly established, the ecosystem which they have supplanted is destroyed, and can be re-created only very slowly if at all.

Studies of vegetation growth in desert *wadis* have shown that there are successional relationships between various plant communities. Elsewhere, desert soils are often too mobile to permit the development of any climax vegetation. The theoretical reconstruction of natural climax types of the desert flora depends therefore, upon studies of localized relics of natural vegetation, experiments in which areas are enclosed to prevent grazing, and the analysis of various types of plant community over extensive stretches of desert.

Soil erosion is followed by retrogressive changes in the habitat, which is rendered more susceptible to this adversity as a result of an artificial reduction in the plant cover. Other retrogressive changes are associated with various geomorphological phenomena, such as the maturation of gravel desert. Increasing sterility in some areas causes further overgrazing in other, more fertile regions. Soils, climate, vegetation and fauna thus interact with one another, producing an unstable, fragile biological environment that tends with misuse steadily to deteriorate.

It may be salutary to realize that the changes initiated by primitive man and continued, today, by unsophisticated societies with simple tools, cannot be reversed by all the might of modern science and technology! A man can kill a mosquito, and this may well be a beneficial act, but he can never create one. Likewise, mankind can destroy the climax vegetation of an ecosystem, and this is not necessarily harmful but, again, he cannot restore it exactly as it was. Savanna may be of greater value to humanity than the forest from which it was produced: the same cannot be said of the desert that has so often been created from savanna and steppe, even in areas of moderately plentiful rainfall.

It is primarily through interference with the soil and vegetation that man-induced desiccation of the landscape occurs. The fragile semi-desert environment is soon injured when concentrations of people and stock accumulate around one of the scarce sources of water, with resulting overgrazing and/or over-cultivation. The exposed soil becomes a hard, compacted surface, and the acceptance and retention of moisture is drastically reduced. Even so, in those areas of Karamoja from which population and game are absent, the recolonization by vegetation of eroded gulleys outpaces further denudation. Indeed, in East Africa the problem of desertification could be solved immediately by reduction in the numbers of stock.[7] In more arid regions, however, the solution is more complex. Nevertheless, where fresh water is available, and along the desert coastline where seawater can be desalinized using atomic or solar energy, urbanization can take place. There could therefore eventually even be a shift in the world population from the temperate towards the arid tropical regions where energy and sunshine are so plentiful.

Wherever civilized man inhabits the desert he plants gardens, bushes, shrubs and even small trees to mitigate the severity of the landscape, provide shelter from the hot winds and add to the amenities of his life. In a short time a small oasis appears, completely artificial and yet an isolated ecological identity. As long as this isolation is preserved, diseases and pests can be kept at bay. Economically it is very well worth while to take the trouble to prevent their accidental introduction. Human ingenuity can transform the desert landscape, at least on a small scale, and scientific knowledge can help to defend hard-earned gains. On a larger scale, the picture is somewhat less rosy.

Various solutions have been proposed to the problem of desert expansion. They include reducing overgrazing by encouraging meat production from camels, which can graze much further from their sources of water than can sheep and goats.[101] Prickly pear might be introduced south of the Sahara as a source of fodder and to reduce excessive run off from rainstorms. Game ranching of ostriches, gazelles and other antelope, instead of over-exploiting the desert by grazing goats and sheep, would again be beneficial.[32] These are aspects of the multiple land use advocated in Chapter 13. Complex problems are seldom responsive to simple solutions: the desert is no exception. There is no single answer to the problem of the world's increasing deserts.

Many things, however, are possible to people who possess the technological capability to send men to the moon and bring them back again to earth. For instance, man could use space satellites to provide comparable multispectral images by utilization of the same sensor over all arid regions: these would provide repetitive data that could be useful for surveying resources. Likewise, photographic images at the proper scale and resolution are invaluable for small and large scale studies. To make the desert blossom may be technically possible but it is usually unrewarding economically and has little of the political and emotional attractions of sophisticated rocketry. Arid regions are well endowed with ultra-violet light, but lack moisture and rich soils. Perhaps their potential for the future will be realized better by the application of industry and tourism than by large-scale agricultural projects.

Bibliography

The following list of references has been restricted to include only the more important publications consulted, and especially those that are well documented. Thus books and review articles have been cited in preference to sources of original research, further information about which can be readily obtained by referring to them.

1. ANON. (1970). *Desalination and its role in water supply*. Central Office of Information, London.
2. ADOLPH, E. F. (1947). *Physiology of man in the desert*. Interscience, New York.
3. ARKELL, A. J. (1949). *Early Khartoum*. Clarendon Press, Oxford.
4. ARNON, I. (1972). *Crop production in dry regions*. Vol. 1: *Background and principles*. Leonard Hill, London.
5. ARNON, I. (1972). *Crop production in dry regions*. Vol. 2: *Systematic treatment of the principal crops*. Leonard Hill, London.
6. BAGNOLD, R. A. (1954). The physical aspects of dry deserts. *In* Cloudsley-Thompson, J. L. (Ed.) *Biology of deserts*. 7–12. Inst. Biol., London.
7. BAKER, S. J. K. (1974). A background to the study of drought in East Africa. *African Affairs*, **73**, 170–7.
8. BAKKER, E. M. VAN ZINDEREN (1967). Upper Pleistocene and Holocene stratigraphy and ecology on the basis of vegetation changes in sub-Saharan Africa. *In* Bishop, W. W. & Clark, J. D. (Eds.) *Background to evolution in Africa*. 125–47. Chicago Univ. Press.
9. BARTHOLOMEW, G. A. (1956). Temperature regulation in the macropod marsupial, *Setonix brachyurus*. *Physiol. Zoöl.*, **29**, 26–40.
10. BARTHOLOMEW, G. A. (1972). The water economy of seed-eating birds that survive without drinking. *Proc. XV Internat. Ornithol. Congr.* (Leiden). 237–54.
11. BERRY, L. AND WHITEMAN, A. J. (1968). The Nile in the Sudan. *Geog. J.*, **134**, 1–37, 15 figs. 4 pls.
12. BODENHEIMER, F. S. (1951). *Insects as human food*. Junk, The Hague.
13. BODENHEIMER, F. S. (1954). Problems of physiology and ecology of desert animals. *In* Cloudsley-Thompson, J. L. (Ed.) *Biology of deserts*. 162–7. Inst. Biol., London.

14. BODENHEIMER, F. S. (1957). The ecology of mammals in arid zones. *In*: *Human and animal ecology. Reviews of research*, **8**, 100–37. UNESCO, Paris.

15. BRIGGS, L. C. (1960). *Tribes of the Sahara*. Harvard Univ. Press, Cambridge, Mass.

16. BRINCK, P. (1956). The food factor in animal desert life. *In* Wingstrand, W. G. (Ed.) *Bertil Hanstrom: Zoological papers in honour of his 65th birthday, November 20th, 1956*. 120–137. Zool. Inst., Lund.

17. BÜCHERL, W. *et al.* (Eds.) (1968–71). *Venomous animals and their venoms*, Vols. **1–3**. Academic Press, New York.

18. BUTZER, K. W. (1966). Deserts in the past. *In* Hills, E. S. (Ed.) *Arid Lands. A geographical appraisal*. 127–44. Methuen, London; UNESCO, Paris.

19. BUXTON, P. A. (1923). *Animal life in deserts*. Arnold, London.

20. CARLISLE, D. B., ELLIS, P. E. AND BETTS, E. (1965). The influence of aromatic shrubs in sexual maturation in the desert locust *Schistocerca gregaria*. *J. Insect. Physiol.*, **11**, 1541–58.

21. CLOUDSLEY-THOMPSON, J. L. (1961). *Rhythmic activity in animal physiology and behaviour*. Academic Press, London.

22. CLOUDSLEY-THOMPSON, J. L. (1962). Microclimates and the distribution of terrestrial arthropods. *Ann. Rev. Ent.*, **7**, 199–222.

23. CLOUDSLEY-THOMPSON, J. L. (1964). Terrestrial animals in dry heat: arthropods. *In* Dill, D. B. (Ed.) *Adaptation to the environment. Handbook of Physiology*, **4**, 451–65.

24. CLOUDSLEY-THOMPSON, J. L. (1965). *Desert life*. Pergamon, Oxford.

25. CLOUDSLEY-THOMPSON, J. L. (1965). *Animal conflict and adaptation*. Foulis, London.

26. CLOUDSLEY-THOMPSON, J. L. (1967). *Animal twilight. Man and game in eastern Africa*. Foulis, London.

27. CLOUDSLEY-THOMPSON, J. L. (1968). *Spiders, scorpions, centipedes and mites*. (2nd ed.) Pergamon, Oxford.

28. CLOUDSLEY-THOMPSON, J. L. (1969). Camel. *Encycl. Americana*. **5**, 261–263.

29. CLOUDSLEY-THOMPSON, J. L. (1969). *The zoology of tropical Africa*. Weidenfeld & Nicolson, London.

30. CLOUDSLEY-THOMPSON, J. L. (1970). On the biology of the desert tortoise *Testudo sulcata* in Sudan. *J. Zool., Lond.* **160**, 17–33.

31. CLOUDSLEY-THOMPSON, J. L. (1970). Terrestrial invertebrates. *In* Whittow, G. Causey (Ed.) *Comparative physiology of thermoregulation*. **1**, 15–77. Academic Press, New York.

32. CLOUDSLEY-THOMPSON, J. L. (1970). Animal utilization. *In* Dregne, H. E. (Ed.) *Arid lands in transition*. 57–72. Amer. Ass. Adv. Sci., Washington, D.C.

33. CLOUDSLEY-THOMPSON, J. L. (1971). Recent expansion of the Sahara. *Intern. J. Environmental Sci.*, **2**, 35–9.

34. CLOUDSLEY-THOMPSON, J. L. (1971). *The temperature and water relations of reptiles*. Merrow, Watford, Herts.

35. CLOUDSLEY-THOMPSON, J. L. (1972). Temperature regulation in desert reptiles. *Symp. Zool. Soc. Lond.*, No. 31: 39–59.

36. CLOUDSLEY-THOMPSON, J. L. (1974). The expanding Sahara. *Environmental Conservation*. **1**, 5–13.

37. CLOUDSLEY-THOMPSON, J. L. (1974). *Desert life*. Aldus Books, London.

38. CLOUDSLEY-THOMPSON, J. L. (1974). *The ecology of oases.* Merrow, Watford, Herts.
39. CLOUDSLEY-THOMPSON, J. L. (1975). *Terrestrial environments.* Croom Helm, London.
40. CLOUDSLEY-THOMPSON, J. L. (1975). Adaptations of Arthropoda to arid environments. *Ann. Rev. Ent.,* **20,** 56–78.
41. CLOUDSLEY-THOMPSON, J. L. AND CHADWICK, M. J. (1964). *Life in deserts.* Foulis, London.
42. COLE, S. (1964). *The prehistory of East Africa.* Weidenfeld & Nicolson, London.
43. COOKE, H. B. S. (1963). Pleistocene mammal faunas of Africa, with particular reference to southern Africa. *In* Howell, F. C. & Boulière, F. (Eds.). *African ecology and human evolution.* 65–116. Methuen, London.
44. CRAWFORD, C. S. (1972). Water relations in a desert millipede *Orthoporus ornatus* (Girard) (Spirostreptidae). *Comp. Biochem. Physiol.,* **42A:** 521–35.
45. CRAWFORD, C. S. AND CLOUDSLEY-THOMPSON, J. L. (1971). Water relations and desiccation-avoiding behaviour in the vinegaroon *Mastigoproctus giganteus* (Arachnida: Uropygi). *Entomologia Exp. & Appl.,* **14,** 99–106.
46. DASMANN, R. F. (1964). *African game ranching.* Pergamon, Oxford.
47. DAWSON, T. J. (1972). Thermoregulation in Australian desert kangaroos. *Symp. Zool. Soc. Lond.,* No. 31: 133–46.
48. DAWSON, W. R. AND BARTHOLOMEW, G. A. (1968). Temperature regulation and water economy of desert birds. *In* Brown, G. W. (Ed.) *Desert biology,* **1,** 357–94. Academic Press, New York.
49. DUISBERG, P. C. AND HAY, J. L. (1971). Economic botany of arid regions. *In* McGinnies, W. G., Goldman, B. J. and Paylore, P. (Eds.). *Food, fiber and the arid lands.* 247–70. Univ. Arizona Press.
50. EDNEY, E. B. (1967). Water balance in desert arthropods. *Science,* **156,** 1059–66.
51. EDNEY, E. B. (1974). Desert arthropods. *In* Brown, G. W. jr. (Ed.). *Desert biology,* **2,** 311–84. Academic Press, New York.
52. EHRLICH, P. R. AND EHRLICH, A. H. (1972). *Population, resources, environment: issues in human ecology* (2nd edn.). W. H. Freeman, San Francisco.
53. FINCH, V. A. (1972). Thermoregulation and heat balance of the East African eland and hartebeest. *Amer. J. Physiol.,* **222,** 1374–9.
54. FORD, J. (1971). *The role of the trypanosomiases in African ecology.* Clarendon Press, Oxford.
55. GHOBRIAL, L. I. (1970). The water relations of the desert antelope *Gazella dorcas dorcas. Physiol. Zoöl.,* **43:** 249–56.
56. GLASER, E. M. (1963). Circulatory adjustments in the arid zone. *In Environmental physiology and psychology in arid conditions. Arid Zone Research,* **22:** 131–51. UNESCO, Paris.
57. GROVE, A. T. (1974). Desertification in the African environment. *African Affairs,* **73:** 137–51.
58. HADLEY, N. F. (1972). Desert species and adaptation. *Amer. Sci.,* **60:** 338–47.
59. HAMILTON, W. J. (1973). *Life's color code.* McGraw-Hill, New York.
60. HAMMERTON, D. (1972). The Nile river—a case history. *In* Oglesby, R. T. (Ed.) *River ecology and man.* 171–214. Academic Press, New York.

61. HARRIS, D. R. (1962). The distribution and ancestry of the domestic goat. *Proc. Linn. Soc. Lond.*, **173**, 79–91.
62. HARRIS, W. V. (1961). *Termites. Their recognition and control.* Longmans, Green, London.
63. HEMMING, C. F. (1966). The vegetation of the northern region of the Somali Republic. *Proc. Linn. Soc. Lond.*, **177**, 173–250.
64. HILLS, E. S., OLLIER, C. D. AND TWIDALE, C. R. (1966). Geomorphology. *In* Hills, E. S. (Ed.). *Arid Lands. A geographical appraisal.* 53–76. Methuen, London; UNESCO, Paris.
65. JACKSON, J. K. (1957). Changes in the climate and vegetation of the Sudan. *Sudan Notes Rec.*, **38**, 47–66.
66. KACHKAROV, D. N. AND KOROVINE, E. P. (1942). *La vie dans les déserts.* (Éd. française par Th. Monod). Payot, Paris.
67. KASSAS, M. (1970). Desertification versus potential for recovery in circum-Saharan territories. *In* Dregne, H. E. (Ed.) *Arid lands in transition.* 123–42. Amer. Ass. Adv. Sci., Washington, D.C.
68. KIRMIZ, J. P. (1962). *Adaptation to desert environment. A study on the jerboa, rat and man.* Butterworth, London.
69. KOCH, C. (1961). Some aspects of abundant life in the vegetationless sand of the Namib desert dunes. *J. S. W. Afr. Scient. Soc.*, **15**, 8–34.
70. LADELL, W. S. S. (1949). The changes in water and chloride distribution during heavy sweating. *J. Physiol., Lond.*, **108**: 440–50.
71. LADELL, W. S. S. (1957). The influence of environment in arid regions on the biology of man. *In Human and animal ecology. Reviews of research*, **8**, 43–99. UNESCO, Paris.
72. LAMBERT, G. E. (1963). Work, sleep, comfort. *In Environmental physiology and psychology in arid conditions. Arid Zone Research*, **22**, 239–72. UNESCO, Paris.
73. LAWRENCE, R. F. (1959). The sand-dune fauna of the Namib desert. *S. Afr. J. Sci.*, **55**, 233–9.
74. LAWSON, G. W. (1966). *Plant life in West Africa.* Oxford Univ. Press, London.
75. LEE, D. H. K. (1968). Human adaptations to arid environments. *In* Brown, G. W. jr. (Ed.) *Desert biology*, **1**, 517–56. Academic Press, New York.
76. LEOPOLD, A. S. (1963). *The desert.* Life Nature Library, New York.
77. LOGAN, R. F. (1968). Causes, climates, and distribution of deserts. *In* Brown, G. W. jr. (Ed.) *Desert biology*, **1**, 21–50. Academic Press, New York.
78. LOUW, G. N., BELONJE, P. C. AND COETZEE, H. J. (1969). Renal function, respiration, heart rate and thermoregulation in the ostrich (*Struthio camelus*). *Sci. Pap. Namib Desert Res. Sta.*, No. 42, 43–54.
79. LOVERIDGE, J. P. (1970). Observations on nitrogenous excretion and water relations of *Chiromantis xerampelina* (Amphibia, Anura). *Arnoldia*, **5**, 1–6.
80. LOWE, C. H. (1968). Fauna of desert environments. *In* McGinnies, W. G., Goldman, B. J. & Paylore, P. (Eds.). *Deserts of the world.* 567–645. Univ. Arizona Press.
81. MACCUAIG, R. D. (1970). Locust control—the economic impact of new technologies. *S.C.I. Monogr.* No. 36, 119–28.
82. MACFARLANE, W. V. (1964). Water and electrolytes of man in hot dry regions. *In Environmental physiology and psychology in arid conditions. Arid Zone Research*, **24**, 43–53. UNESCO, Paris.

83. MACFARLANE, W. V. (1964). Terrestrial animals in dry heat: ungulates. *In* Dill, D. B. (Ed.). *Adaptation to the environment. Handbook of Physiology*, 4, 509–39. American Physiological Society, Washington, D.C.

84. MCGINNIES, W. G. (1968). Appraisal of research on vegetation of desert environments. *In* McGinnies, W. G., Goldman, B. J. & Paylore, P. (Eds.). *Deserts of the world.* 379–566. Univ. Arizona Press.

85. MAYHEW, W. W. (1968). Biology of desert amphibians and reptiles. *In* Brown, G. W. jr. (Ed.) *Desert biology*, 1, 195–356. Academic Press, New York.

86. MINTON, S. A. JR. (1968). Venoms of desert animals. *In* Brown, G. W. jr. (Ed.) *Desert biology*, 1, 487–516. Academic Press, New York.

87. MONOD, T. H. (1954). Modes 'contracté' et 'diffus' de la végétation saharienne. *In* Cloudsley-Thompson, J. L. (Ed.) *Biology of deserts*, 35–44 Inst. Biol., London.

88. MOREAU, R. E. (1963). Vicissitudes of the African biomes in the late Pleistocene. *Proc. Zool. Soc. Lond.*, 141, 395–421.

89. MOREAU, R. E. (1966). *The bird faunas of Africa and its islands.* Academic Press, London.

90. NYE, P. H. AND GREENLAND, D. J. (1960). The soil under shifting cultivation. *Tech. Commun. Bur. Soils*, No. 5, 1–157.

91. PIERRE, F. (1958). *Écologie et peuplement entomologique des sables vifs du Sahara nord-occidental.* Centre nat. Recherche scientifique, Paris.

92. POLUNIN, N. (1960). *Introduction to plant geography.* Longman, London.

93. PRADHAN, S. (1957). The ecology of arid zone insects (excluding locusts and grasshoppers). *In Human and animal ecology. Reviews of research*, 8, 199–240. UNESCO, Paris.

94. RAINEY, R. C. (1963). Meteorology and the migration of desert locusts. *W.H.O. Tech. Note*, No. 54: 1–115.

95. RAJULU, G. S. AND KRISHNAN, G. (1968). The epicuticle of millipedes belonging to the genera *Cingalobolus* and *Aulacobolus* with special reference to seasonal variations. *Z. Naturf.* B 23, 845–51.

96. REITAN, C. R. AND GREEN, C. R. (1968). Weather and climate of desert environments. *In* McGinnies, W. G., Goldman, B. J. and Paylore, P. (Eds.) *Deserts of the world.* 19–92. Univ. Arizona Press.

97. RIVNAY, E. (1964). The influence of man on insect ecology in arid zones. *Ann. Rev. Ent.*, 9, 41–62.

98. RUSSELL, E. W. (1968). Some agricultural problems of semi-arid areas. *In* Moss, R. P. (Ed.) *The soil resources of tropical Africa.* 121–35. Cambridge Univ. Press, Cambridge.

99. SARGENT, F. II (1963). Tropical neurasthenia: giant or windmill? *In Environmental physiology and psychology in arid conditions. Reviews of research. Arid Zone Research*, 22, 273–314. UNESCO, Paris.

100. SCHMIDT-NIELSEN, B., SCHMIDT-NIELSEN, K., HOUPT, T. R. AND JARNUM, S. A. (1956). Water balance of the camel. *Amer. J. Physiol.*, 185: 185–94.

101. SCHMIDT-NIELSEN, K. (1956). Animals and arid conditions: physiological aspects of productivity and management. *In* White, G. F. (Ed.) *The future of arid lands.* 368–82. Amer. Ass. Adv. Sci., Washington, D.C.

102. SCHMIDT-NIELSEN, K. (1964). *Desert animals. Physiological problems of heat and water.* Clarendon Press, Oxford.

103. SCHMIDT-NIELSEN, K. (1972). *How animals work*. Univ. Press, Cambridge.
104. SCHMIDT-NIELSEN, K. AND SCHMIDT-NIELSEN, B. (1952). Water metabolism of desert mammals. *Physiol. Rev.*, **32**: 135–66.
105. SCHREIDER, E. (1963). Physiological anthropology and climatic variations. *In Environmental physiology and psychology in arid conditions. Reviews of Research. Arid Zone Research*, **22**: 37–73. UNESCO, Paris.
106. SHAW, J. AND STOBBART, R. H. (1972). The water balance and osmoregulatory physiology of the desert locust (*Schistocerca gregaria*) and other desert and xeric arthropods. *Symp. Zool. Soc. Lond.*, No. 31, 15–38.
107. SHINNIE, P. L. (1967). *Meroe*. Thames & Hudson, London.
108. SHKOLNIK, A., BORUT, A. AND CHOSHNIAK, J. (1972). Water economy of the beduin goat. *Symp. Zool. Soc. Lond.*, No. 31, 229–42.
109. SIMONS, M. (1967). *Deserts—the problem of water in arid lands*. Oxford Univ. Press, London.
110. STEBBING, E. P. (1954). Forests, aridity and desert, *In* Cloudsley-Thompson, J. L. (Ed.) *Biology of deserts*, 123–8. Inst. Biol., London.
111. TAYLOR, C. R. AND LYNN, C. P. (1972). Heat storage in running antelopes: independence of brain and body temperatures. *Amer. J. Physiol.*, **222**, 114–17.
112. TEMPLETON, J. R. (1972). Salt and water balance in desert reptiles *Symp. Zool. Soc. Lond.*, No. 31: 61–77.
113. TERCAFS, R. R. (1962). Observations écologiques dans le massif du Tibesti (Tchad). *Rev. Zool. Bot. Afric.*, **66**, 107–26.
114. TRESHOW, M. (1970). *Environment and plant response*. McGraw-Hill, New York.
115. TYNDALE-BISCOE, H. (1973). *Life of Marsupials*. Arnold, London.
116. UVAROV, B. P. (1957). The aridity factor in the ecology of locusts and grasshoppers of the Old World. *In Human and animal ecology*, **8**, 164–87. UNESCO, Paris.
117. WADE, N. (1974). Sahelian drought: no victory for Western aid. *Science*, **185**, 234–7.
118. WALLÉN, C. C. (1966). Arid zone meteorology. *In* Hill, E. S. (Ed.) *Arid lands. A geographical appraisal*. 31–52. Methuen, London.
119. WALOFF, Z. (1966). The upsurges and recessions of the desert locust plague: an historical survey. *Anti-Locust Memoir*, No. 1, 1–111.
120. WALTON, K. (1969). *The arid zones*. Hutchinson, London.
121. WARREN, A. (1970). Dune trends and their implications in the central Sudan. *Z. Geomorph.*, Suppl. **10**, 154–86.
122. WEINER, J. S. (1971). *Man's natural history*. Weidenfeld & Nicolson, London.
123. WINSTANLEY, D. (1973). Rainfall patterns and general atmospheric circulation. *Nature, Lond.*, **245**, 190–4.
124. ZEUNER, F. E. (1958). *Dating the past*. (4th edn.) Methuen, London.

Index

Ablepharus spp., 95
aborigines, 113–15, 118, 121, 153
Acacia spp., 29, 47, 53, 54, 59, 62, 63, 66, 129, 164
A. bussei, 54
A. decurrens, 67
A. mellifera, 29
A. raddiana, 29
A. senegal, 29, 67
A. seyal, 29
acclimatization, 119
Acinonyx jubatus, 109, *see also* cheetahs
Acer spp., 47
Achatina spp., 113
Acheulian culture, 36
Adansonia digitata, 29
addax, 70, 93, 100, 105, 111–12, 154
Addax nasomaculatus, 93, 105, *see also* addax
Aden, 26, 129
Adesmia bicarinata, 74
Adrar, 23, 45
aeolian deposits, 16, 20, 26
aestivation, 74, 83
Agave spp., 64
A. atrovirens, 67
A. fourcroydes, 67
A. lechuguilla, 66
A. sisalona, 67
A. tequilana, 67
Agkistrodon halys, 146
agricultural crops, 158–60
Aïr, 26, 45, 167
albedo, land surface, 41
Alexandersfontein, 28
alfalfa (lucerne), 159, 161
Algeria, 6, 9, 10, 15, 16, 19, 52, 56, 109, 127, 141, 152, 155, 161, 166
alluvial deposits, 13–16
Alnus spp., 47
Alternaria spp., 136
Alysicarpus spp., 166
American desert, 3, 4, 11, 15, 26, 104, 109, 139, 140, 144, 167
Amitermes spp., 129
A. desertorum, 129
A. messinae, 129
A. vilis, 129
A. wheeleri, 129
Ammophilus arenaria, 9
Amphibia, 72, 79, 80, 83, 84
Anacanthotermes spp., 129
Anastatica sp., 59
Andes, 68
Androctonus australis, 144
anklé, 17
Ankole cattle, 41
Anopheles spp., 140
A. gambiae, 141

antelopes, 52, 73, 108, 138, 154, 171, *see also* gazelles
antibiosis, 137
Antilax paludinosus, 50
Antilocapra americana, 104, 156, *see also* pronghorns
ants, 11, 59, 74, 114, 143
apes, 116, 120
apocrine glands, 116, 117
aphids, 131
aposematic coloration, 98, 149
Arabs, 113–15, 118, 121, 130, 155
Arabian desert, 3, 16, 101, 104, 129, 154, 166
Arachis hypogaea, 159
Arachnida, 70, 71–2, 74, 78, 95, 114, *see also* species
arborviruses, 141
Arenivaga spp., 86
aridity, 9–10
Aristida spp., 59, 94
Arizona, 6, 7, 9, 11, 16, 43, 130, 150
arroyos, 15
Artemisia spp., 20
artesian wells, 42, 161
Arthropoda, 70, 149 *see also* species
Arunta, 114
Arvicanthis sp., 50
asps, 146, 147
asses, 73, 100, 106, 108, 137, 158
Aswan, 143
Atacama desert, 3, 4, 139
Atlas mountains, 10, 12, 47, 51, 161
Atrax robustus, 144
Atriplex spp., 85
Australia, 23, 101, 128, 131, 153, 160
Australian desert, 3, 4, 6, 7, 15, 16, 64–5, 77, 104, 109, 113
Australopithecines, 39
Austroicetes cruciata, 129

Baghdad, 7
Baja California, 4, 161
bajadas, 13
barchan dunes, 16, 17, 18, 19
barley, 156, 161
Bartonella bacciliformis, 139
beans, 158, 159
Bedouin, 154, 155
beetles, 59, 60, 72, 73, 74, 78, 80, 86, 97, 98, 131, 143, 149
Bellefonds, L. de, 52
Berbers, 113
berseem clover, 159
Beta vulgaris, 159

bilharzia (schistosomiasis) 142, 163
Bilma, 77
Bindibu, 64–5, 114–15
biological control, 141
Bir Mighla, 9
birds, 82, 84, 85, 87, 97, 141
Biskra, 18
bison, 38
black widow spiders, 144
blackflies, 143
block tectonics, 22
Boerhaavia repens, 58
bollworms, 130, 132
Bombylius sp., 98
Botucatu sandstone, 26
Bouteloua aristidoides, 58
bristle-tails, 59, 86, 94
brown recluse spiders, 144–5
brown soils, 14, 20
Buddelundia albinogriseus, 77
buffaloes, 50, 112, 138
bullae tympanicae, 98
burrowing, 71–3, 84, 87
Bushmen, 64–6, 113–5, 121, 153
Buthidae, 144

Cacti, 60, 63, 75, 131, *see also* *Opuntia* spp.; prickly pear
Cactoblastis cactorum, 13
California, 7, 38, 130, 131, 142, *see also* Baja California
Callitroga americanus, 133
camel-spiders (Solifugae), 71–2, 74, 78
camels, 63, 68, 70, 74, 75, 84, 100–4, 106, 107, 108, 110–11, 116, 138, 155
Camelus bactrianus, 100–4
C. dromedarius, 100–4, *see also* camels
canals, 130–1, 142
Capra falconeri, 110
C. hircus, 110
C. ibex, 110
Carboniferous period, 23, 26
Carnegiea gigantea, 60
carnivores, 88, 109–10
carotid rete, 93
Carpathians, 155
Carpodactus mexicanus, 85
Cassia senna, 64
castor beans, 159
cattle, 11, 37, 41, 43, 50, 110, 138, 152, 153–4, 159
Cedrus spp., 47
Cenchrus spp., 166
C. ciliaris, 166
C. setigerus, 166
centipedes, 70, 72, 97, 143, 149
Centruroides spp., 144
Cerastes spp., 95–6

C. cerastes, 146
Ceratophyllus silanteri, 137
Cerballus spp., 72
cercariae, 142
Chad, *see* Tchad
Chalcides ocellatus, 72
cheetahs, 52, 109
chemical defences, 148–50
chernozems, 21
chestnut soils, 14, 20
chick peas, 158
Chile, 60, 166
Chihuahuan desert, 3, 33, 43
China, 20, 38, 114, 127, 159
Chiromantis xerampelina, 79
chironomid midges, 143
Chloris spp., 166
Chortoicetes terminifera, 128, 133
chotts, 15
Chrysopogon fulvus, 166
chubaseos, 11
chuckwallas, 85
cicadas, 149
Cicer arientinum, 158
circulatory adjustments, 116–17
Circulifer tenellus, 131
Citellus spp., 87, 92, *see also* ground squirrels
C. leucurus, 85
citrus trees, 69, 129, 131
cleidoic eggs, 84
climate, 44–50
clothing, 121
Coachella Valley, 142
coastal deserts, 4
cobras, 145–8
Coccidiodes immitis, 140
coccidiomycosis, 140
Colomb-Béchar, 69, 130
Colorado, 9, 43, 68, 131, 156
coloration, animal, 72, 97–9, 105, 141
Colubridae, 145
Commiphora africana, 29
C. myrrhae, 64
continental movements, 24–5
Cossidae, 144
cotton, 132
Côte d'Ivoire (Ivory Coast), 33
cowpeas, 159
coyotes, 109
creosote bushes, 62, 67
Cretaceous period, 23, 24, 25, 44
crickets, 129, 149
Crotalinae (pit vipers), 146
Crotalus spp., 146
C. cerastes, 91, 95–6
Cryptolaemus montrouzieri, 131
cucumber beetles, 131
Culex spp., 141
Culicoides spp., 138
Cupressus spp., 47
C. dupreziana, 68
cutworms, 131

Cynomys ludovicianus, 156

Dams, 143, 161–3
Darfur, 29, 68
Dasycerus cristicauda, 87
date palms, 19, 42, 68, 69, 130, 155
Death Valley, 7, 26
Deccan shield, 23
Dermacentor spp., 139
desalination, 163–4
desert sores, 139
Desmodium spp., 166
Devonian period, 26
dew, 9, 55, 60
Diabrotica balteata, 131
diapause, 94, 135
Diceros bicornis, 112, 157, *see also* rhinoceroses
dingoes, 109
Diodorus, 51
Dipodomys spp., 92
D. merriami, 81
Dipsosaurus dorsalis, 80–1
Dipus spp., 91
Dociostaurus moroccanus, 128
dogs, 107, 108, 109, 115, 154–5
Dongola, 51, 52, 104
donkeys, 70, 106, 138, *see also* asses
dourine, 138
doves, 85, 94
draa, 16
dreikanter, 13–14
dryland farming, 157–8
duikers, 36
dune stabilization, 164–5
dunes, 9, 12, 16–19, 26, 28, 164–5
dysentry, 140

Earias insulana, 132
ears, 88, 95, 98
East Africa, 29, 40, 170
eccrine glands, 116, 117
Echis carinatis, 146
Egypt, 6, 15, 50, 109, 111, 130, 132, 158, 161, 162–4
El Alamein, 15
El Azizia, 7
El Djem, 53
El Gueisi, 54
eland, 112, 157
Elapidae, 145–6
Eleodes spp., 149
elephants, 47, 50, 51, 53
Ennedi, 45
Entamoeba histolytica, 140
ephemerals, 57–8
epizootics, 137–8
Equus asinus, 106, 157
E. hemionus, 106, 138
E. kiang, 106
E. onager, 106
Eragrostis pilosa, 58
Eritrea, 63
ergs, 16, 95
Erkowit, 6, 9

erosion, 13, 18, 22, 53, 54, 55, 110, 165
Ethiopia, 40, 41, 158, 159, 161
Eucalyptus spp., 164
Euphorbia spp., 64, 75
E. abyssinica, 9
E. antisyphilitica, 66
evapotranspiration, 9, 10
excretion, 83–5, 116
explosive heat death, 103, 117
eye gnats, 141

Facaratia hassleriana, 66
Felis cougar, 109
F. leo, 109, *see also* lions
fire, 29, 36, 37
fleas, 70, 78, 86, 137
flies, 74, 133, *see also* species
forage, 159
forest peoples, 38–41

Galeodes granti, 78, 79, *see also* camel-spiders
Gambusia spp., 141
game ranching, 156–7
Gastrimargus musicus, 129
Gazella dorcas, 93, 105, *see also* gazelles
gazelles, 11, 50, 52, 70, 75, 93, 100, 111–12, 138, 152, 171
geckoes, 72, 90, 95
Geoffroea spp., 66
gemsbok, 105, 138
geomorphology, 22–6
gerbils, 111–12
gerenuks, 111–12
Gherib, 155
Gila monsters, 145
giraffes, 50, 51
glacial periods, 26, 27, 45, 47
Glossina spp., 138, *see also* tsetse flies
Glycine max, 159
goats, 11, 28, 32, 53, 59, 63, 106–7, 110, 138, 151–2, 154, 171
Gobi desert, 3, 22, 23, 100, 104, 110, 138
grasses, 29, 33, 38, 50, 58–60, 67, 110, 154, 166
grasshopper mice, 87
grasshoppers, 11, 72, 85, 114, 123–9, 149
Great American desert, 3, 4, 11, *see also* American desert
Great Australian desert, 3, 4
Great Basin desert, 3, 4, 66
Great Palaearctic desert, 4, 9, 129, 140, 141, *see also* Arabian, Gobi, Indian, Kara Kum, Sahara, Takla Makan, Thar and Sind deserts
Grewea spp., 29
ground nuts, 159
ground squirrels, 50, 85, 87, 92, 94, 138

Gryllotalpa gryllotalpa, 129
Gryllulus servillea, 129
Guinea savanna, 29, 33
Guir, 23
gum arabic, 67

Haboobs, 10
haematocrit ratio, 117
hafirs, 152, 153
hair, 108, 120
hammada, 16, 23
Hanno, 51
hares, 50, 87–8, 138
harmattan, 10
hartebeests, 138
Haute Volta (Upper Volta), 33
heat exchange, 118
heat stroke, 121
hedgehogs, 98
Helianthus annuus, 159
Heliothis armigera, 132
Helix aspersa, 114
H. pomatia, 114
Heloderma horridum, 145, 149
H. suspectum, 145, 149
Helwan, 6
Hemilepistus reaumuri, 72, 77
henbane, 67
henequen, 67
Hepialidae, 114, 131
hibernation, 83
Hippelates collusor, 142
hippopotamuses, 47, 50
Hodotermitidae, 129
Hoggar, 12, 22, 26, 45, 47, 68
Holocene epoch, 45
Homo erectus, 39
Hordeum vulgare, 158
horses, 116, 138
hyaenas, 109
Hyalomma domedarii, 78
hydroponics, 164
Hyocyamus muticus, 67
hyperthermia, 83, 93–4, 102, 112
Hyphaene thebaica, 29
Hystricidae, 150

Ice ages 26, 27, 45, 47
Icerya purchasi, 131
Idrisi, 51
iguanas, 80–1
Indian desert, 42, 43, *see also* Thar desert
Indians, American, 38, 113, 114–15
Indigofers spp., 166
industry, 167
insecticides, 141
In Salah, 9, 19
interglacial periods, 26
Iran, 18, 43, 101
Iranian desert, 3, 10, 16, 129
Iraq, 16, 104, 159
irrigation, 137, 142, 159, 160, 161–3
Isoberlinia spp., 29
I. doka, 29
Israel, 67, 132, 136

ixtle, 66

Jackals, 139
Jacobson's organ, 146
Jaculus spp., 91
Jassidae, 131
Jebel Marra, 68
jerboas, 73, 75, 87, 91–2, 96, 139
Juniperus spp., 47, 166
J. procera, 42
Jurassic period, 26

Kajiondo, 152
kala-azar, 139
Kalahari desert, 3, 15, 27, 64, 95, 113, 114
Kalotermitidae, 129
kangaroo-rats, 73, 81, 84, 87, 91–2, 96
kangaroos, 96, 104, 107
Kara Kum desert, 68, 164
Karamoja, 54, 170
Karoo, 42–3
khamsin, 10
Khartoum, 6, 7, 40, 47, 50, 52, 57
Kordofan, 28, 40, 104

Lagomorphs, 138, *see also* hares
Lamyra sp., 98
Larrea divaricata, 67, *see also* creosote bushes
Las Cruces, 43
Lathyrus sativum, 159
Latrodectus spp., 144
L. hasselti, 145
Laurasia, 24
lechwe, 50
Leishmania spp., 139
leishmanisasis, 139
Lens culinaris, 159
lentils, 159
Leptis Magna, 52
Leptadenia pyrotechnica, 29
Levantina guttata, 113
Libya, 7, 10, 15, 16, 18, 47, 109, 127, 154–5, 161
lichens, 60, 93
Limicolaria flammata, 50
Limnea spp., 142
lions, 51, 53, 109
Lithocranius walleri, 112
Little Kharas, 22
lizards, 60, 72, 73, 78, 83, 85, 86, 90, 91, 95, 97, 145
Locusta migratoria, 78, 127, *see also* locusts
Locustana   septemfasciata, 127
locusts, 75, 78, 83, 114, 123–9, 131, 132–4, 149
loess, 20, 21
Lower Californian desert, 4, *see also* Baja California
Loxocheles spp., 144–5
lucerne, 159
Lupinus spp., 159
lynxes, 109

Mabuya spp., 95
M. quinquetaeniatus, 90
macchia, 47, 165
Macropus robustus, 107
maize, 158
malaria, 140–2
Mali, 33, 42, 127
man, 70, 78, 82, 107–8, 113–22, 139–48
manna, 114
Marmota spp., 137
Mastigoproctus giganteus, 78, 85, 149
Mastomys spp., 137
Mauretania, 47, 167
Medicago sativa, 159
Melanoplus spritus, 129
Meloidae, 143
Melophorus spp., 114
Mega-Chad, 47
Megaleia rufa, 107
Meroë (Merowe), 51
Mesolithic deposits, 50
mesquite, 62
Mexico, 7, 43, 66, 129, 139, 144, 145, 148, 159, 166
microclimates, 11–12, 72, 93, 120
Microtermes spp., 130
Micruroides euryxanthus, 145
millet, 153, 158
millipedes, 70, 72, 78, 86, 143
minerals, 166–7
Miombo savanna, 30, 33
mites, 72, 86
Mojave desert, 3, 4, 166
Mollusca, 47
Mullugo cerviana, 58
Moloch horridus, 87
Mongolia, 166
Mongols, 113
mongooses, 50
monkeys, 116, 139
Morocco, 6, 52, 128, 130
mosquitoes, 131, 140
mouflon, 52
mule-deer, 104
mulgara, 87
Müllerian mimicry, 98

Nagana, 138
Naja haje, 146
Najacoccus serpentinus, 114
nalas, 15
Namib desert, 3, 4, 60, 64, 72, 94
Nemadi, 154–5
Neobatrachus spp., 74
Neolithic artefacts, 44, 50
Nerium oleander, 68
neurasthenia, 119
Nevada, 166
New Mexico, 7, 9, 43, 131, 167
Niger, 18, 127, 167
Nigeria, 33, 36, 41
nightjars, 11, 73
Nile, 45, 49, 50, 52, 53, 68, 101, 141, 161, 162–3
Noctuidae, 132

nomadism, 41, 54, 66, 110, 114–15, 119, 121, 153–5
Nomadacris septemfasciata, 127
Nubia, 50, 51, 163

Oases, 19, 57, 68–9, 110, 130, 140, 141, 161, 164, 167
Odocoileus hemionus, 104
Oestridae, 138–9
Olduvai Gorge, 27
Olea spp., 47
oleander, 68
olives, 52, 68
Oncopera fasciculata, 131
Onotragus megaceros, 50
Onychomys spp., 87, 149
Ophiobolus graminis, 137
Opuntia spp., 64, 67, *see also* prickly pear
O. ficus-indica, 63
O. inermis, 63, 131
Ornithodorus savignyi, 78
orographic precipitation, 4
oroya fever, 39
Orthoporus armatus, 78, 86
oryx, 50, 70, 93, 100, 104–5, 112, 154
Oryx spp., 93, *see also* oryx
O. algazel, 104
O. gazella, 105
O. leucoryx, 104
Oryza glaberrima, 158
O. sativa, 158
ostriches, 52, 85, 93, 94, 112, 154, 157, 171
Otala lactea, 113–14
Oued Rhir, 69
Ounianga, 50
overgrazing, 19, 28, 53, 54, 109–10, 156
owls, 11, 73

Pachydactylus hasselquisti, 72
Pakistan, 10, 66
Palestine, 129
Palmatogecko spp., 95
pampas, 165
Pangaea, 24
Panicum antidotale, 166
panting, 82, 90, 108
Papago, 115
Paraneotermes simplicicornis, 130
Parlatoria blanchardi, 130, 131
Paspalum spp., 158
Pasteurella pestis, 137–8
P. turalensis, 139
pastoralism, 151–3
Patagonian desert, 3, 4, 109, 153
pathogens,
    animal, 137–9
    human, 139–43
    plant, 136–7
peas, 158
pedalfers, 15, 21
pedocals, 15, 20, 21

Pekin man, 39
Pennisetum spp., 158
Permian period, 24, 26
Peru, 60, 68, 139, 159, *see also* Atacama desert
pests, 123–35
phagostimulants, 133
Phalaenoptilus nuttalli, 82, 94
Phaseolus lunatus, 159
P. vulgaris, 159
phenology, 74–5
Phlebotomus spp., 139
Phoenicoccus marlatti, 130
Phoenix, 7
Phoenix dactylifera, 68, *see also* date palms
Phrynosoma cornutum, 91
Phytophthora spp., 136
pigeon-peas, 159
pigmentation, 119–20
Pinus spp., 47
P. edulis, 166
P. monophylla, 166
Pisum arvense, 158
P. sativum, 158
plague, 137–8, 156
Plasmodium spp., 140
Platyedra gossypiella, 130
Platymeris rhadomanthus, 143
playas, 15
Pleistocene epoch, 27, 28, 45, 47, 48, 169
Pleuroderma nebulosa, 83
Pliny, 51, 101
Pliocene epoch, 26, 44
podsols, 21
poikilotherms, 73, 81
poison, 72
pollen analysis, 47, 50
polymorphism, 126
poor-wills, 82, 94
Populus spp., 165
porcupines, 150
Porosagrotis orthogonia, 131
prairie dogs, 150
prairie soils, 21
Pre-Cambrian basement complex, 22, 23
prickly pear, 63, 67, 131, 170, 171, *see also Opuntia* spp.
Prodenia spp., 134
pronghorns, 66, 104, 156
Prosopis spp., 66
P. velutina, 62
protein synthesis, 102, 106
Psammomys obesus, 87
Psammophis spp., 145
Psammotermes hybostoma, 129
psychological adaptation, 119, 121–2
Puccinia spp., 136
P. graminis, 136
P. sorghi, 136
pulses, 158–9
pumas, 109
Punans, 38
Pygmies, 38

Qoz, 16, 28
Quattara depression, 15

Quercus spp., 47
quokkas, 107

Rabbits, 87–8
railways, 18
rain, 1, 4, 6–7, 9, 13, 20, 21, 35–6, 41, 44, 45, 53, 54, 67, 132–3, 152, 153–4, 155, 164, 165
rain-shadow deserts, 4
Rallus longirostris, 156
rats, 50, 84, 87
rattlesnakes, 146–8, 150
Redunca redunca, 139
Reduviidae, 143
reedbuck, 139
reg, 15, 16
reptiles, 83, 86–7, 89–90, 93, *see also* species
Reticulitermes lucifugus, 129
rhinoceroses, 51, 112, 157
Rhinotermitidae, 129
rhourds, 16
rhythms,
    daily, 71–4
    seasonal, 74–5
rice, 158
Ricinus communis, 159
rinderpest, 138
Rio Grande, 57, 68
Roadlia cardinalis, 131
rodents, 60, 73, 79, 84, 92, 94, 138, 139, *see also* species
Romans, 53, 101
Rudolf, Lake, 53
rumen, 101–2
Russia, 20, 139
rusts, 136–7

Saccharinum spp., 166
S. officinarum, 159
safflower, 132, 159
saggias, 162
Sahara, 3, 4, 10, 12, 15, 16, 18, 22, 23, 26, 27, 29, 39, 40, 41, 44–54, 56, 57, 63, 68, 95, 104, 125, 127, 129, 130, 139, 141, 144, 153, 155, 156, 161, 171
Sahel savanna, 30, 33, 35, 41, 47, 141, 152, 157–8
Saiga tatarica (saiga), 96, 105–6, 138, 156–7
salinity, soil, 15
salt glands, 80, 85, 94
Salvadora persica, 27
sandgrouse, 85
Sanga cattle, 41
San Luiz Potosi, 7
Sauromalus obesus, 85
savanna, 29–38, 169, 170, *see also* types
scale insects, 130, 131
Schistocerca gregaria, 75, 83, 123–7, 132–3, *see also* locusts.
Schistosoma spp., 142
S. mansoni, 142
Scolopendra spp., 143
Scorpionidae, 144

scorpions, 59, 60, 71–2, 74, 78, 95, 143–4, 148
screes, 13
screw worms, 133
sebkhas, 15
seed dispersal, 58–9
seif dunes, 16, 17
selima, 16
semi-desert soils, 20–1
serir, 15, 16
Sesamum indicum (sesame), 159
Setonix brachyurus, 107
shahali, 10
Shaheinab, 50
Shambat, 6
sheep, 11, 43, 50, 53, 106–7, 110, 138, 154, 156, 171
shifting cultivation, 33–8
Shoshonean tribes, 66
side-winding, 95–6
sierozems, 14, 20, 21
Silurian period, 26
simoom, 10
Simulium damnosum, 143
Sind desert, 139
sirocco, 10
sisal, 67
Sistan desert, 43
skinks, 72, 90, 95
slaves, 155, 159
sleep, 122
snails, 50, 113–14, 142
snakes, 73, 78, 83, 87, 91, 95–6, 97, 145–8, 150
soils, 13–21
Solifugae, 71–2, 79, 95, 149, *see also* camel-spiders
Somalia, 42, 53, 106, 125
Sonoran desert, 3, 43, 77
sorghum, 40, 41, 142, 145, 158
Sorghum sudanense, 159
Souf, 19
soy beans, 159
spiders, 72, 74, 85, 97, 144–5
Spinifex spp., 65
spiracles, 75, 78, 79, 80
Spirobolus spp., 166
springbok, 138
starlings, 156
steatopygia, 65
stellar dunes, 17
stomata, 59, 75, 80, 85
Stomoxys spp., 138
Strabo, 51
Strategus julianus, 80
stridulation, 149–50
Struthio camelus, 93, 94, 157, *see also* ostriches
Sturnus vulgaris, 156
sub-elytral cavities, 78, 80
Sudan, 8, 9, 11, 16, 30, 40, 50, 104, 105, 110–11, 132, 139, 162
Sudan grass, 159

Sudan savanna, 29, 33, 35
sugar crops, 159
sunflowers, 61, 159
sweating, 70, 79, 91, 102, 107–8, 113, 115–16, 118, 121
Syncerus caffer, 112, *see also* buffaloes
Syrrhaptes paradoxus, 85

Tabanidae, 138, 139
Taenioptygia castanotes, 85
take-all fungus, 137
Takla Makan desert, 3
Tamanrasset, 6
tamarisk, 18, 19, 68, 114
Tamarix aphylla, 68
T. gallicae, 68
tanning agents, 64, 67
Tanytarsus spp., 143
Taoudeni, 47, 55
Tarentola annularis, 90
Tashkent, 9
Tassili, 23, 50, 51
Tata, 130
Tatera spp., 137
Tchad (Chad), 6, 127, 130
technology, 120–2
Teda, 155
temperature, 7–9
Tenebrionidae, 78, 80, 86, 94, 143, 149
tequila, 67
termites, 74, 114, 129–30, 134, 149, *see also* species
Termitidae, 129
Testudo sulcata, 92–3
Tethys sea, 24
Texas, 63, 66, 130, 141
Thar desert, 3, 23, 43, *see also* Indian desert
Themeda spp., 166
thermoregulation, 89–93
Thryonomys arkelli, 50
T. swinderianus, 36
Thylacinus cynocephalus, 109
Thysanoptera (thrips), 131
Thysanura, 59, 86, 94
Tibesti, 12, 22, 26, 45, 50, 68
Tibu, 154
ticks, 78, 80, 86, 139, 145
Tilia spp., 47
Timbuktu, 153
Tit, battle of, 155
tornillos, 11
tortoises, 81, 83, 92–3
Touggourt, 18
Tourat, 130
tourism, 167–8
Trabutina mannipara, 114
trachoma, 139
transchumance, 155
transpiration, 70, 75, 77–83, 89, 90
transverse dunes, 17
Triassic period, 24, 26

Tribulus spp., 57
Trifolium alexandrinum, 159
Trimerorhinus spp., 145
Trimorphodon spp., 145
Triticum spp., 158
trypanosomiases, 41, 138
Trypanosoma brucei, 138
T. congolense, 138
T. equiperdum, 138
T. vivax, 138
tsama melons, 63, 65
tsetse flies, 41, 54, 138, 153
Tuareg, 118, 121, 155
Tunisia, 15, 155
turalemia, 138, 139
Turkestan desert, 3, 9, 20, 101
Typhlops spp., 95

urine, 83, 84, 85, 93, 102, 106, 108, 119
Uromastix acanthinurus, 72
Ustilago zea, 136
Utah, 15, 167

Vegetation, 55–69
Venezillo arizonicus, 77
venoms, 143–8, 149
vetches, 159
Vicia spp., 159
V. faba, 158
Vigna mungo, 159
V. unguiculata, 159
Viperinae (vipers), 145–8
vultures, 11

Wadi Halfa, 8, 9
wadis, 6, 14, 15, 32, 52, 56, 57, 66, 169
Wad Medani, 54
wallabies, 104
wasps, 74, 98, 143, 149
Welwitschia mirabilis, 60, 61
wheat, 158
wind, 5, 10–11, 18, 19, 28
witchetty grubs, 114
woodlice, 70, 72, 77, 79–80, 83, 97

Xerophytic plants, 60–3
Xenopsylla brasiliensis, 137
X. cheopis, 137
X. philoxera, 137
X. pirei, 137

Yellow soils, 14, 20
Yucca spp., 63
Y. filamentosa, 80
Yuma, 6, 8

Zea mays, 158
Zebu cattle, 41, 106–7
Zenaidura macroura, 85, 94
Zizyphus spp., 66
Zootectus insularis, 50